A History of *The Vale*

Schenectady's Historic Rural Cemetery

Don Rittner

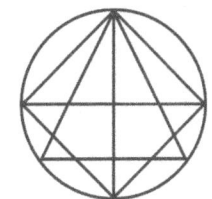

Square Circle Press

Schenectady, New York

**A History of The Vale:
Schenectady's Historic Rural Cemetery**

Published by
Square Circle Press LLC
PO Box 913
Schenectady, NY 12301
www.squarecirclepress.com

© 2015 by Don Rittner.
All rights reserved. No part of this publication may be reproduced or transmitted in any form or by any means, electronic or mechanical, except brief quotes extracted for the purpose of book reviews or similar articles, without permission in writing from the publisher.

First American paperback edition 2015.
Printed and bound in the United States of America on acid-free, durable paper.
ISBN-13: 978-0-9856926-8-1
ISBN-10: 0-9856926-8-5
Library of Congress Control Number: 2016938517

Publisher's Acknowledgments
Cover ©2015 by Square Circle Press; design by Richard Vang. Black and white cover images, courtesy of the author. Color images courtesy of Richard Vang.

Unless otherwise noted, all interior images are courtesy of the author.

Dedicated to

Bernie and Barbara McEvoy

Two Tireless Volunteers

Table of Contents

Preface, vii

Introduction, *3*

Burial Practices in Schenectady before The Vale, *8*

The Rural Cemetery Movement, *17*

The Development of Vale Cemetery, *20*

Special Areas in Vale Cemetery, *42*

Appendix 1: 101 Notables in Vale Cemetery, *57*

Appendix 2: General Electric Employees in The Vale, *183*

Appendix 3: Burials in the Union College Plot, *184*

Appendix 4: Vegetation Planted in Vale Cemetery, *188*

About the Author, 201

Preface

This book is divided into four chapters and four appendices. Chapter One explains the burial conditions of the city before the development of Vale, while Chapter Two gives a brief explanation of the Rural Cemetery Movement. Chapter Three is the story of how Vale became a reality, and Chapter Four describes some of the special areas in the cemetery.

Appendix 1 provides brief biographies and other information about 100 notable people buried at Vale. Appendix 2 gives a list of General Electric employees, while Appendix 3 lists those residents of the Union College plot. Appendix 4 has multiple lists of vegetation that have been planted in various sections of the cemetery.

Vale Cemetery is a working cemetery and is operated by a non-profit organization that maintains it, mostly by volunteers. You can help continue to make Vale successful by considering having Vale be your eternal resting place, or you can adopt a grave of one of the notables in the book by making a donation each year in his or her name. By purchasing this book you have already made a small donation to the cemetery, as all the royalties for this book go directly to the Cemetery Association.

I would like to thank Bernie and Barbara McEvoy for their trust in me to bring to light some of the eternal stories from a selected group of Vale residents. Acknowledgments also go to the Vale Cemetery Board; Chris Hunter, Archivist at Schenectady Museum of Innovation and Science; Brown School; Frank Taormina; Dr. Hargan Thomsen; Marlene DesChamps, Union College Archives; Paul Carnahan, Librarian, Vermont Historical Society; Brooke A. Manrique, Public Relations, SI Group; Laurie McFadden, Herrick Librarian and University Archivist, Alfred University's Susanne Greenhagen; Jim Gandy, Assistant Librarian/Archivist, New York State Military Museum; Timothy Ware; Mike Reid, KU Memorial Unions; Efner Research Center. Apologies to those omitted.

Don Rittner

Historic Postcard of original entrance to Vale Cemetery from Nott Terrace. The path to the left goes to the lakes.

A History of
The Vale

Introduction

For death is no more than a turning of us over from time to eternity.

—*William Penn*

In the Capital District of New York State there exist three major cemeteries attributed to the "Rural Cemetery Movement" of the early 19th century: Albany Rural Cemetery (1844), designed by Maj. D.B. Douglass; Oakwood Cemetery (1848) in Troy, designed by John C. Sidney and John Boetcher; and Schenectady's Vale Cemetery (1857), designed by Burton A. Thomas and John Doyle. All were expressions of a growing movement to rid urban areas of overcrowded and unsanitary graveyards, as well as create more "park-like" reposes for the dead. They also provided a means for anyone who could afford a burial an eternal resting place that did not matter what religion or socioeconomic status one belonged to. Among the millionaires and notables could be found the small business owner, tailor, soldier or iron worker. It was a democratization of death.

When Vale Cemetery was originally designed it was located on the eastern end of the city of Schenectady, and indeed was rural. It was part of the sandy Pine Barrens that stretched all the way to Albany. There was little residential development in the area, and State Street and upper roads were impassable in the spring due to the soaked and rutty mud laid down by carriage wheels and, later, early automobiles. Expansion of residential and commercial development after the 1930s engulfed the area around the cemetery, and it is now an integral part of the city.

Vale is not only a beautiful and well laid out cemetery—it is also a history lesson. While many of the cemetery's residents are spending their eternal rest in peace, many of the residents buried at Vale represent people that have made major notable contributions to American history in science, politics, military, literature, education, business and invention, and a host of other disciplines. Laid out among the 33,000 residents at Vale are many names found in history books. The purpose of this book is to illustrate one hundred of these notable figures, with their biographies and contributions, in celebration of the continued operation of the 100-acre cemetery—one biography for every acre.

There are many types of materials that make up headstones, and most of these types can be found in Vale. For an enjoyable geology lesson, try to locate ones made from sandstone, slate, limestone, soapstone, field stone (blue stone, graywacke), cast iron, stainless steel, granite, bronze, marble, field boulders, cast zinc or even wood. These monuments are usually inscribed with the name, birth and death dates, and sometimes a few words about the deceased, and often contain much more in the form of symbols or iconic forms, clues about what the deceased did, or was proud of during his or her lifetime. (See the images on the following pages.)

Those that do contain symbols or icons can tell something about what the grieving family felt, or proudly promote a membership in a society, an award or recognition, a military affiliation or a religious or fraternal connection. There is a very good web site that describes the meaning of many of the symbols you will find as you explore the graves at Vale. Go to the United States Genealogy & History Network at *http://msghn.org/usghn/symbols.html*.[*]

There is also another good web site that explains the abbreviations found on graves at *http://msghn.org/usghn/abbreviations.html*.

The Vale (Vale Park), that is the wooded ravine of Cowhorn Creek that runs through the cemetery and is impounded into two lakes, is a great retreat for nature loving, hiking or biking. An extension of a county-wide bike trail now runs through the cemetery grounds, beginning at the Nott Street entrance, and exiting at Brandywine Avenue.

---

[*] All web site addresses in this book were accurate at the time they were recorded.

The James G. Haigh Monument. "Dog Lion" visited every day and when he died, workmen paid to have this statue of him.

The Magee monument allows you to rest and contemplate.

A headstone in the form of a tree trunk often meant "brevity of life." These are members of Woodmen of the World.

"A Friend of Bill W's" meant that the deceased was a member of Alcoholics Anonymous (AA). There are many interesting bits of information on a headstone besides the name and dates of the deceased.

Not all gravestones are made from stone. From 1874 to 1914 the Monumental Bronze Company in Bridgeport, Connecticut produced zinc gravestones, called "white bronze," though they were more blue-gray in color, and were popular for their durability. Peak sales were in the 1880s. Originally invented by M.A. Richardson in 1873, he contracted with William W. Evans, and the rights were sold to Wilson, Parsons & Company, which incorporated as the Monumental Bronze Company in 1879. They were made for only 40 years. World War I required the use of all zinc for the war effort and the company never recovered after the war.

Joseph Yates Peek (1843-1911) may have been a pessimist with this statement, or could be referring to the death of his early Dutch roots in Schenectady.

Burial Practices in Schenectady before *The Vale*

The First Organized Cemetery - Dutch Reformed Church

The Dutch founding of Schenectady in 1661 began with fifteen families from nearby Albany, located sixteen miles to the east through the sandy Pine Barrens which separated the two 17th-century communities.

Among the many hurdles these early residents faced as they settled the frontier village was the burial of their dead. The burial of loved ones was the responsibility of the immediate family, although the church often played a major role. In 17th-century Schenectady, the dead would often be buried in the backyard or another location on the property or even, in some cases, in the cellar of the home. It is known that Adam Vrooman, one of the survivors of the 1690 Schenectady massacre, had his private burying ground inside the village on his pasture lot on the north side of Front Street (#35), which was 46 feet long by 9½ feet wide.

Once a house of worship was built, the establishment of the church cemetery became a priority, but burial there was often not free.

In Schenectady during the 17th and early 18th centuries, The Dutch Reformed, Presbyterian, and Episcopal congregations were the earliest denominations represented in the stockade village and each had their own cemetery near their respective churches.

The earliest church building after Schenectady's founding belonged to the Dutch Reformed, and was erected not far from Cowhorn Creek and the Albany Road, now State Street, near the intersection of Church and Water Streets. The church was located on the south side of the Albany Road, outside the south gate, and contained a grave yard on the west side. The church became a blockhouse after the massacre of 1690.

A new stockaded settlement called the King's Fort was built on the banks of the Mohawk River near present-day Schenectady County Community College after the 1690 massacre, and the settlers there utilized a blockhouse for a church. Burials were likely done outside the smaller fortification, and later may have been near the new church that was built a few yards east of the fort.

There is evidence to indicate a makeshift graveyard was created after the massacre near the intersection of Church and present-day Front streets (then Front Street headed north and was known as the river road to Niskayuna), as shown on the 1698 Wolfgang Romer Map. Over the years, skeletons identified as massacre victims have been uncovered near that intersection. Skeletons were also found in many parts of the original village bounds, which may indicate that no formal burying ground existed before the massacre or that there was no time after the massacre to properly bury the dead in the makeshift cemetery. Another conjecture is that the dead were buried in the yards of the burned out properties.

Burials under the church were available for those that could afford to pay for the privilege.

A Dutch church and cemetery is located at the same location, prior to the massacre, on the later Romer Map of 1698, which suggests that the church did not burn. It measures 25 feet square, the same size as a blockhouse of the time.

The congregation outgrew the original first church building and a petition was made to build a new and bigger church. The petition was granted, funded and was built at the same location in 1703. It was 56 feet north and south and 46 feet east and west, Amsterdam Measure (an Amsterdam foot is 11 inches). The burying ground adjoined the church on the west side, and was 15 feet wide and 56 feet long. It was enlarged south to 84 feet towards Cowhorn Creek, the rear line being 44½ feet. The church was likely built of stone, and after it was abandoned in 1734, it was used as a fort. It was removed entirely in 1754.

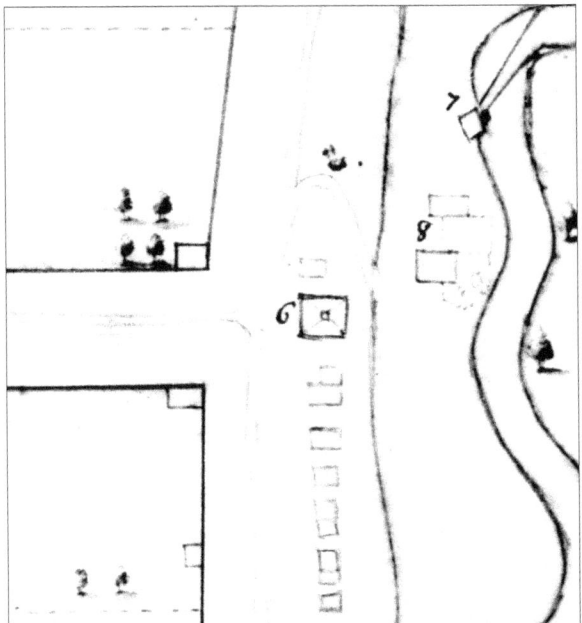
The 1698 Romer Map shows the Dutch Church (number 6) and the cemetery to the east of it (small rectangle).

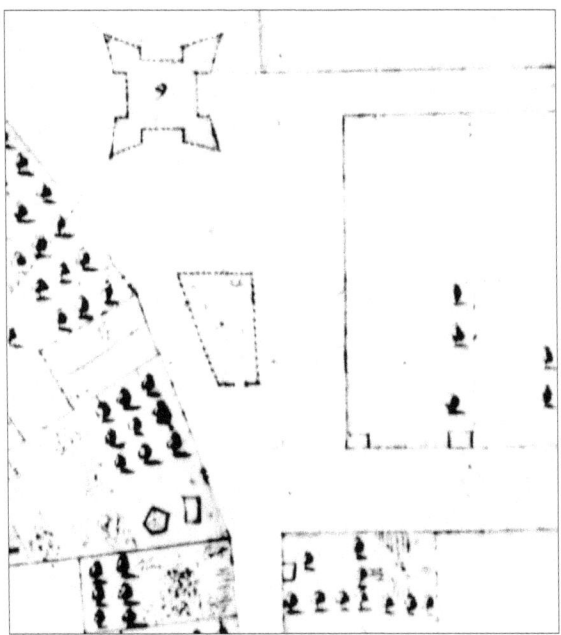
The 1698 Romer Map shows a possible cemetery (middle) that may have been used to bury the dead from the 1690 massacre. Several skeletons were found near here in 1902.

In 1792 a new academy and dwelling house were proposed to be built on the vacant land where the church formerly stood. The property was eventually leased to Arent S. Vedder for building purposes, with conditions that the site could never be dug up, unless it was for a building or insertion of fence posts and that any foundations be laid out father west from where the old church's west wall stood. Ultimately nothing was developed on this land because the site was not suitable for building, especially after being a burial ground for fifty years. The burying ground appears to have been abandoned in the 1840s. A cistern was being constructed at that time, and bones were found from the 1720s burying ground and discarded. The final disposition of this first cemetery is not known, since several 19th century homes, including inventor George Westinghouse's home, were eventually built on the property later in the century. The Dutch church moved to the center of Union and Church streets in 1734, and was 80 feet long north and south, and 56 feet wide. It was the site of the erection of the Liberty Flag in 1774, a sign of independence during the beginning of the American Revolution. This church stood until 1814, when it was moved to the present location at the northeast corner of Union and Church streets.

The Dutch church moved to the center of Union and Church streets in 1734.

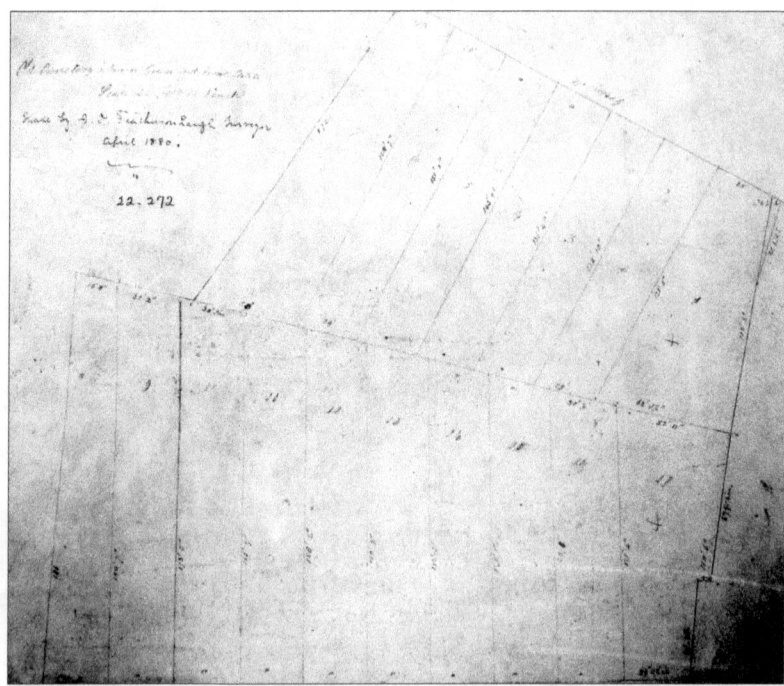

Layout of the Green and Front Streets Burial Ground in April 1880. The graves were reburied at Vale Cemetery.

While it is not found in written records, the burying ground near the original church site may have still been used during this period. The earliest record of a new cemetery at Green and Front streets, near the old Fort Crosby, was in a deed given by the patentees of the town to the church, dated August 1, 1721. The oldest headstone was set in 1722. However, an older gravestone considered the oldest ever found from the village was taken out of a cellar wall nearby, where it had been used after serving its original purpose. The gravestone had inscribed on it "1690" and the name of Hendrick Jansen Vrooman, who was the son of Jan Vrooman.

The Green Street cemetery was later removed, after being neglected for many years, to Vale Cemetery in 1879.

Second Village Cemetery:
Saint George's Episcopal Church

With the financial help of Sir William Johnson, ground was broken in 1759 for the construction of St. George's Church on Ferry Street next to the fort. Religious services began in 1763. A cemetery was placed on the west and north sides of the church where it currently remains. For a short time, the Presbyterians shared St. George's Church. The earliest headstone dates to 1788.

Third Village Cemetery
First Presbyterian Church

The First Presbyterian Church formed in 1769 and built a small wooden church on Union Street. The present building was built in 1809, with later additions in 1834 and 1859. The cemetery was placed along the east and west sides of the church.

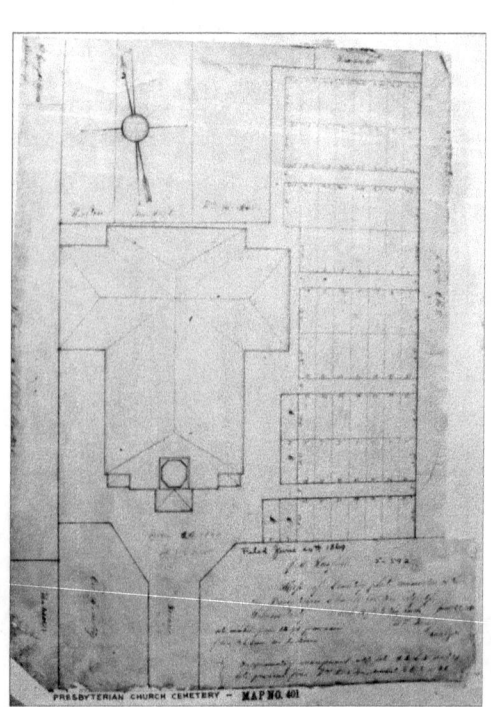

Map of the cemetery lots in the Presbyterian Church filed June 24th, 1869.

Fourth Village Cemetery - First Methodist Episcopal Church

The Methodist religion began in Schenectady in 1770, when traveling preacher George Whitefield stopped to pray among a few gathered to hear him. There is some history of Methodist lay preacher Thomas Webb, who was stationed in Albany as Barrack Master in 1766, perhaps visiting Schenectady and preaching the Word in front of a bolting flour mill on the east side of Church Street, near Union. The year 1807 is the official date for the beginning of Methodism in Schenectady. Rev. Benjamin Akin preached to a few in the home of Richard Clute on Green Street. The church was officially organized in 1808, and a church was built on the northeast corner of Liberty and Canal streets, the cornerstone laid on July 28th, 1808. A church cemetery was created there. When the church was sold and a new church built on Liberty Street in 1835-36, the bodies were taken up and reburied in the rear of the new church. This burial ground was used until 1846, when a new burial site was purchased "on the Albany turnpike." The cemetery ran from State Street to Albany Street, bounded by Martin Street, and was directly across from where the State Street entrance of Vale Cemetery would be developed later in the century. This site was used until 1873. The Liberty Street church closed the previous year and was sold to the Catholic Church. It is assumed that the burials were removed from the site and re-interred at Vale. However, in 2012 several unmarked headstones—and one with the inscription "Gertrude Bancker Frank, Died June 12, 1849. The wife of Jacob Frank. The daughter of John and Gertrude Bancker. Aged 22 years."—were uncovered in the backyard of a resident's house on the Albany Street side of the former burial site. Research uncovered that she was reburied in Vale.

The church purchased land from Giles S. Barhydt next to Vale Cemetery to be used for the burial of the poor of the church and relocating the remains from the former church lot. This new cemetery was offered to Vale on June 7, 1891 at no charge, but then the offer was rescinded in August.

New Cemeteries and Unknown Graves

As the city of Schenectady grew in size and population, and as new citizens representing other religions made the city their home, cemeteries were needed to accommodate them. On November 7, 1812 the city council approved a resolution to appoint a committee to

> ... designate a suitable place for the Burial of the dead & that Mr Boyd, Mr. Walker, Mr Rosa, & Mr. Dunlap be the said committee. Mr. Boyd proposed certain resolutions relative to the mode to be adopted in the leasing of the common lands in case a law should be passed to that affect, which were read, thereupon.

A piece of the city's "common land" on Albany Hill (now Hamilton Hill) was chosen during the first quarter of the 19th century near Hamilton Street, Paige Street, Summit Avenue and Westover Street. Westover Street was then called Cemetery Street and created for that purpose. It fronted the cemetery lots. It was also known as Cemetery Lane in 1899. It was changed to Westover around 1914. (See the Swits Map of 1824 on the next page.) Originally it was four sections, but was expanded to seven by 1824.

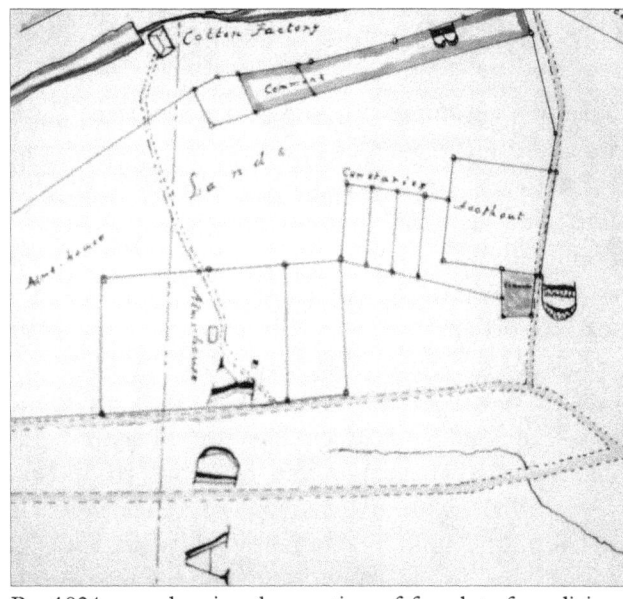

Pre-1824 map showing the creation of four lots for religious denomination cemeteries by the common council on Albany Hill.

On May 26, 1821, the Council passed a resolution:

Resolved that the alms house committee be & they are hereby directed to enquire & examine whether any encroachments have been made by the superintendent of the Alms House upon the Burial ground or upon private property & that they report to this board at their next meeting.

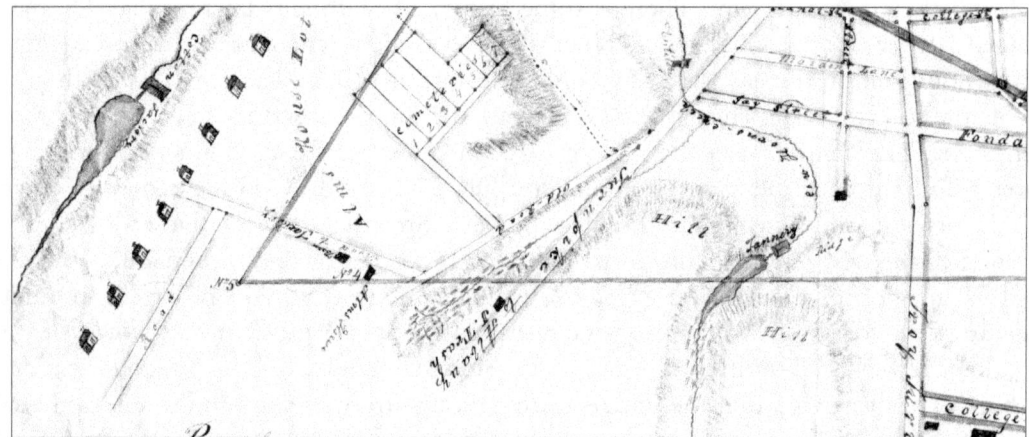

The 1824 Nicholas Swits Map of Hamilton Hill shows the location of the first public cemetery sections given by the city to various religious denominations but later expanded to seven sections.

On September 29, 1821:

Resolved, that the commissioners of Highways be & they are hereby authorized & empowered to agree with Mr. Oothout in relation to the road leading to the Burial places given by the city to the several churches & that they report their proceedings to this board at their next meeting.

While it was reported to be given to several denominations, recent maps only show sections used by the Baptists and Catholics.

The old city Alms House for the Poor, established around 1815, had a cemetery on a triangular plot of land adjacent to the county fair grounds at Emmet and Factory streets (now Craig Street), from 1840 to 1890.

Unknown Graves

Skeletons continued to be found periodically throughout the original village, later the city and the surrounding land. In 1854, when Lafayette Street was being excavated and pitched as a street, fifty-seven skeletons were found, all victims of the Revolutionary War. They were buried in the rear of a hospital lot. They were re-interred at Vale, and a monument was erected in their honor in August 1859.

On June 24, 1902, three Native American and three Dutch skeletons were exhumed near the location of the North Gate of the original village near Front and Church streets, likely victims of the massacre.

In November 1925, seven skeletons were found in a cellar that was being dug for a house on Mumford Street. They were believed Native in origin, as an old Schenectady map indicated an ancient Native burying ground in the area.

In 1933, while excavating a sand bank on Crane Street in Mount Pleasant, two skeletons and additional bones were found, and it was thought to be a Native American gravesite or an old family plot. The bones were determined to be over 100 years old, most likely of people of European descent, since no artifacts were found with them.

Fifty-seven Revolutionary War soldiers were recovered from Lafayette Street excavations in 1854 and buried under this monument in 1859.

In May 1941, five skulls and assorted bones were found in a common grave in the backyard of 418 Paige Street. In 1943, four skeletons were unearthed on the old Shopmyer Farm on Van Antwerp Road.

In June 1965, workers digging a trench for a natural gas pipe near the southwest corner of Broadway and State streets found parts of four skeletons. They were found in a flexed position with artifacts, a clay pipe with the initials "MG," and layers of bark around them, more than likely indicative of being Native American. The Initials "MG" are puzzling because of two different attributions: one could be for Miggiel Gillisz of Gouda in 1667; the second supposition that it was for Thomas Sparnaay, whose burial was as late as 1865. If indeed they were from the earlier date, they were likely victims of the 1690 massacre, if not simple earlier deaths by natural causes.

Three of these skeletons (1, 2, 3) are Native Americans while the remaining are Dutchmen exhumed on June 24, 1902, near the site of the North Gate (Ferry and Church Streets), massacre victims.

In July 1974, workers digging for a new sewer pipe found the remains of a mass burial ground on Hamilton Street near Hulett Street. The burial ground was thought to have been a mass burial of cholera epidemic deaths of 1832. The remains were brought to Vale.

An abandoned cemetery with nineteen headstones was found on Florence Street, north of Albany Street, on what was the old Vrooman Farm. The oldest headstone was dated 1811, the newest 1902.

Many of the headstones from the old Dutch cemetery on Front and Green streets never made it to the Vale re-internment. Several can be found in the gardens and walkways of the homes of Stockade residents, such as 48 Washington Avenue and 3 Front Street.

It is likely that more remains will be found over the years.

The Schenectady Poor House had its own burial plots not far from the Hamilton Hill burial lots of the 1820s. Some of these may have been reburied at Vale's Potter's Field.

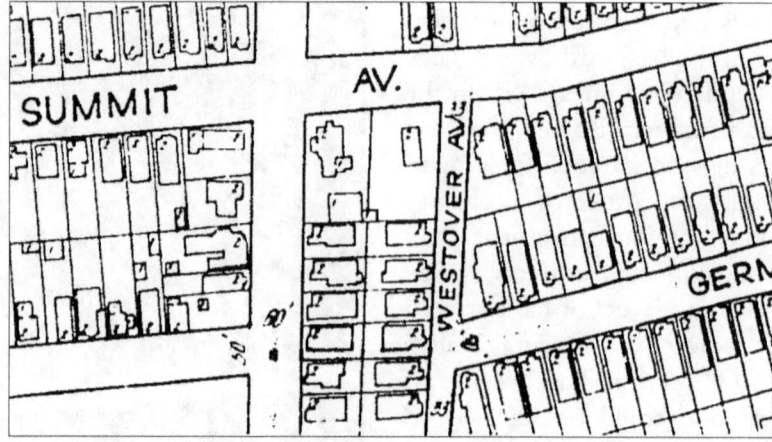

By 1914 the burial site on Cemetery Lane, then Westover Avenue, now Westover Place, was replaced by twelve duplex houses between 1900-1914, no doubt needed for the influx of immigrants to the city seeking work at nearby General Electric and American Locomotive. Six two-family houses still occupy the Westover side, while only four now occupy the Hamilton Street side.

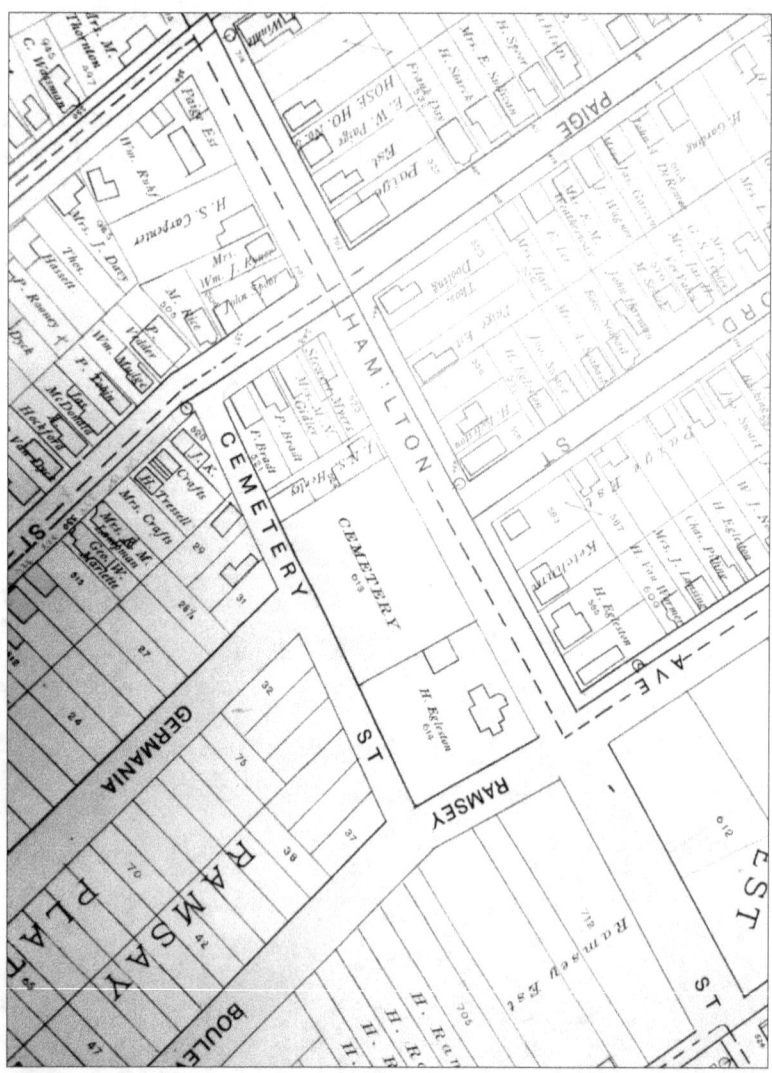

In 1905 the middle section (Catholic) of the Hamilton Hill grave site was still listed as a cemetery. The house on the former Baptist burial lots is still standing as 361 Summit Avenue.

Burial Practices in Schenectady Before The Vale

Former cemetery site of the First Methodist Episcopal Church "on the Albany turnpike" from 1846 to 1873. The cemetery ran from State Street to Albany Street and was bounded by Martin Street. It was directly across from where the State Street entrance of Vale Cemetery would be developed later in the century. In 2012 several unused and one named headstone were recovered from the backyard of a house on Albany Street. This Sanborn map is dated 1894.

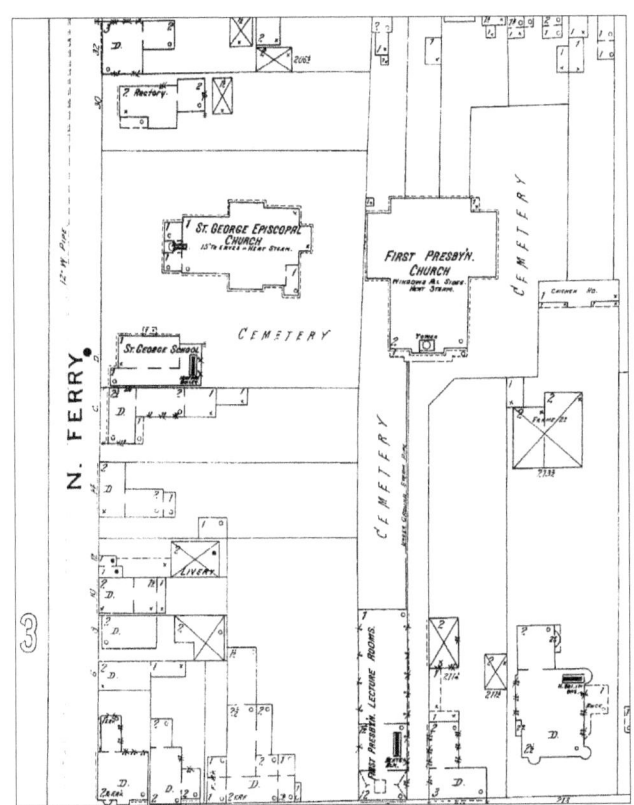

Location of St. George's and First Presbyterian Church cemeteries in 1884.

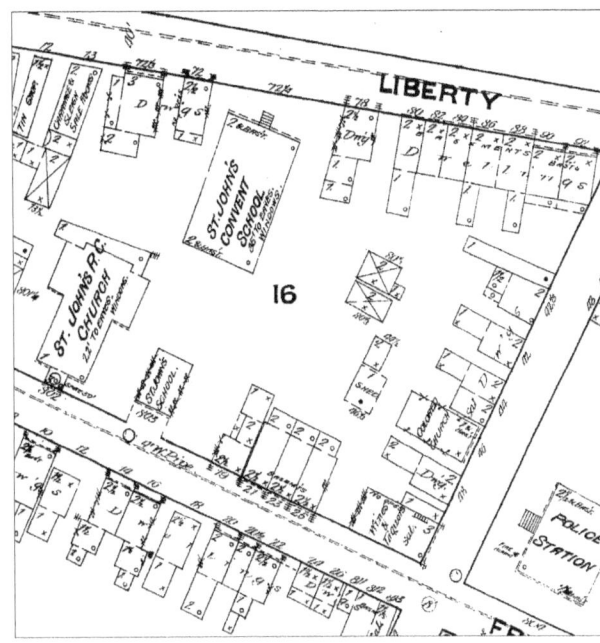

Location of former First Methodist Episcopal Church in 1884, later taken over by St. John's Catholic Church.

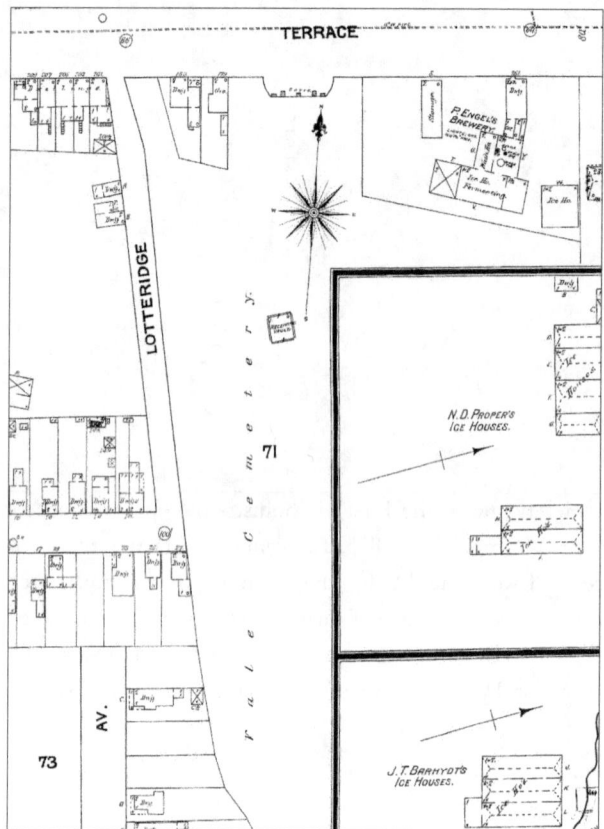

Early receiving vault location at Nott Terrace in 1889.

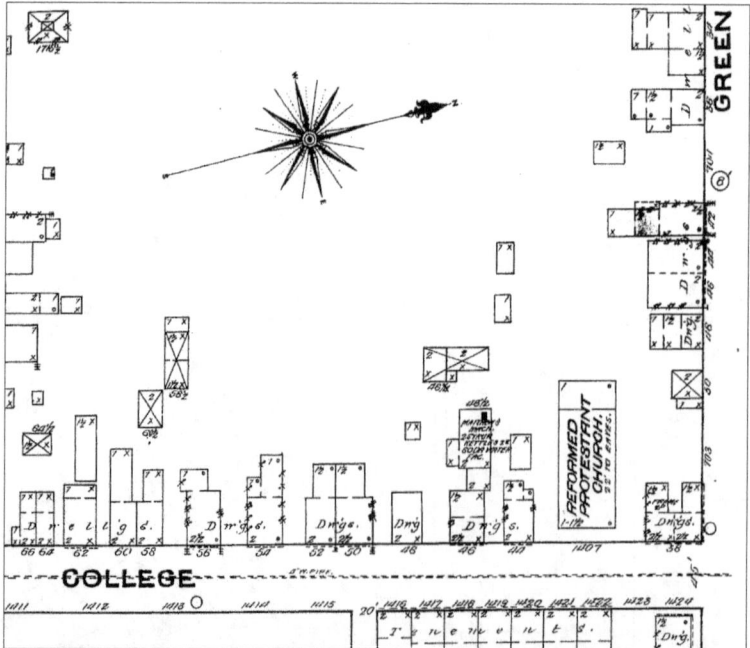

Third Evangelical Protestant Reformed Church location on North College Street near Green Street in 1884.

The Rural Cemetery Movement

The idea of a rural cemetery was suggested as early as 1711 by Sir Christopher Wren, but it wasn't until 1804 that the first landscaped cemetery, the Père Lachaise Cemetery in Paris, was created. In turn, the beginning of the 19th century saw the views of American cemeteries begin to change. In 1835, Stephen Duncan Walker published a series of papers called <u>Rural Cemetery and Public Walk</u> (Sands & Neilson, Baltimore, 1835). Walker had given a series of lectures on the formation of a rural cemetery in Baltimore, similar to one at Mount Auburn, not far from Boston, which was the first American rural cemetery, built in 1831. He wrote:

The improvement and embellishment of grounds devoted to public uses is deserving of special consideration, and should interest the ingenious, the liberal and tasteful in devising ways and means for the accomplishment of so desirable an object.

He further wrote:

I refer to the establishment of a public Cemetery, similar in its designs to that of Père la Chaise, in the environs of Paris, to be located in the suburbs of this metropolis. A suitable regard for the memory of the dead is not inconsistent with the precepts of religion, or of our duty to the living. The place of graves affords to the serious and contemplative, instruction and admonition. It teaches us "what shadows we are, and what shadows we pursue." It is there that the heart is chastened, and the soul is subdued, and the affections purified and exalted. It is there that ambition surveys the boundaries of its powers, of its hopes, and its aspirations; and it is there that we are constrained to submit, that human distinctions, and arrogance, must terminate. I would render such scenes more alluring, more familiar and imposing, by the aid of rural embellishments.

A winter scene at Vale.

Walker suggested and advocated for the creation of a public rural cemetery and a public walk in the same location. These were not quite the reasons for establishing cemeteries in the previous centuries. The cemeteries were usually under the control of local churches that could be temporary and where the cemeteries could be neglected, crowded and often abandoned. The burials were often on top of each other. The "public" cemetery, so reasoned, would be more permanent and better maintained. This was a period when cities were often crowded, dirty and lacked public parks. Walker goes on to say:

A public burial ground, under the auspices of the corporation, when once established, would doubtless be preferred as a place of sepulcher, to the grounds attached to churches in consideration of its permanency as a mortmain possession; being exempted from the liability of removal, or the necessity of future disinhumanation which upon the recent plan, frequent occurs, and to which they will always be subject depended as they now are on the wants of the congregation, to whom they belong; and as often to the caprice of trustees, or those, by whatever name they may be distinguished, who have the control and direction of church temporalities.

In supporting his argument, Walker then wrote about the Boston public cemetery experiment:

Boston, always in the lead in taste, literature, and refinement, has laid out and constructed a cemetery upon an extensive, classic and munificent basis—seventy acres of land have been appropriated to this object, of a capacity sufficient to supply her population for generations to come. A part of these extensive grounds, the Horticultural Society of Massachusetts have turned into an experimental garden. It has been laid out by practical engineers, in a manner tasteful and scientific; the society have planted trees and formed groves, and Flora and Pomons, have breathed an Eden of beauty and blooming over the landscape. The proceeds of the sale of the lots will be applied to the completion of the proposed embellishments, which includes in its prospectus Egyptian Gateways, Gothic and Grecian towers, Doric Temples, Ionic Vaults and a granite Cenotaph, emblematic and commemorative of our venerated Washington. The revenue arising therefrom is expected to be adequate to those purposes, and although considerable time will elapse ere the details of the scheme will be completed, it will doubtless be regarded by posterity as a moral legacy worthy to be transmitted from one generation to another.

Family plot at Vale surrounded by cedar pines. The stone at the stairway entrance bears the words, "Some are fallen asleep." (Courtesy of Richard Vang.)

In his book, <u>Designs for Monuments and Mural Tablet Adapted by Rural Cemeteries, Church Yards, Churches and Chapels</u> (Bartlett and Welford, Philadelphia, 1846), John Jay Smith, one of the founders of the Laurel Hill Cemetery in Philadelphia, expressed the need for organized and aesthetically pleasing cemeteries in what was to become known as the "Rural Cemetery Movement."

Smith states that:

The main object of a burial-ground is, the disposal of the remains of the dead in such a manner that their decomposition, and return to the earth from which they sprung, shall not prove injurious to the living, either by affecting their health, or shocking their feelings, opinion, or prejudices. A second object, still an important one, is, or ought to be, the improvement of the moral sentiments and general taste of all classes, and more especially of the great masses of society.

The secondary object of cemeteries, that of improving the moral feelings, will be one of the results of the decorous attainment of the main object; graveyards lose their monitory virtue when they are covered with weeds, and left to nature. "Why," says Washington Irving, "should we thus seek to clothe death with unnecessary terrors, and to spread horrors around the tomb of those we love? The grave should be surrounded by everything that can inspire tenderness and veneration for the dead, or that might win the living to virtue. It is the place, not of disgust or dismay, but of sorrow and meditation.

His third point was that churchyards and cemeteries were scenes not only "calculated to improve the morals and the taste, and by their botanical riches to cultivate the intellect, but they serve as historical records."

By the mid-nineteenth century the rural cemetery movement was widespread in America. "Rural" actually meant a burial ground located on the outskirts of a city that was based upon the romantic idea of the English landscape gardens that were popular at the time in Europe. Unlike the previous views of burial grounds, the rural cemetery was considered a regular and must-do adventure for a tourist—especially in the early days, when it was more park-like than graveyard—with winding roads, wrought iron bridges and plenty of nature to enjoy.

The development of Vale Cemetery was made possible due to the partly growing rural cemetery movement, but also because of the deplorable conditions of existing cemeteries in the city.

Postcard view of Valley Lake emptying into a new lake to the west towards Nott Terrace.

A heron fishing on one of the small lakes in The Vale. (Courtesy of Richard Vang.)

The Development of Vale Cemetery

By 1850 the Albany (Hamilton) Hill cemeteries were near full and the condition of the old burying ground on Green and Front Streets was in deplorable shape. Members of the Schenectady City Council, at the urging of citizens, decided that something had to be done about the lack of public burial space. However, it took a few more years before anyone could agree on a plan. There was a growing need by many of the religious denominations in the city to have a burial place for their deceased, and they petitioned the Common Council to set aside acreage for them. The cemetery lots formerly given on Albany Hill were already near capacity.

The city owned a parcel of land of about 41 acres in the upper eastern part of the city, called the City Hospital Farm, that was assessed for a value of $2,000. It was also known as the "best partridge feeding and homing ground anywhere near here." On February 17, 1846, a petition by laborer George Chism of Lafayette Street was submitted to rent the farm. On Dec 17, 1851, city Alderman Potter introduced a resolution that was accepted to grant a piece of land to the "German Church for a burial place, reported in favor of selling to petitioners one acre of ground from the hospital farm." It was the same year that city engineer Henry Ramsay prepared a map for possible cemetery use of the same area.

Common Council announcement on March 1, 1854 to read a petition to create a public cemetery.

On March 21, 1853, Alderman Yates reported from the select committee relative to a new location of burial grounds, stating that they "had not effected it, and asking to be discharged," which was granted. In other words they never looked into the matter.

On March 1, 1854, a petition was introduced by Alderman Fuller from A.C. Paige, George McQueen, J. Trumbull Backus, and others, that the Common Council appropriate lands for a public cemetery. That request was referred to the Committee on Lands.

On September 6, 1854, a petition by William Wolff and others asked the Common Council to assign to members of the Third Reformed Dutch Church a suitable piece of ground as a burial for their dead. That request was tabled.

On October 4, 1854, Alderman Arthur W. Hunter declared,

Whereas a map of a proposed cemetery has been laid before this board by the committee on public lands and buildings, of the late Common council, therefore, Resolved, That the subject be referred to the present committee on public lands and buildings, to report to this board.

The resolution was carried.

On November 1, 1854, the city council heard the results of the committee to create a public cemetery. The report gives a good insight as to what the city administrators were thinking. Alderman Hoag, from the Committee on Lands and Public Buildings, submitted the following report and resolution in regard to a public cemetery.

PUBLIC CEMETERY

The Committee on lands and public buildings, to whom was referred the subject of establishing a public cemetery, respectfully report, that they have come to a determination, favorable to the project. Many reasons may be urged in support of this determination, among; which it is thought proper to mention the following:

At this late day, when knowledge is so extensively spread among all classes of the people, the committee deem it but a work of supererogation to cite the considerations which have induced almost every city and town in Christendom to abandon the practice of burying the dead in church-yards surrounded by the dwellings of the living—a practice unknown to the world before the third century of the Christian era - persevered in from that time until within a late period - by custom and superstition and now universally condemned, as deleterious to the public health, and in direct conflict with the rules that the science of the present age has prescribed for its preservation. On this branch of the subject, it will in the opinion of the committee, be quite sufficient to state, that the present number of residents in this city, and the constant increase of its population, as well as a due regard to an enlightened public sentiment amid the preservation of the public health, require that there should be no needless delay on the part of the common council, in procuring a place for depositing the bodies of the dead beyond the corporate limits of the city, and in passing an ordinance that thereafter no interments, without special leave shall be made within those limits.

In pursuance of the task imposed upon them, the committee have personally examined the lands designated as "Cemetery Grounds," on the map prepared by the City Surveyor, Henry Ramsey Esq., and are of the opinion, that in regard to surface, nature of the soil, facility of access, beauty of location, and susceptibility of adornment, they are preferable to any other lands in this vicinity. The site includes parts of the respective farms of Messrs. W. K. Fuller and John Myers and contains about one hundred acres. It can now be purchased for about forty dollars per acre, on a credit of ten-or twelve years, secured by city bonds payable at any time/within, that period; with interest annually. An extension of the credit of the city to the comparatively trifling amount of about four thousand dollars, is therefore, so far as respects this matter, all that will be needed to raise our city to a level with the progress of the age, and place it in the same rank with the other cities of the State.

The committee feel no apprehension that in making this purchase, the city will be exposed to the hazard or loss, but on the contrary, if the results of like enterprises in other places afford data for accurate judgment, they have no hesitation in asserting, that it will be productive of great revenue, and ultimately not only repay the cost but under proper management, leave a large surplus, and furnish the means of making such other public improvements as my from time to time be called for. To prove the justness of this assertion, it may here be proper to make a brief statement of facts and figures.

The learned in this matter say, that one hundred acres of ground, deducting one-third for walks, roads and adornments, will serve as a cemetery for a population of fifteen thousand for a period of five hundred years, before it will become necessary to disturb the ashes of the dead to make room for new graves. The ground selected by the committee, as has already been stated, contains about that number of acres and it is submitted to the wisdom of the Common Council to determine whether its area is sufficient to meet the prospective growth of the population of the city. It will, no doubt, meet the wants of the present population and their descendants for a long term of time, even after deducting therefrom, by the way of gift to each of the religious denominations of the city, the average space of three acres to be used by them respectively in substitutions of their present graveyards. This deduction, reckoning the different denomination at ten, would leave seventy acres undisposed of. If then from this remainder one third be taken for walks, roads and ornaments purposes, there will be left 46 2/3 acres to be subdivided into cemetery lots and sold to individual purchasers. The size of these lots or subdivisions, according to the example of other places, should be one-rod square, which would give 160 lots to the acre, or 7,413 lots for the whole number to be thus sold. Lots of less than half this size, viz. 8 by 16 feet square, have been sold by the Episcopal Church in this city, at fifty dollars a piece. In the public cemeteries of our neighboring cities, the prices have ranged from twenty-five dollars to fifty dollars, per rod square, and upwards. Lots of like size, the committee think, would readily sell in this city at twenty dollars each, and that at least an area of three acres might be sold at that rate within the next two years. At this price, which is five dollars less than the lowest sum charged elsewhere, each acre would yield a return of three thousand two hundred dollars, and the whole for the 7,413 lots would ultimately bring into the city treasury the large sum of $148, 260. But if no more than two acres should be so disposed of within the next two years, the returns to the treasury would then be $6,400, a sum adequate not only to pay the liability of the city for the purchase money, but to meet all necessary expenses in laying out and preparing the ground for market, and also, to surround the whole plot with a living hedge.

Lands, when once devoted to cemetery purposes, with the title vested in a personal corporation, become immensely valuable, and sell for high prices - a fact which may, perhaps find its solution in the natural repugnance which, mankind in general feel to the mere thought of having their ashes and the ashes of their kindred desecrated.

The excellent moral effects of such institutions are too obvious to need much comment. They inevitably lead to the encouragement of the arts and the cultivation of a correct taste, while at the same time they constantly remind us that is but one rest land, and that it behooves us at all times to be ready to depart to that place "where the wicked cease from troubling and the weary are at rest."

With these remarks the committee beg leave to submit the accompanying resolution.

Caspar F Hoag
Nicholas Cain
Nicholas Yates

Resolved, That his Honor, the Mayor, be and he is hereby authorized to purchase lands designated as "Cemetery Grounds" on the map lately made by Henry Ramsay, Esq., City Surveyor, at a price not exceeding forty dollars per acre; and that on the receipt of proper deeds of conveyance of the same for the use of the city, he execute city bonds in payment there're, redeemable at any time, within ten years, with interest annually.

Report received and ordered published.

Alderman Hunter moved, as an amendment, that the whole subject be postponed till the next meeting of the Board.
    Lost

Alderman Hand moved, as an amendment, that the whole subject of a public cemetery be postponed until the first meeting of this board in May next, and that the question of cemetery or no cemetery be submitted to the people of this city at our next charter election for their decision.
    Lost

Alderman Chadsey moved the adoption of the resolution offered by the committee, and the ayes and noes being called resulted as follows:
    Ayes – His Honor, the Mayor, and Ald. Barker, Chadsey, Chequer, Consaul, Cain, Fuller, Hunter, Hoag, McQueen, Putnam, Powell, Vandebogart and Yates [14]
    Nays – Ald. Hand [1]
    Carried.

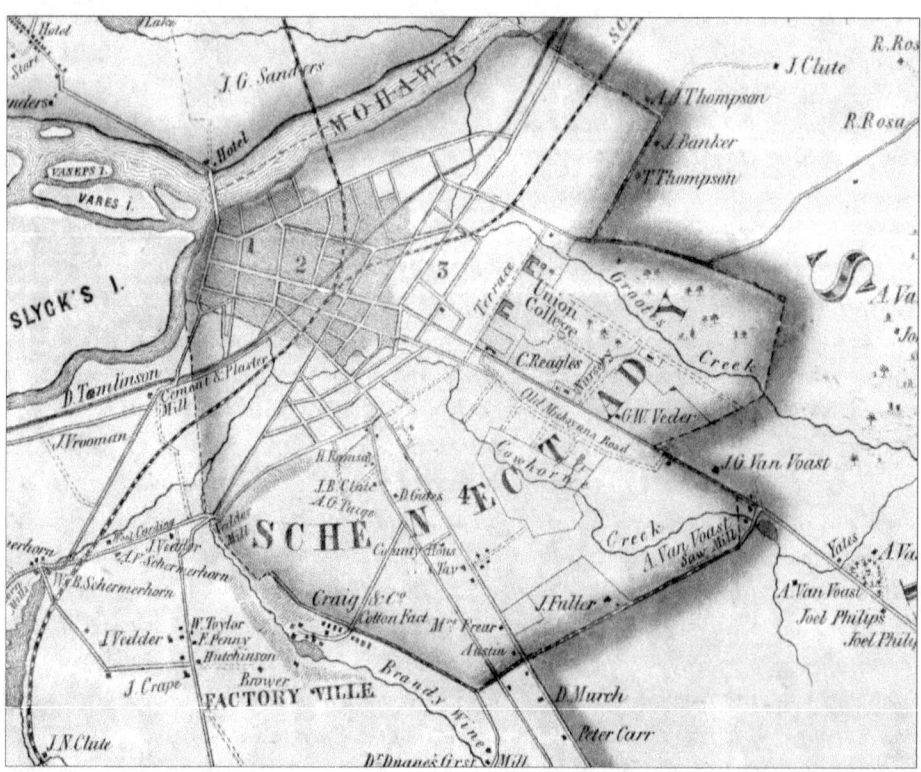

The 1856 Fagan Atlas Map shows the original boundaries of the Schenectady Hospital Farm site and original dimensions of Vale Cemetery as proposed. Old Niskayuna Road is present day Eastern Avenue. The word Cowhorn encompasses the hospital site and it was this stream that was dammed up to form three lakes.

On December 6, 1854, Alderman Fuller made a motion that the

... committee on lands and buildings be and are hereby authorized and requested to employ some suitable person to make a proper map and survey the Cemetery Grounds, laying out the same into burying lots and walks and roads, after the most approved plan of landscape gardening adapted to Cemetery grounds, and that they submit the same to this board for their approval, as soon as practical.

In the meantime, on March 12, 1855 a petition was read by Alderman Chadsey for the Hebrew Society asking the council to grant them a burial place "in the Cemetery." It was referred to the committee on lands and buildings.

On March 19, 1856, Alderman William Van Vranken introduced a resolution that passed to let the Cemetery Farm for the ensuing year, upon such terms, as they shall deem most advantageous to the city. The city began advertising in the local newspaper that it had a farm for sale that it had purchased for a cemetery and that it would be sold as a whole or in parcels. The members of the city's Committee on Lands and Buildings were listed as contacts: William Van Vranken, Hiram Champion, and Walter McQueen. This appears to be the city's hospital farm.

On June 4, 1856, Alderman Van Vranken from the Committee on Lands and Buildings reported in favor of granting the Third Reformed Dutch Church one acre of ground for a burial place, to be laid out adjoining the grounds granted to the German Methodist Church, they paying the expenses of laying out, surveying and fencing the same. This is the same church that requested the plot back on September 6, 1854, but which was tabled.

On July 2, 1856 the council passed a resolution

That the committee on public lands be and are hereby directed to examining the Hospital farm, with a view to laying out the same into a public cemetery, and report at a future meeting of this board.

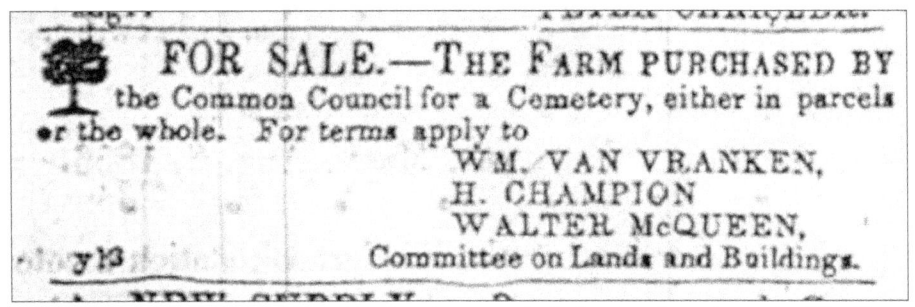

January 22, 1856 *Schenectady Cabinet* advertisement declaring lots for sale on the City Farm lot.

On December 3, 1856 Alderman Van Vranken presented the following report on the cemetery, which was accepted:

Your committee, to whom was assigned the duty of examining the Hospital Farm, as to its location and adaption for a Rural Cemetery, beg leave to submit the following report:

> After an examination of the grounds known as the City Hospital Farm your committee deem it the best location in this vicinity and in very way well adapted for the use and purposes of a Rural Cemetery, its location being near the city, and so accessible at all seasons of the year. With its never failing stream, and ravine adorned with trees and shrubbery, its level and undulating grounds, give it decidedly the preference of any grounds in our vicinity, In fact it seems to be the very spot nature designed for the repose of our dead. Nature has done much of the work in adorning and beautifying the grounds; a little assistance in the way of fencing and grading some of the principal avenues and walks, will make it very desirable as a place of burial, and ultimately be a source of revenue to the city, and meet the wants and wishes of a great

portion of our citizens. The grounds we deem sufficient size to meet the wants of our growing population for many years to come.

All of which is respectfully submitted

Wm. Van Vranken
P. Dorsh
Committee on lands and buildings.

It appears the farm was rented previously to the county for a period of years, as Councilman Van Vranken ordered on January 21, 1857 that the treasurer collect from the county the rent "due on the Hospital Farm, for the three years past."

The former City Hospital Farm of about 38 acres was finally selected to be the new cemetery. The physical attributes of the farm fit well into what was then the growing Rural Cemetery Movement: wooded ravines, flowing water via the Cowhorn Creek and a natural setting. The Vale, or Cowhorn Creek Ravine, to the north of the property, rises some 68 feet from the bottom of the ravine (272 to 340 feet above sea level), while the rest of the property is slightly undulating. It was also known as the best partridge feeding and homing grounds anywhere in the region.

Original entrance to cemetery from Nott Terrace about 1912.

On June 2, 1857 Mayor Benjamin V.S. Vedder was authorized to create a cemetery committee and was given authority to grade roads, walks and lots for the purpose of a public cemetery. This select committee was put in charge of designing the cemetery.

There was an access road into the hospital farm on Nott Terrace, called Entrance Avenue, but the committee petitioned the First Dutch Reformed Church for an easement from State Street to the burial lot, and petitioned Union College for an easement through some 17 acres known as the College Vale, a burial property for their faculty. This gave access to State Street and Nott Terrace (then called College Terrace), with Nott Terrace acting as the main entrance point.

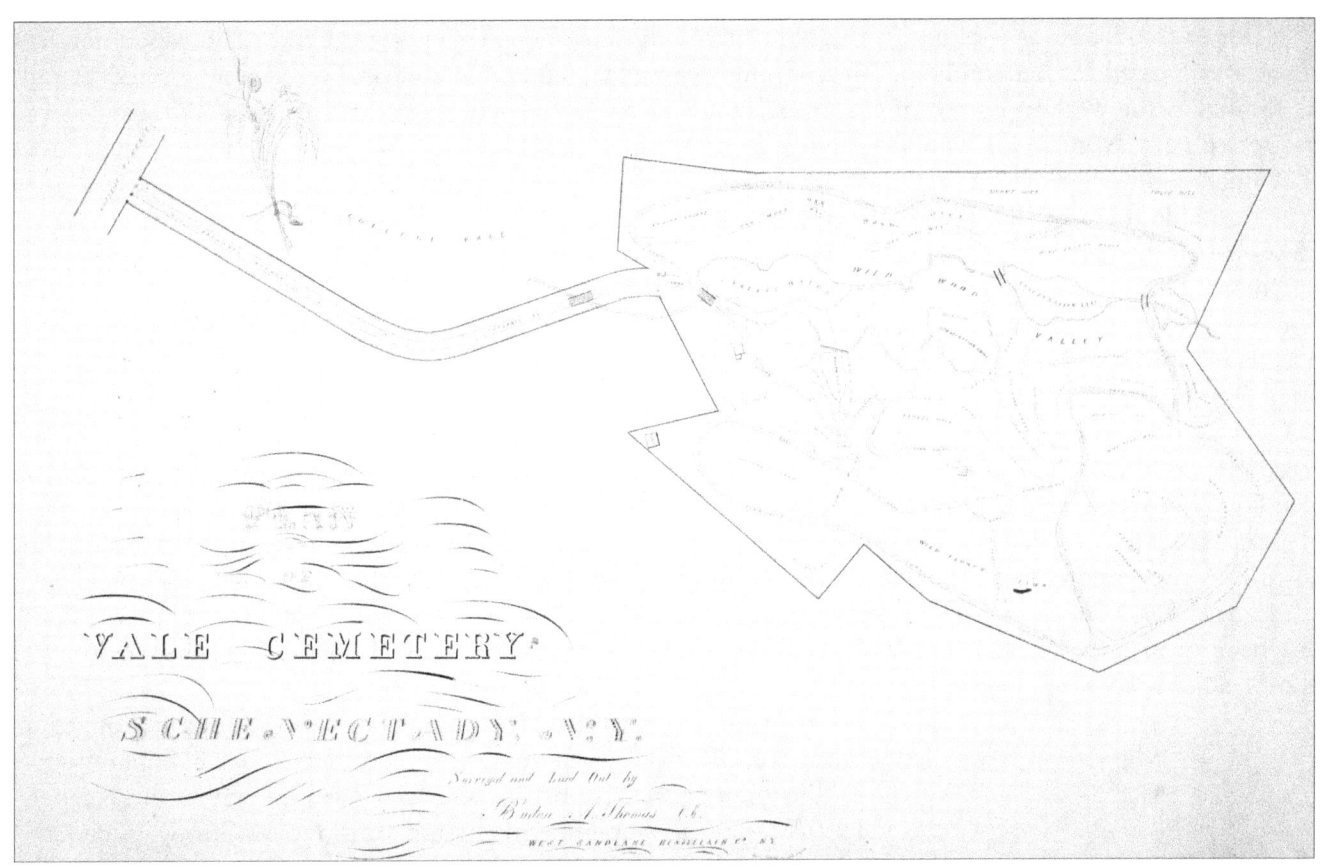

Official map of Vale Cemetery drawn by Burton Thomas in 1857. (Courtesy of the New York State Archives.)

The cemetery committee members authorized on June 16th were Arthur W. Hunter, Charles S. Vedder and John B. Marsh. They hired Burton Arnold Thomas (1809-1880), a well-known surveyor from West Sand Lake, New York, who laid out the Albany Rural Cemetery in 1844, and John Boyle to supervise the landscaping of the new cemetery. Thomas prepared a map plan of the cemetery, which served as the blueprint. Thomas identified and named most of the features and roads and designed a one-way scenic tour route around the cemetery. Three ponds were created by damming up parts of Cowhorn Creek: the larger pond, Valley Water, furthest west, followed by Consecration Lake and Lake Schenda to the east.

Thomas was commissioned by the city on June 21, 1857, and work began on June 24th. During the following months, many of the city residents visited to see the work in progress.

The property was divided into "lawns," "hills," "dells," "groves," "ridges" and "gardens," with a system of roads, trails and paths or walkways.

The hills included Cottage Hill, Bower Hill, Oak Wood Hill, Laurel Hill, Cypress Hill, Landscape Hill, Roseland Hill and Tulip Hill; the lawns included Primrose Lawn, Wild Flower Lawn, Wild Rose Lawn, Violet Lawn, Crescent Lawn and Sunny Side Lawn; the dells included Sylvan Dell and Green Wood Dell; the ridges included Pine Forest Ridge; the groves included Consecration Grove; and the glens included Wild Wood Glen.

Streets and paths included Entrance Avenue, Oak Wood Way, Ravine Walk, Garden Walk, Collage Hill Avenue, Meadow Avenue, Bower Hill Way, Magnolia Path, Sylvan Dell Walk, Wild Flower Avenue, Hearse Way, Green Wood Avenue, Evergreen Walk, Dell Wood Avenue, Tour Cross Way, Crescent Way, Linden Way, Elm Wood Way and Wild Rose Way. Many of these still exist, while some have fallen into disuse.

A Mount Hope was named near the northern edge of the cemetery, while Indian Mound was located southeast of Cypress Hill. It is not known if this was an actual Native American burial mound, or simply named for one. Native American burial mounds were known to exist in the Capital District region and many in New York State are attributed to the "Mound Builders," a Native American culture that flourished along rivers in the northeastern and mid-western United States from 200 B.C.E. to 500 C.E. The naming of this location as Indian Mound is peculiar, as it has no connection to any of the other names, and if one existed, it was leveled.

A porter's cottage was located on the Nott Street entrance near Valley Water Lake. The superintendent's cottage was located further south and up from the vale ravine, where the crematorium is now located. A stable was located in the western corner of the property not far from the superintendent's cottage. A receiving vault was located near Cypress Hill, with an entrance path called Hearse Way.

A small pond called Sylvan Water was located south of Valley Water and was connected to a spring.

A driveable tour through the cemetery was drawn on the map in hatches and labeled "Tour." It took the visitor around the perimeter of the cemetery, and near the spring and pond near Bower Hill.

Union College burial grounds were also located on the map.

On August 4, 1857, a 66-foot corridor (one chain wide) was created, and the gate was initially erected where the cemetery property began, a quarter mile from Nott Terrace. This entrance way was called appropriately "Entrance Avenue."

Over 1,000 trees were planted on the property.

Lots were ready for sale on September 1, 1857. On September 25th the Common Council named the new cemetery "Vale Cemetery." By 1866, it was also known as "Valley Cemetery."

Vale Cemetery was dedicated on October 21st, in a ceremony under weather conditions that were windy and cold. A procession of about 3,000 people began at 10 a.m., led by the local Schenectady cornet band, along with eight extras from the Cook's Band of Albany, and followed by the Common Council, clergy, large delegations from St. George's Lodge and Mohawk Royal Arch Chapter of Freemasons, and three lodges of the Odd Fellows, all dressed in full regalia.

Rev. Julius H. Seelye was a member of the 44th Congress, from 1875–1877.

A seated stage was furnished for members of the Common Council and clergy, along with: Burton A. Thomas, Surveyor; Peter Dorsch, Superintendent of the Work; John Doyle, Landscape Gardner (also known as the Keeper of the Vale); J.W. Greene, Superintendent; and Anthony M. Strong, Secretary of Albany Rural Cemetery.

An opening prayer was delivered by Rev. Elbert Slingerlands of Scotia, followed by singing of the invocation hymn by the combined choirs of the city and led by Mrs. S.B. Marsh. The hymn was written by Charles S. Vedder. Scripture from the Old Testament, Gen. 3:8-19, was read by Rev. Dr. Jonathan Backus, and from the New Testament, 1 Cor. 15, by the Rev. Montgomery Goodale of Amsterdam. The choirs sang the hymn "I Would Not Live Alway," and a poem written by Mrs. M.C. Myers was read. The address was delivered by Rev. Julius H. Seelye, pastor of the First Dutch Reformed Church (1853-1858). The consecration Prayer was given by Union College's Dr. Nott. A benediction was given by Rev. Dr. Hickok.

The first burial took place on November 9, 1857, with the burial of four-year-old Noah Vibbard Van Vorst, son of G.H. and H. Van Vorst. The burial was overseen by Rev. William Payne of St. George's Episcopal Church, who remarked that the boy was "the first of a great multitude who through the coming years would rest in 'God's Acre.'"

The minutes of the Vale Cemetery Association reported the first burial:

The First Burial in Vale Cemetery took place on Monday, Nov. 9th, 1857. The little son of [Gardiner] B. Van Vorst, an early and warm friend of the cemetery, was the first occupant. On the following page will be found the account of this event, as it appeared in the Schenectady Evening Star, *of Nov. 10, 1857.*

The First Burial

The first burial in Vale Cemetery.— "The Vale" has at length an occupant. Monday witnessed the first funeral procession that ever wound through its quiet walks—the vanguard of a mighty army that shall hereafter break its solitudes. The first inhabitant of our beautiful City of the Dead—so soon to compete with our living city in the number of its inhabitants—has lain down forever in its sacred shades. Under our obituary head we record the death of the little son of Gardiner B. Van Vorst, of this city, aged four years. He was a bright, intelligent boy, and had been—with his parents—a frequent visitor to the new cemetery, and had manifested, for so young, an unusual interest its progress, expressing a preference for particular spots, and actually selecting one for his father to purchase. It was for his beloved boy that the first grave was opened in "The Vale." A very large concourse followed the body to the Cemetery, and as the solemn tones of the Burial Service of the Episcopal Church rose upon the air, after the procession had entered the grounds, the scene presented was most solemn and impressive.

The service was read by the Rev. Mr Payne, of St George's Church, who improved the occasion by an eloquent and beautiful allusion to the circumstances under which it took place. The remarks of Mr. Payne were so timely and appropriate, that we cannot refrain from giving his very words, as nearly as they can be recalled:

Friends and Brethren:-We stand around the first grave ever opened in this new and beautiful Cemetery. And most fittingly, in the ordering of Divine Providence, it is the grave of a child—one of those little innocents of whom the Savior hath said "of such is the Kingdom of God," and whose death, we are sure, is the prelude always to their eternal happiness. Here lies the body of Noah Vibbard Van Vorst, a very interesting and dearly beloved boy. His spirit has returned to God who gave it; but his dust has returned to the earth as it was, where it shall sleep till that morning when all they are in their graves, both small and great, shall awake at the sound of the Redeemer's voice. This little grave be of sad and touching interest not only to the bereaved parents, who doubtless will often bedew it with their tears, and to their sympathizing friends, of whom so many are present, and who will often visit again the resting place of a well-remembered lovely child; but also to our citizens generally, and to our children and children's children after us, who shall point to this little hillock as the beginning of what then will have become a thick planted field of the dead. We see before us the first fruits of a great harvest which Death, for years and centuries to come, will gather within these shades; and the first fruits, too. We trust, of a more joyful harvest, which the Victor of the Grave shall garner out of these valleys and hill sides when He shall come to sift the wheat from the chaff. So, the solemnity of this day sanctifies this Vale more than ever in our eyes, giving to it, as it were, a new consecration; and now, if not before, we shall feel that it is a sacred place, that is holy ground, having begun to receive the precious dust of loved departed ones. Softly fall the turf over their heads, and dear to us be the earth which covers them. Let us garnish their sepulchers; let us tread lightly amid their ashes, and let us learn to think recently, as well as affectionately, of the ground where we may shortly lie.

And may the grace of Lord, Jesus Christ, and the love of God, and the fellowship of the Holy Ghost be with us evermore. Amen.

Four-year-old Noah Vibbard Van Vorst became the first resident of Vale on November 9, 1857.

In fact the first five burials were all under the age of 20. Besides Noah Van Vorst, Francis Louisa Consaul, six months old, died a few weeks later on November 27, 1857. The other three were reburials: John Consaul, aged two years, who died on October 7, 1857; Ann Eliza Reagles, who died on July 20, 1854; and George Reagles, just twenty-one days old, and who died on July 25, 1854.

VALE CEMETERY.

NAME OF DECEASED.	PLACE OF BIRTH.	LATE RESIDENCE.	AGE OF DECEASED.	DATE OF DECEASE.	Married or Unmarried
Noah V Van Vorst	Schenectady	Schenectady	4 years & 9 days	Nov 8th 1857	
John Consaul	Schenectady	Schenectady	2 - 8 mos & 30 days	Oct 7 1857	
Francis Louisa Consaul	Schenectady	Schenectady	6 mo. 21 days	Nov 27 1857	
Ann Eliza Reagles	Schenectady	Schenectady	19 yr. 9 mo.	July 20 1854	Married
George Reagles	Schenectady	Schenectady	21 days	July 25 1854	
Alma Beckly	Ballston Saratoga Co NY	Schenectady	56 ys. 1 mo. 8 days	April 23 1858	Married
Arthur W Tichenor	Schenectady	Schenectady	8 ys. 2 mos. 5 days	April 12 1858	
Jennie L Smits	Schenectady	Schenectady	3 ys. 4 mos. 4 days	March 19 1858	
Alida Onderkirk	Schenectady	Schenectady	21 days	August 5 1854	
Ida M Onderkirk	Schenectady	Schenectady	1 yr. 11 mos	December 7 1857	
Charles E Onderkirk	Schenectady	Schenectady	6 mos	December 11 1857	
Charles W Barker	Schenectady	Schenectady	2 ys. 6 mos	November 14 1857	
Betsey Wessels Moore	Schenectady	Schenectady	65 ys	November 21 1857	Married
Madaline Hulett	Schenectady	Schenectady	9 ys. 4 mo. 2 days	November 4 1857	
Herbert Seely Hulett	Schenectady	Schenectady	3 yds. 3 mos. 6 days	December 3 1857	
George A Collamer	Plattsburgh NY	New York	1 yr. 1 mo. 29 days	July 5 1854	
Charles N Collamer	Terre Haute Ia	Terre Haute Ia	1 yr. 5 days	July 28 1857	
John Phillip Morgan	Schenectady	New York	3 ys. 5 mos	August 12 1857	
Charles Morgan	Schenectady	New York	2 ys. 1 mo	April 7 1858	
Jane Hawthorn	Ireland	Schenectady	70 ys	June 14 1858	Unmarried
Catharine G Clement	Schenectady	New York	47 ys. 4 mos. 2 days	June 29 1858	Married

The first five burials at Vale were under the age of 20.

On January 5, 1858 the city's cemetery committee reported that they purchased a fence around the grounds and a dam was built across the Cowhorn Creek to create a large ornamental lake. It was soon determined by the city that they could not afford to own a public cemetery and decided a private organization should take charge of operating the cemetery. According to Vale's board minutes,

> Opposition to it began to be developed on the ground of the legal right of the Common Council to expend the amount necessary to improve the Cemetery grounds, and from the year that it would increase the taxes, and become a source of taxation in the future to the city.

Postcard view of Valley Lake in 1913.

In January 1858, the city's cemetery committee published the following report:

Report

In entering upon the duty to which they were appointed by the Common Council, the committee were fully aware of the delicacy and difficulty of the task which they assumed, yet feeling, in common with the whole community, the necessity of a public cemetery, and believing that the city had within its own boundaries, and in its own possession, grounds singularly well adapted for Cemetery purposes, and cheered by the unanimity of the Board and throughout the community upon the subject, they entered upon the duty with alacrity. The Committee have endeavored heretofore, by every frequent reports, to make public their progress as far as possible, and thus to gratify that public interest so natural and so just with regard to such an undertaking.

The chief point of difficulty which the committee anticipated in the beginning, was the fact that, although the Common Council had power to give title to lots sold, yet had not power to give a Cemetery title, without organizing the Cemetery under the General Cemetery Law, or procuring a special act of the Legislature for that purpose, and that, until this was done, the full price of the lots sold could not be reasonable demanded. This would for a time necessarily embarrass the committee for the funds necessary to carry on the work. As this embarrassment could only be a temporary one, however, and as the demand for progress of the undertaking, and for the preparation and sale of lots was so urgent, the committee did not feel at liberty—as they certainly did not desire—to disappoint public expectation by delaying the work in the least. The anticipated embarrassment of the committee in the respect mentioned, has been to some extend realized, more from the grounds it has given for misrepresentation, however, than from any other cause. Through the cordial cooperation of all city authorities, of the purchases of lots, and of the citizens generally, every other difficulty has been obviated.

As the committee have heretofore reported, they were fortunate in securing the services of Burton A. Thomas, of Sand Lake, as surveyor of the work; Mr. Peter Dorsch, as overseer of the actual labor, and with the competent assistants employed under their direction, the work proceeded with a rapidity that excited general surprise. As it progressed the Cemetery was visited by crowds daily, and if the committee had so wished, it would have been doing violence to manifest public sentiment to check its rapid progress.

The committee take no credit to themselves in saying that the work could not have been more thoroughly, beautifully and economically performed that it was under the direction of the gentlemen above mentioned. The fact that when the season of work closed the Cemetery was so far completed that lots were sold sufficient to cover the entire expense of the labor performed, is a sufficient commentary upon the diligence and faithfulness of the workmen to whom it was entrusted.

Soon after the commencement of labor at the Hospital Farm, the difficulty of securing a convenient and becoming entrance to the grounds was a matter of much anxiety to the Committee. Their anxiety was speedily and agreeably relieved by the gift from Rev. Dr. Nott of an avenue sixty-six feet in width, through Vale—an act of generosity characteristic in the giver, and for which it remains yet for the city to make suitable acknowledgement. By this avenue, the value of the Cemetery was increased many fold, and though the completion of it through to connect with the Cemetery farm was an expense which the committee had not before contemplated, yet they had no hesitation in believing that such an increased outlay would be many times returned by the greatly augmented value thus given to the Cemetery.

The committee have received many offers to sell the Cemetery to private individuals, at a price very much in advance of the estimated value of the grounds before their adaptation to Cemetery purposes was understood. They have not listened to nor reported these offers, believing that the sale of the property would neither be for the benefit of the city, nor the Cemetery itself. The sale of lots already has indicated how large a pecuniary return may be received by the city in retaining and prudently managing the enterprise. And great as has been the rapidity with which the lots have been disposed of, the committee feel confident that nothing comparatively has been done in that direction, compared with what will be done during the coming spring and summer. There are now as large a number of applications for lots as there have been at any time, and if the committee should publish the names of the applicants—as some of them have requested—for lots in the spring, the list would present a record as gratifying as it would be indicative of the future prosperity of Vale Cemetery.

The heaviest expenses that will ever be required upon the Cemetery have been already incurred. The two most important items- a suitable fence surrounding the whole grounds, and a firm dam across the stream that runs through them, for the purpose of forming a large and ornamental lake—have been met at the beginning and when to these are added the fact that the heavy grades necessary have all been made, with one exception, and that still the amount of money pledged for lots is handsomely in advance of the expenditure, notwithstanding the shortness of the time given for the choice and purchase, owing to the lateness of the season, the committee cannot but feel that the city has reason for the sincerest satisfaction at the support which has been given to the project.

The expenses of the coming year must be much less than those of the past, while the proceeds will be more than double, with the additional advantage that the purchasers of lots may then receive at the beginning a full Cemetery title—one which can not be seized under execution, and which will be a possession forever, and the price of those lots will immediately be realized by the city.

The committee take occasion to say that they began their action with regard to the Cemetery under competent legal advice, have continued it with the same sanction, and are now supported by the highest legal authority.

With these remarks, which the committee have thought due to the public interest in the Cemetery, if not themselves, they beg leave to submit the following detailed report of their action. The amount of moneys reported as the proceeds of lots sold, is pledged as soon as the deeds are given—a portion of it only has actually been paid—the committee not claiming the full amount due until they were able to put the purchasers of lots in full possession of Cemetery lots. The sales, however, are conclusive—the names given as a pledge of their reliability:

C. Vibbard	12-1/2 Lots,	$625.00
James R. Craig	9-1/2 "	475.00
J.Y & G. Y. Van Debogart	6 "	400.00
C. Reagles,	6 "	300.00
C.S. Vedder,	10	500.00
A.A. Vedder,	5-1/2	275.00
Dr A.M. Veeder,	7-1/2	375.00
Peter Dorsch,	4	200.00
Andrew Frame	3	150.00
Mrs. H. H. Yates,	3	150.00
Van Vorst & Benson,	2	100.00
A. W. Hunter,	2-1/2	100.00
J. Sedgwick,	2-1/2	125.00
E.O. Jenkins,	1	50.00
Mordecai Myers,	1	50.00
John B. Marsh,	1-1/2	75.00
J. Magoffin,	1	50.00
Marvin Strong,	1-1/2	75.00
A. Doty,	2	100.00
James E. Van Horne,	3	60.00
Nathaniel Drullard,	3	60.00
Isaac Reagles,	3	60.00
D.W. Consaul, Glen and Blackburn,	3	60.00
	93	$4315.00
Hospital Building,		48.00
Total Sales,		$4363.00
Amount received from City Treasurer,		1685.00
Amount received from lots,		406.25
Total receipts		$2091.25
Amount dispersed and audited by Common Council,		1945.75

for Labor in full to December 1st, Consecration expenses,	62.50	
Incidental expenses	29.98	
Total disbursements,		$2038.22
Fencing audited by Common Council,		1028.51
Amount Due not audited:		
Vedder & Co., for lumber,	163.19	
J.O. & J. Horsfall, for lumber,	180.00	
C. Reagles & Son,	210.12	
Burton A. Thomas,	175.00	
Peter Dorsch,	193.00	
John Hilts	127.28	
H. Eggleston	24.00	
H.S. Edwards,	35.54	
F. Mahew,	3.75	
D.C. Gage,	4.00	
Bill of labor in December,	50.25	
		1166.13
Total expenses,		$4232.87

Your committee have endeavored to obtain the bills for all expenses incurred by them in the work upon the Cemetery, and believe every item is included in the bills offered this evening by the committee on accounts. The bill of Thomas, the surveyor, not yet having been received, the exact amount is not yet known. It will, however, vary but little from the figures as above.

The Committee call attention to the fact as shown by the above that the Cemetery has paid its own expenses for the first year—a fact unprecedented, they believe, in the history of cemeteries.

All of which is respectfully submitted.
Signed,

> *A.W. Hunter,*
> *C.S. Vedder,*
> *John B. Marsh,*

The difficulty referred to as the matter of giving cemetery title to the lots, was sought to be obviated by a Special Session of the Legislature. This, however, met with much opposition, and to relieve the matter of all embarrassment, the lot owners whose names are mentioned in the above Report resolved to organize themselves into a Cemetery Association, under the General Cemetery Law, and purchase the ground from the Common Council. The organization was approved on Friday February 26, 1858, under the name of "Vale Cemetery," and the following Directors were chosen, and drew for the terms mentioned.

For one year
John B. Marsh
Dr. Alex M. Vedder
Edward McCamus

For two years
Chauncey Vibbard
Jos. Y. Vandebogart
Peter Dorsch

For three years
James E. Van Howe
Charles S. Veeder
Arthur W. Hunter

James E. Van Howe was chosen President, Joseph Y. Vandebogart, Vice President, Dr. Alex M. Veeder, Treasurer, and Edward McCamus Secretary.

On the 2d day of March following, a proposition was made to the Common Council for the purchase of the Cemetery grounds with the improvements. The offer was to give to the Common Council $5000 for the Cemetery as then improved, and pay any unsettled demands in the cemetery. The offer was not accepted by the Common Council, but a resolution was adopted authorizing the Cemetery Committee to sell the grounds for $800, over and above all expenses and liabilities on account of them, reserving to the city a sufficient space for the burial of the Poor, the Association deducting from such expenses and liabilities the amount of monies received on amount of sales.

The Association acceded to these terms, and Vale Cemetery passed into the hands of "Vale Cemetery Association," by whom the work of improvement has been rapidly advanced, and the sweep of the project placed beyond a [???].

The minutes also has the following somewhat conflicted information regarding the formation of the cemetery association:

Schenectady Feb. 25 1858
On the above date the persons below named met for the purpose of forming themselves into a Cemetery Association subject to "An Act for the incorporation of Rural Cemetery Associations.

Msz Chauncy Vibbard	*Giles Y. Van De Bogart*
James E. Van Horne	*Peter Dorsch*
John Frame	*Andrew Frame*
Joseph Y. Van De Bogert	*Christopher Reagles*
Edward McCamus	*John B. Marsh*
A.W. Hunter	*Y.B. Van Vorst*
Charles S. Veeder	*Alex M. Veeder*

The meeting then arranged by appointing Chauncy Vibbard chairman and Giles Y. Van De Bogart Secretary, by the vote of all said persons. By a unanimous vote of the meeting it was agreed that the corporate name of the cemetery shall be "Vale Cemetery" and that nine (9) shall be the number of Trustees to manage the concerns of the association.

The meeting then proceeded to elect nine Trustees by ballot and the following persons received the unanimous vote:

James E. Van Horne	*Chauncy Vibbard*
Alex M. Veeder	*Joseph Y. Van De Bogert*
Edward McCamus	*A.W. Hunter*
John B. Marsh	*Charles S. Veeder*
Peter Dorsch	

The chairman and Secretary then proceed to divide the Trustees by lot, into three classes. Those of the first class were <u>Alexander M. Veeder</u>, <u>Edward McCamus</u>, and <u>John B Marsh</u> and to hold their office for one year from the first Monday in March 1858.

Those in the second class were <u>Chauncy Vibbard</u> <u>Joseph Y. Van Bogert</u> and <u>Peter Dorsch</u>, and to hold their office for two years from the first Monday in March 1858.

This in the third class were <u>A.W. Hunter</u>, <u>James E. Van Horne</u> and <u>Charles S. Veeder</u>, and to hold their office for three years from the first Monday in March 1858.

The meeting further agreed that the annual meeting for the election of Trustees shall be held on the <u>first Monday in March in each year hereafter</u>. <u>All of which proceedings</u>, of said meeting, held on the day first above stated. At the City of Schenectady in the State of New York by the persons above named, residents of the city, and as above set forth. And hereby certified to the undersigned Chairman and secretary thereof in presence of Section of 2 of the act above mentioned.

Dated Schenectady February 27th AD 1858.

Giles Y. Van DeBogert
Secretary

C. Vibbard
Chairman

There were conditions set upon the sale and that included a plot set aside for burial of the poor—known as Potter's Field. The first board meeting was held on February 27, 1858 at the bookstore of Giles Y. Van Debogart at 89 State Street. They passed a resolution authorizing the association to offer the city $5,000.00 for the purchase of the cemetery. The city rejected that offer since they wanted $800.00 over what the city initially had spent to build the cemetery which totaled $4,643.61. The final sale price of $5,445.61 was accepted by the cemetery association. The association received a credit of $454.25 from lots that were sold but not used by the city. After one year in operation the association made $4,821.39 from sale of burial lots.

The success of the cemetery made it necessary to expand the acreage, and in 1863 two tracts were purchased from Union College near the Nott Terrace entrance. More land was added from property Union College owned along the Cowhorn Creek, including the 3.5-acre Union College Burial Grounds on the northwest part of the grounds, and land from Jonathan Levi. The road and 17 acres raised the total acreage of the cemetery to 58 acres. The entryway from Nott Terrace was modified to run totally on the south side of Cowhorn Creek, a new lake was formed west of Valley Lake, fences removed, an old power house renovated to be a temporary receiving vault and all incorporated into the larger cemetery plan. Prices for lots were agreed upon with various grades costing $40.00, to as low as $16.00 per lot. Ironically, it was decided that no one could bring in refreshments, nor bring dogs into the grounds. Children had to be accompanied by parents. No "improper persons" were allowed. Horses had to be fastened and carriages could not move faster than a walk. In addition, no firearms were allowed and no smoking on the grounds. John Doyle was hired as keeper of the cemetery for an annual salary of $410.00, payable monthly "during good behavior." He lived in the "Keeper's house" rent free. Doyle did not last long and was fired in January 1859 for neglect of duty. It appears he was hired right back. He was fired again in August 1864 for being drunk and neglect of duty. William Carl then replaced Doyle.

In 1862, the cemetery association attempted to have the German Methodist, German Reformed Dutch and Universalist societies' cemeteries on its southern boundaries transferred to their control, as they had been originally part of the city farm. The Universalists agreed in 1863, but both German congregations declined the offer for purchase.

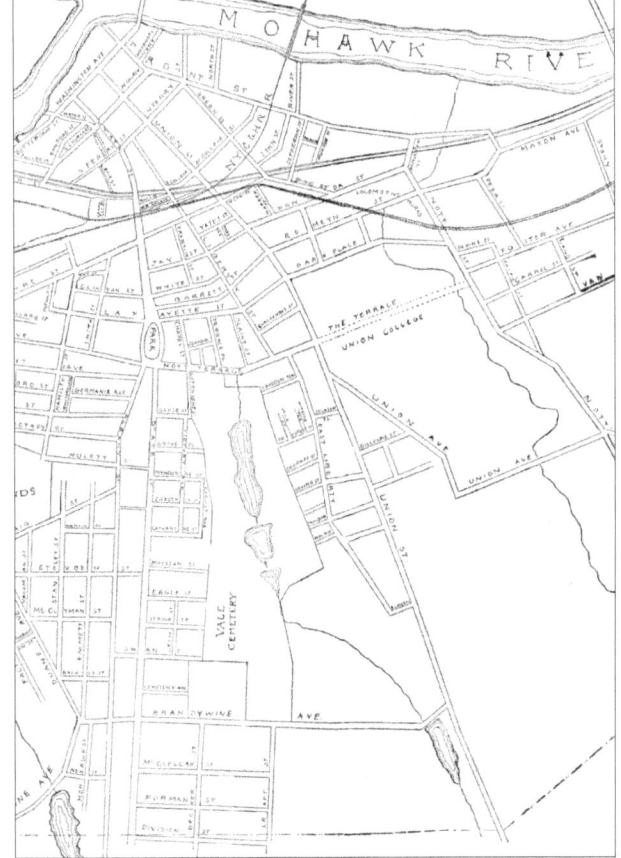

An 1899 city map shows Vale's three man-made lakes.

The 1875 Bailey & Company Map of Schenectady shows one entrance to Vale from the corner of Eastern Liberty Street (now Eastern Avenue) and Nott Terrace along with the Nott Terrace first entrance. Upper State Street was then East Avenue. The State Street entrance is not on the map. The cemetery lakes are shown.

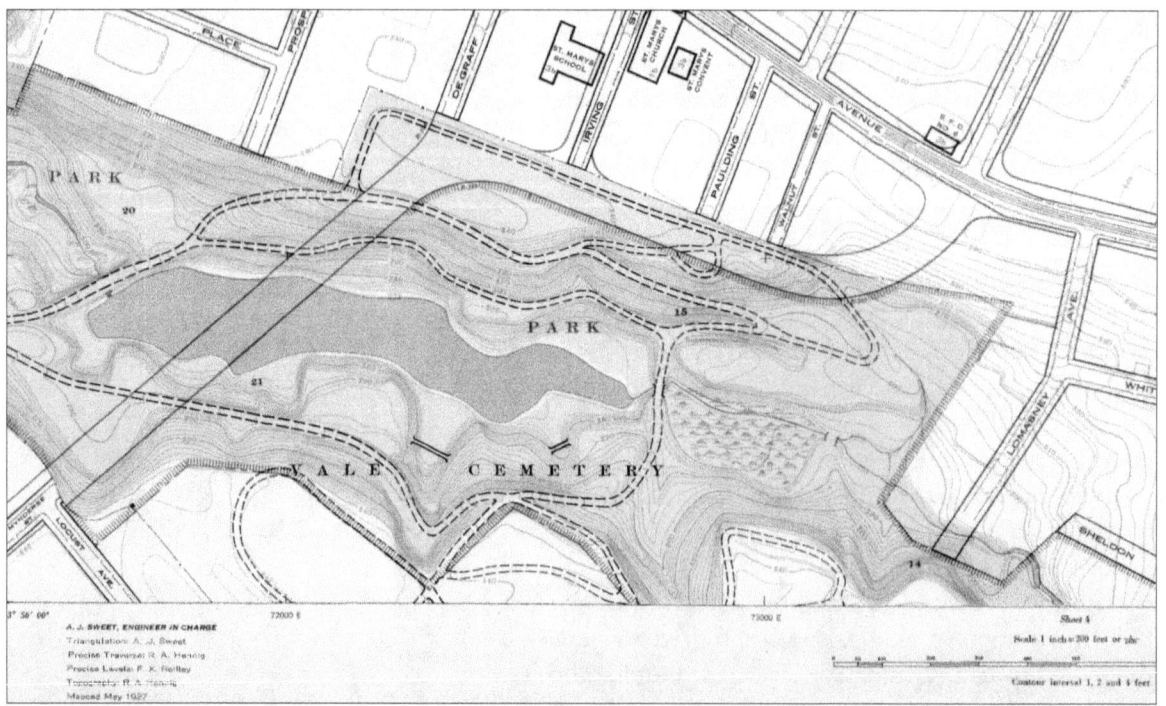

Topographic view of Vale lakes in 1927 showing location of bridges and road system. The eastern-most lake had already disappeared.

The Development of Vale Cemetery

In 1863, Union College agreed to sell 17 acres at $200.00 an acre, with additional reservations and conditions.

In 1867, land off State Street was purchased from the Dutch Reformed Church, and the Estate of Barent Mynderse in 1869, bringing the total to 100 acres for cemetery use. The sale by the Dutch Church had a stipulation that the old burial grounds in the Stockade had to be reinterred on the property. An entrance via DeGraff Street was also added.

More acreage was added over the years that brought the total up to 300 acres. In 1884 Section M (number 1-3) was added to the original rural cemetery of Sections A to X. It was influenced by the "Lawn Park" landscape style, developed by the renowned Prussian landscape architect Adolph Strauch (1822-1883), who did Spring Grove Cemetery (Cincinnati) and Graceland Cemetery (Chicago). The Lawn Park movement was a result of the growing feeling that the Rural Cemeteries were too overdone, crowded and elitist, and had a high cost of maintenance. Strauch was ordered to remove much of his earlier design at Spring Grove, such as raised mounds, ornate gates and gardens, and established this new design that dominates park design today. In 1886, two iron bridges were purchased by the Westinghouse & Company, for a few dollars short of $1,000.00. A year later the cemetery committee was looking at getting control of the water connecting the cemetery pond and building reservoirs to hold back water during dry times. The area above the cemetery was known as "Dickey Baums Fly." It appears it was not successful.

The cemetery group also hired Albany architect Albert Fuller to design a new gateway at Nott Terrace in 1888. The iron work came from the famous Albany foundry James McKinny & Son. It was decided in September 1889 that a new gatekeeper's house should be built at the State Street entrance, and hired the Albany architectural firm of Ogden & Wright to design it. It was finished the following year. The old keeper's house was rented in 1897 to Alex Sherman who, in lieu of rent, would labor for the association when asked. To make additional money for the association, ice was sold from the pond during the winter.

An unidentified worker at the Caretaker's house.

Horse and carriage waiting beside the Caretaker's house on the State Street entrance in October 1899.

Entrance to Vale from State Street showing Caretaker's house and entrance before 1940.

Two views of the early State Street entrance before 1940.

An unidentified man in a carriage in 1930. It might be the Vale Superintendent.

An unidentified man in a carriage at Vale in 1930 (possibly Harry Arning, President of the Vale Cemetery Association).

In 1905 a new chapel and vault was built a few feet from the main entrance on Nott Terrace, replacing an earlier vault at that location. The $10,000.00 project was carried out by J.A. Bradshaw, who was the superintendent of Vale for some 30 years. It was built by Lew Jeffers. The chapel could hold about sixty persons seated, was heated and had electricity. The vault could hold 200 bodies. There was a small trolley car system to carry the caskets within the vault.

"New Chapel, Vale Cemetery, Schenectady, N.Y."

In the late 19th century an eastern section, AN-IN, was added that was an influence of the "City Beautiful" movement, and later the Memorial Park Plan (c. 1912-1949). This section was extensively planted with ornamentals (see Appendix 4 for listings). The Memorial Park was designed for cemeteries to be run as a business and for maintaining the park as an open expanse of green, with central place monuments and regulated grave markers. This began with Forest Lawn in California in 1917, designed by Dr. Hubert Eaton. His philosophy was to have "a great park, devoid of misshapen monuments and other customary signs of early death." It didn't become popular until after World War II.

Vale has all three major styles: Rural Cemetery, Lawn Park, and Memorial Park designs in the 300-acre cemetery.

In 1872-73 an earlier caretaker's house was built on the northwest part of the cemetery overlooking the lakes by John Willis, who was paid $800.00 for the task. The two-story house was later razed to make way for a new crematorium. Before it was torn down it appears that a floor plan was drawn and contents listed. The house can be seen on the 1882 Burleigh panorama of Schenectady (see following page). The current Superintendent's office was built in 1889-90.

In 1858 the city sold the cemetery to the Vale Cemetery Association for $5,445.61. A non-profit volunteer organization currently maintains the cemetery. In 1969, seven acres of the cemetery fronting Nott Terrace were sold. In 1973, the City of Schenectady purchased 37.5 acres of the "Vale" from the association for $300,000.00, for park purposes. It currently has swings and other accommodations for children.

Today, there are more than 33,000 graves in Vale's 100 acres, and there is still ample room for many more. Vale Cemetery is still a working cemetery and is managed by a group of dedicated volunteers.

The 1882 Burleigh Map shows the State Street entrance but much of the northern part of the cemetery is cut off from the map. The Caretakers house is shown located where the crematorium stands today. The Nott Terrace entrance shows a chapel at the entrance.

Enlargement of the original Caretaker's house now razed and replaced by the crematorium.

Above: Aerial view of Vale Cemetery showing entrance on Brandywine Avenue (far right). The Vale (Cowhorn Creek) can be seen as the dark band running from middle right to upper left. St John's Cemetery is the square. Below: Current layout of Vale Park and Vale Cemetery. It is no longer a "rural" cemetery, as the City of Schenectady expanded around it after the 1930s.

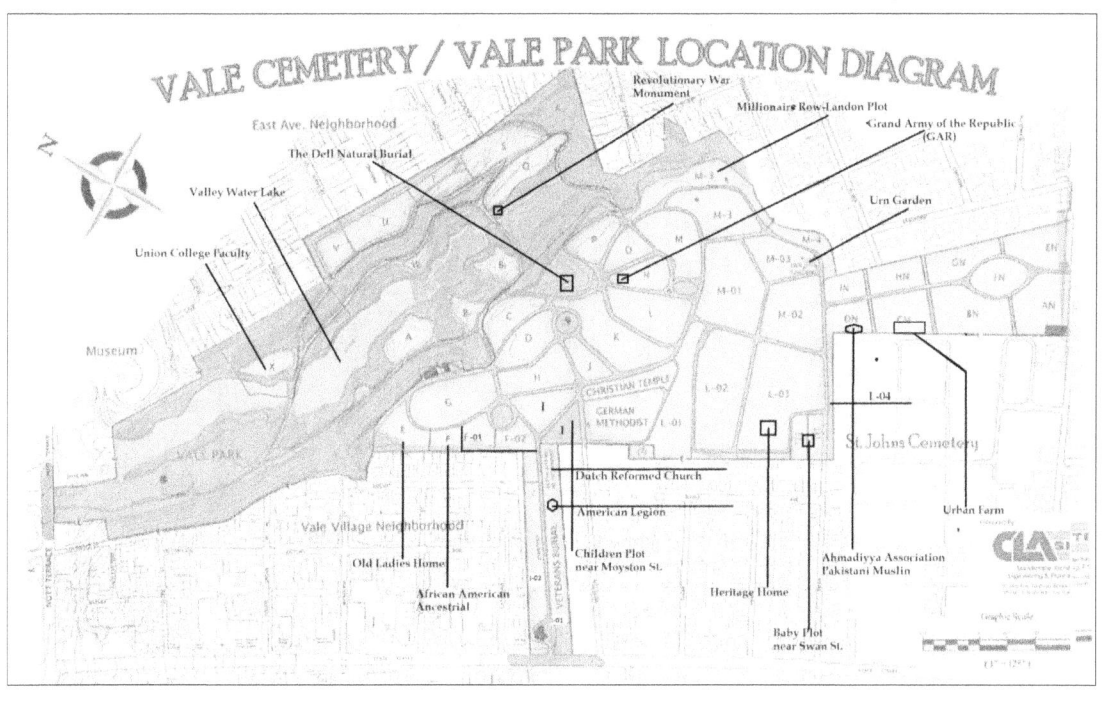

Special Areas in Vale Cemetery

The Vale

Cowhorn Creek, which originally began in the sandy pine barrens to the west, flows through Vale Cemetery, eventually finding its way to the Mohawk River. It is one of many such streams that drain the sandy pine barrens that sit between the Mohawk and Hudson Valleys. It is likely that it was in the area around the Vale that Arendt Van Curler, founder of Schenectady, first saw the beauty of the Mohawk Valley and wrote it was "the fairest land the eyes of man ever rested upon."

This valley of the Cowhorn Creek, with its abundance of native wildlife and flora, has been modified over the years with the building of the lakes, sewer lines and other human disturbance. However, it still retains much of its its natural setting, and is a great place to commune with nature, hike and take photographs. In 1973, 37.5 acres of the Vale on Nott Terrace were sold to the City of Schenectady as a park.

The Union College Plot

Known as the College Plot, one of the most unusual benefits of teaching at Union College is a free burial plot. Nestled among pines and oaks and overlooking Valley Water Lake, it was not the first choice of Union College. Urania, the wife of college president Eliphalet Nott, wanted the site to sit along the Hans Groot Kill east of the North College. President Nott decided on the Vale Cemetery location in 1863 when he sold the land totaling 17 acres to the cemetery association for $200 an acre, and reserved the 3.5-acre site for college use. There are currently over 200 plots and several notable figures who reside there.

Local historian Frank Taormina, a 1950 graduate of Union, compiled a list of the residents and they are listed in Appendix 3 with his permission.

Entrance to the Union College Plot.

World War Veterans

The American Legion purchased a plot in 1918 (called the American Legion Plot and later the Indigent Veterans Plot), which contains about 90 graves. This "Old GAR" plot is in Section O. On May 22, 1948, a burial plot for veterans of World War II was selected in Vale by members of the County Board of Supervisors veteran's committee and several veteran's organizations. It was selected between the State Street boundary and the World War I veterans plot, just to the right of the State Street entryway. It includes 10 lots, which will allow for about 120 graves. The GAR and Spanish War veteran's burial grounds are adjacent to the new plot. The WWII plot was to hold about 12 graves for the use of veterans that did not serve during wartime. At that time, about one-fourth of the space reserved, purchased by the county 30 years earlier principally for veterans of WWI, had already been used.

The World War Veterans Plot is located just south of the Dutch Reformed Church Plot.

Potter's Field

In 1858, when Vale was sold to the cemetery association, a section in the eastern part of the cemetery was set aside as a condition of the sale. There are 778 headstones, along with pieces of others, with dates that range from 1830 to 1942.

Each has a story not told. While most have the name and date of death, there are stones that only have "Unidentified Man/Woman" inscribed. Some were reclaimed when identified later. Periodically a newspaper story gives some glimpse of who they were.

For example, on April 17, 1911, it was reported that a woman who had been buried in Potter's Field was later identified by her husband. The woman, Mrs. Edward Clifford of St. Johnsville, drowned in the Mohawk River east of the city. She had disappeared the previous November and no traces of her were ever found. The description of the woman, and two rings and clothing matched the husband's description. Since the husband had no money, she was allowed to stay.

On June 6, 1932, an unidentified man about 60 years old was struck and killed on the Amsterdam road by a car driven by Roy Thompson of the Hotel Amsterdam, in Amsterdam, New York. The dead man was buried in Potter's Field.

On July 10, 1936, George Hayden, who had died in the county home at Glenridge, had been buried in Potter's Field. He contracted food poisoning while at the home, but was not diagnosed for several days. He had been working as a checker at the D&H railroad station, and was found along the roadside of the Schenectady-Saratoga highway. Without this knowledge, his wife had been searching for him for a month. He was exhumed, identified by his wife, and reburied at Vale.

On August 10, 1936, the body of a man killed a year prior from being struck by a New York Central train near Washout Road in Glenville was later identified as John F. Landers of Springfield, Massachusetts. He was identified by fingerprints and from a label on a necktie that had a Springfield haberdashery on it.

Ironically, while Potter's Field is for the indigent, in the front row lies the gravestones for a man named John Millions, who died February 10, 1934.

On June 28, 1941, it was reported that a person only known as H. Davis, who drowned in the Mohawk River on June 19, was buried in Potter's Field.

Perhaps the most celebrated resident in Potter's Field is Native American (Mohawk) James Cuff Swits, who has a profile of his face carved on his stone (see page 151).

There are more than 700 residents in Potter's Field.

One of several markers for unknown persons.

James Swits, a local Native American, was well-known to Schenectadians during the 19th century (see page 151).

African-American Burial Plot

Originally African-Americans were buried in a field along the east side of Veeder, between State and Hamilton streets. In September 1859, a discussion was held at the Vale Cemetery board meeting concerning the establishment of a "colored section" in the cemetery, with a price of $25 for each lot. This was in response to a petition submitted four days prior by members of that community. In October 1863, Lawyer Alonzo Paige of 42 Washington Avenue was sold a number of lots in the western section, just past the State Street entrance, to establish a new section for this purpose. In March 1864, bodies were removed from the Veeder Avenue cemetery and reinterred at Vale in this plot.

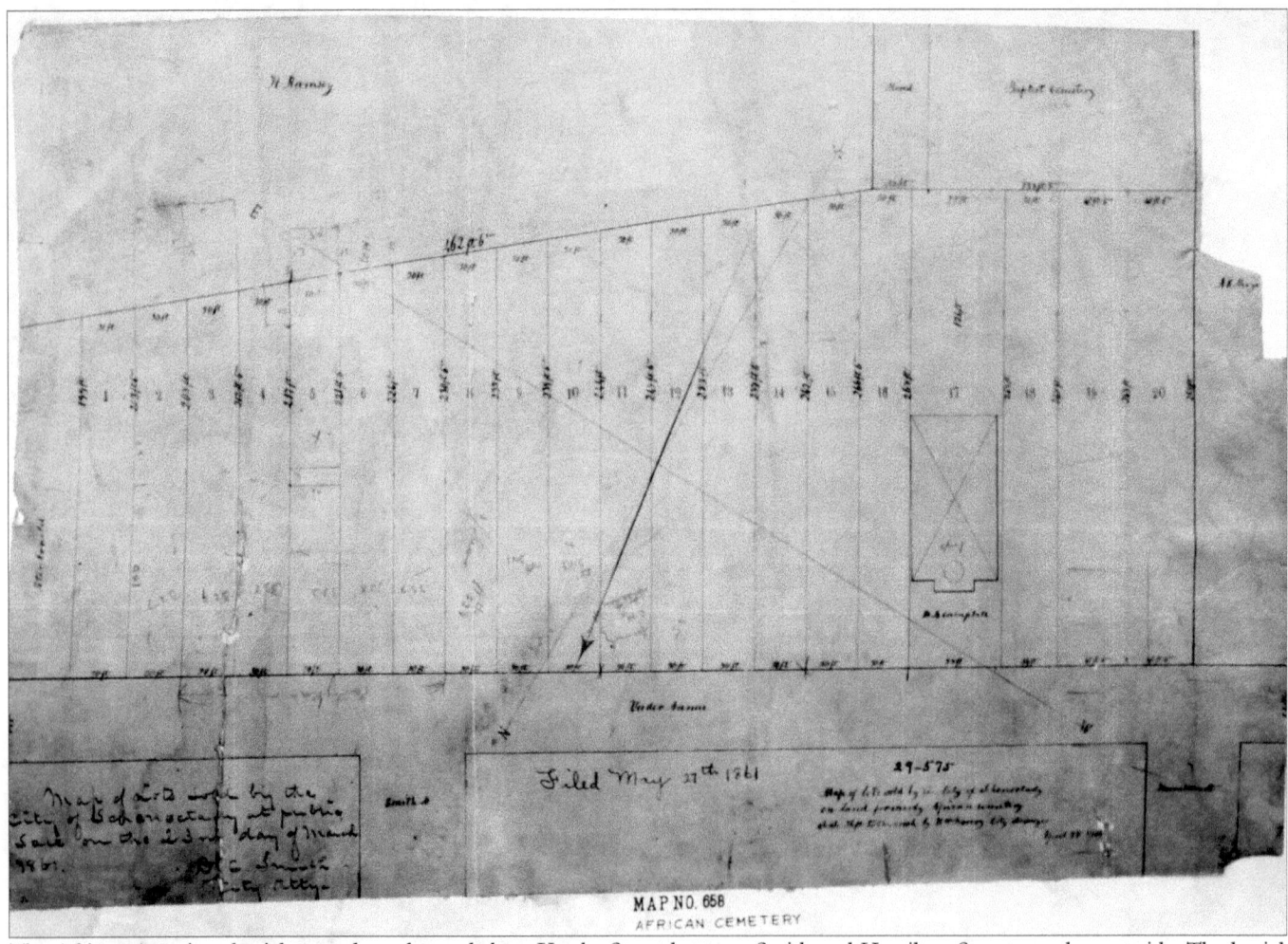

The African-American burial ground was located along Veeder Street between Smith and Hamilton Streets on the east side. The burial lots extended east and connected with the other city burial lots belonging to the Baptists and Catholics along Cemetery Lane. Summit Avenue did not extend north to Albany Street at this time. This map shows the African-American lots for sale on March 23, 1861. The bodies were removed in 1864 and residential homes were built on the lots. The road labeled on top is Cemetery Street.

The African-American Plot was originally on the east side of Veeder Avenue.

The Old Ladies Home Plot

A short distance to the right of the African-American Burial Plot is a small section (E to L-5) dedicated to the Old Ladies Home. Established in 1868 by an organization known as the Haven of Rest, the first home began as the Home of the Friendless on Green Street in Schenectady's Stockade area. In 1901 the name was changed to the Old Ladies Home, and a new building was built in 1905 on the old Troy-Schenectady Turnpike, now 1519 Union Street. A century after its founding, the name was changed to the Heritage Home for Women.

There are 19 residents of the home buried there. The first burial was Betsey Holdrich Smith in 1884, with the last being Caroline Campbell in 1917. As the home grew they added plots in Section L-3 in lots 165, 166, and 193. Fifteen women are buried there, the first being Hannah Southard in 1905, the last being Elsa C. Fahrenburg in 1978. A second monument was laid in this section on June 1, 2014 (see next page).

The Old Ladies Home Plot.

Second monument erected in the Old Ladies Home Plot on June 1, 2014.

Crematorium

In 1995 a crematorium was added to the offerings of the cemetery. In its first year, 58 cremations took place. The number jumped to 400 the following year. From 1995 to 2013, a total of 14,581 cremations took place. It has two retorts with a third to be added in the future.

The Crematorium replaced the original Gatekeeper's house.

German Plot

It would not be inaccurate to write that the German Lutheran section of Vale was the original beginning of Vale Cemetery. As previously written, on Dec 17, 1851, Alderman Potter introduced a resolution to grant a piece of land to the "German Church for a burial place, reported in favor of selling to petitioners one acre of ground from the hospital farm." It was the same year that city engineer Henry Ramsay prepared a map for possible cemetery use of the same area. The section is filled to capacity, and the small vault remains locked and not in use.

On September 4, 1852 the City of Schenectady sold to the German M.E. Church a plot of land with the following dimensions:

- 3 chains 86 links 255 ft South
- 2 Chains 4 links 162 ft East
- 5 Chains 7 links 334 ft North
- 2 Chain 26 links 150 ft West Moyston Street.

This acre of land was located east of Moyston Street. A vault was erected on the same side of the street at the terminus.

An additional plot of land was sold to the German church on January 7, 1897, when the Trustees of the First Baptist Church sold a nearby section of their property 80 feet front and rear, and 285 feet deep. In 1911 Vale Cemetery sold the roadway (Moyston Street) to the church.

The Funeral Car, a trolley equipped for bringing a deceased person to the cemetery, came up Albany Street and over to Moyston Street, stopping near the German Plot vault at the end of the street.

It was equipped with a large door in the front so that a casket could be moved inside. The funeral coaches were elaborately designed to maintain the air of a funeral and respect for the dead. Rather than leather seats, there were wicker chairs located around the catafalque in the center. Plush carpets covered the floors and windows were draped in black. After the casket was loaded into the car, the mourners took their place around the interior and the car moved slowly from its origins to the cemetery. The motorman dressed in black. Before the trolley, the casket would be delivered in a special hearse wagon by horse.

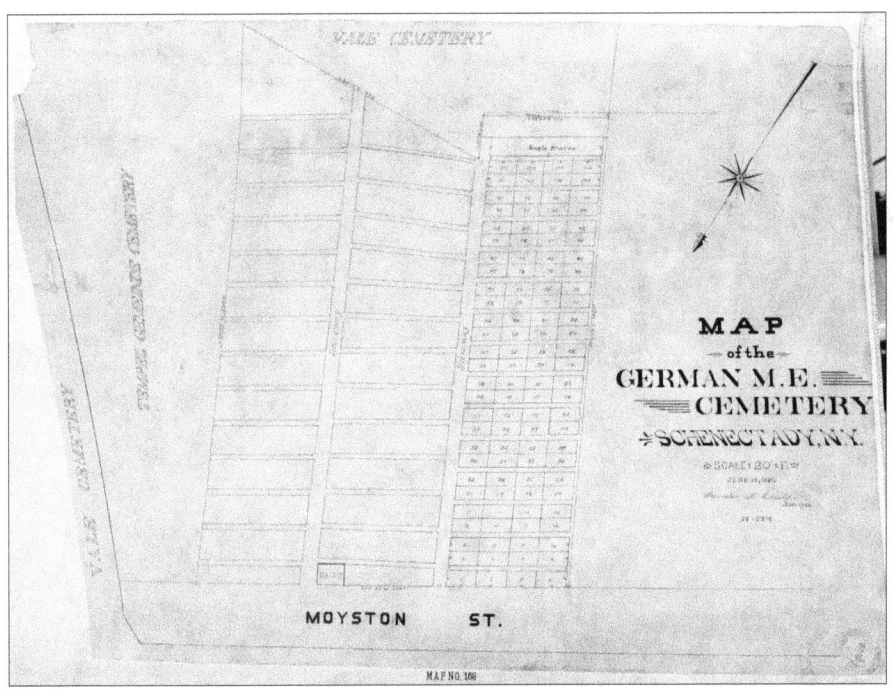

Map of the German M.E. Cemetery, dated June 15, 1897.

Temple Gemeinde Cemetery (Christian Temple Plot)

(German, *Tempelgesellschaft*) (also known as *Deutscher Tempel* or *Jerusalemsfreunde*)

This plot of cemetery land, laying adjacent to the German M.E. cemetery plot, belonged to "The Temple Gemeinde" Church. The church was located on College Street, and was a branch of the German Temple Society that was organized in Germany by Rev. Dr. Christoph Hoffman. Hoffman was a Lutheran clergyman. Gottlieb W. Hoffmann, the father of Christoph Hoffmann, had founded the separatist settlement of Korntal near Stuttgart. The German Temple movement grew out of the religious ferment in mid-19th century Württemberg.

The doctrine of the church stated that "The only source of revelation for the members of the Society is exclusively the Bible, without ecclesiastical traditions and human doctrines, as far as they are in contradiction to the will of God, as interpreted by the members of this Society."

The Schenectady congregation was organized in May 1854 by Rev. W. Wolf and incorporated in New York State as the Third Evangelical Protestant Reformed Dutch Church. They had both a church and a school. In 1854 Rev. W.F. Schwik took the leadership. In 1856 they purchased what was known as the old Lancaster School and converted it into a chapel. A school room was added in the rear and later used as an apartment for the Sexton and his family. They then built a larger church not far from the old one, toward Green Street, and was dedicated on September 1, 1867.

In 1867, the Rev. Schwik started the first German newspaper in Schenectady, *Die Reichs Posanne*, a religious, social and political semi-monthly, and published it for seven years until his health prevented him from continuing.

At the end of 1867, the congregation withdrew from the Classis of Schenectady and declared itself independent of the General Synod of the Reformed Dutch Church, though they retained their legal name. They later then decided to change their name to The Temple Gemeinde on Dec 25, 1884, with 200 members. They later became known as the Christian Temple.

The German Plot vault next to Moyston Street.

Methodist Plot

A small Methodist plot was located in the rear of the pastor's house at the end of Catherine Street, and later incorporated into the cemetery.

Baptist Plot

The Baptist Plot was placed at the end of the drive from the State Street entrance on the western corner. It may be the remains taken up from the old Baptist plot on Hamilton Hill.

The Green Plot

The latest addition to Vale Cemetery is the "The Dell," a new plot large enough for 200 burials, set aside for "natural" burials. Before the advent of embalming, expensive and elaborate caskets and funeral homes, saying goodbye was less complicated. The deceased was washed, dressed, and placed in a wooden box or other container and buried.

In recent years there has been a move to go back to the simpler ways, and Vale has become only the sixth cemetery in New York State to be accredited to offer this form of burial. Plans include fencing the area, the planting of weeping willows and flowering fruit trees, access for the handicapped and becoming a cooperative Audubon Bird Sanctuary. There are no insecticides or herbicides used on the Dell. Sheep and goats are allowed to graze and mow the plot.

The "Dell."

According to Vale,

People concerned about the environment have begun looking at "The American Way of Death." After death the body is embalmed using gallons of formaldehyde (a know carcinogen) and placed in a casket of exotic wood or metal. This is placed in a concrete vault and buried. A large carved granite or bronze marker is placed at the site. The area of the burial is scrupulously maintained by frequent mowing and applications of herbicide and fertilizer.

An environmentally friendly alternative is "green burial." There is no chemical embalming, but organic products may be used. Burial is in a biodegradable container of wood, wicker or cardboard. No concrete vault is used. The burial site may become a wildflower meadow, a bird-butterfly habitat. Only a small flat marker is placed there or the global positioning satellite coordinates are recorded.

Reinterred Green Street Cemetery (Dutch First Reformed Church)

Some would say it was the deplorable condition of this original cemetery on Green and Front streets that led to the movement to create Vale. As part of the deal to buy land from the church, Vale agreed to reinter the graves from the Dutch Church lot into the new Vale Cemetery in 1879.

The Dutch Reformed Church plot originally on Green Street and Front Street was removed to Vale in 1879.

Millionaires Row (Landon Plot)

In the section known as the "Millionaires Row" or Landon Plot, several wealthy people are buried, such as Levi Case, George Featherstonhaugh, Alexander Vedder McGee and others.

Bike Trail

The new trail that runs through Vale Park is part of a larger trail that connects Central Park, Vale Park and downtown Schenectady, where the trail intersects with the Mohawk-Hudson Bike Trail, which runs nearly 40 miles along the shores of the Hudson and Mohawk Rivers, from downtown Albany to Rotterdam. It is also frequently used by runners and walkers.

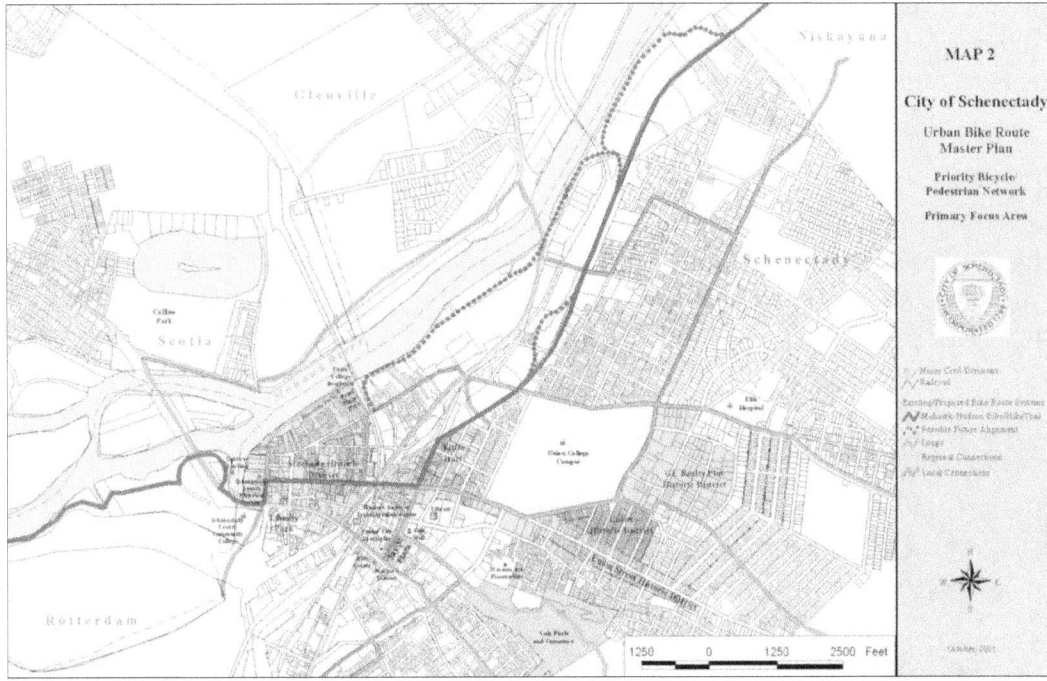

Map showing bike trail through Vale Cemetery. From the City of Schenectady Urban Bike Route Master Plan.

Nott Terrace entrance is now part of a county-wide bike trail through the park and cemetery.

Vale Urban Farm

An innovative urban farm is being tried in the newest section of the cemetery by Transition Schenectady, a group of people that have created local initiatives based on ideas by Transition US, a grassroots, non-profit organization that provides inspiration, encouragement, support, networking and training for Transition Initiatives across the United States. People, mostly from the Vale neighborhood, contribute eight hours per month of garden work in exchange for a percentage of what is grown. Each person who contributes volunteer work on the large plot is given a 10-foot by 10-foot plot. Produce from the garden, grown without pesticides and herbicides, is also donated to the Schenectady Day Nursery and City Mission's meal programs. Crops include tomatoes, collard greens, peppers, cabbage, radishes, lettuce, broccoli, arugula and spinach.

Vale Park

In 1973 the city purchased 37.5 acres of the "Vale" from the association for $300,000 for park purposes. It currently has swings and other accommodations for children. The first burial vault was located here when the cemetery opened in 1857.

Nott Street entrance to Vale Park. (Courtesy of Richard Vang.)

Ahmadiyya Muslim Community

The newest area of the cemetery is dedicated to the Pakistani Muslim group and is in the eastern section of the cemetery. There is currently one burial.

Wooden bridge near Valley Lake.

Valley Lake.

Appendix 1: 101 Notables in Vale Cemetery

This section contains biographical information on 101 notable residents of Vale Cemetery. They are given in alphabetical order, with the known birth and death dates, and their locations (if known). The plot locations are somewhat problematic, as the catalog is maintained on file cards and over the years different notation systems were used to record them. In addition, Union College uses a different notation index for their plot.

Ernst Frederick Werner Alexanderson

January 25, 1878 - May 14, 1975
Location: M1 #87 A

Ernst, who went by the name Alex, was born in Uppsala, Sweden, the son of a judge and professor of Greek. He graduated from the Royal Institute of Technology in Stockholm in 1900 and did post-graduate work at the Technical University in Berlin. He came to America in 1902. While in Germany he read books on AC current written by Charles Steinmetz; he wanted to work for Charles Steinmetz and moved to Schenectady to meet him. He worked for the C&C Electric Company as a draftsman before he found his job at General Electric in 1902. He is considered to be "the father of radio and television."

In 1906, on Christmas Eve, he played his experimental alternator and broadcast Christmas music, which could be heard by Navy ships and shore stations as far south as Arlington, Virginia. He even played the violin, making it the first AM radio broadcast in entertainment. The alternator in Varberg Sweden is still fired up each July 4th, Alexanderson Day, in his honor. It was placed on the UNSECSO World heritage list in 2004. His Alexanderson alternator was used between 1906 and the 1930s for long distance radio transmission.

During WWI he perfected a 200-kilowatt alternator that was installed at the transatlantic Marconi Company station in New Brunswick, New Jersey. Both President Woodrow Wilson and Franklin D. Roosevelt, then Assistant Secretary of the Navy, used it for transmitting messages to the war theaters in Europe.

On October 20, 1918, the first important practical test was conducted with the transmission of President Wilson's ultimatum to Germany that helped bring the war to a close. Wilson then asked G.E. to organize an American company to use the alternator, and the Radio Corporation of America (RCA) was created, with Alexanderson named as its chief engineer in 1919. He later went back to G.E. before he retired in 1948.

In 1923, Alexanderson was the first to use what we now call an "Amber Alert," when he recovered his 6-year-old son Verner from kidnappers near the Canadian border. He and his wife went on WGY radio and pleaded for his release, and a caretaker in a resort in northern New York

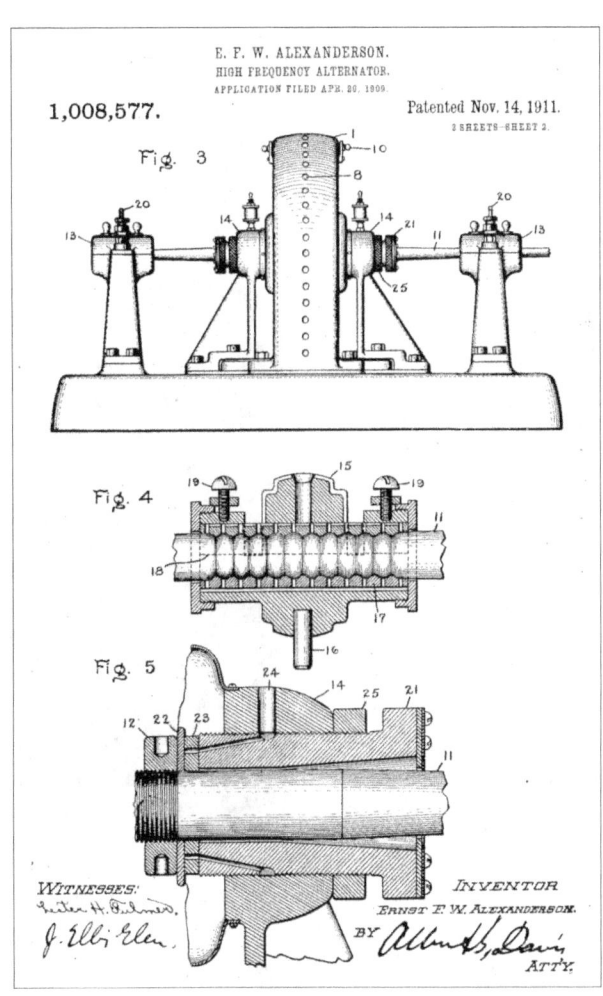

Patent drawing for Alexanderson's alternator. (Courtesy of Museum of Innovation and Science, Schenectady.)

recognized the two kidnappers by the description used on the radio. Spiritualists and mediums had told them they were being held in spite and for ransom by kind kidnappers.

In 1926 he sent the first fax transmission, a handwritten note from New York to his father in Sweden. Two years later he sent a fax around the world in two minutes.

He held 340 patents and was the most prolific inventor, only passed by Edison and Thompson, the founders of G.E.

Alex was ready to promote television as early as 1922, but G.E. managers told him to get radio off the ground first. As a pioneer in television, the first home reception of a TV program took place in his home at Adams Road in 1927, using high-frequency neon lamps and a perforated scanning disc. He gave the first public demonstration of television on January 13, 1928, and on September 11, the first broadcast of a professional television drama: "The Queen's Messenger." In 1930, at Proctors Theater in Schenectady, the theater orchestra was led by the conductors' image on a 7-foot screen. His 321st patent granted in 1955 was for a color television receiver that he developed for RCA.

His inventions in radio included the multiple-tuned antenna, the vacuum tube radiotelephone transmitter, the tuned-radio frequency receiver, the magnetic amplifier, the electronic amplifier, the directional transmitting antenna and the anti-static receiving antenna. He filed his last patent in 1968 at age 89.

In 1983, he was inducted into the National Inventors Hall of Fame, and in 2002 the Consumer Electronics Hall of Fame. He was elected to the Royal Academy of Science in Sweden. He also received the Medal of Honor from the IRE in 1919, Knighthood in Poland in 1924, The Edison Medal from the American IEE in 1944 and the Royal Danish Medal in 1946.

The WGY Players were the first to broadcast a staged performance over television in 1928. (Courtesy of Museum of Innovation and Science, Schenectady.)

Howland S. Barney

March 23, 1822 - November 14, 1904
Location: T #31 HB

H.S. Barney Co. was the superstar of State Street in Schenectady for over 100 years. Customers flocked to H.S. Barney Co. until competition from suburban malls led to the demise of the State Street store in 1973.

The biography from the book <u>New York State Men: Biographic Studies and Character Portraits</u> by Frederick Simon Hills (1910) states:

Barney's Department Store on lower State Street in the 19th century.

Merchant, was born in Minaville in the town of Greenfield, Saratoga County, N.Y. March 23, 1822, and was a son of Dr. Zadoc H. Barney, a physician of that town. It was the father's wish that the son should succeed him in his practice, but when fourteen years of age the boy removed to Schenectady and entered the employ of Sidney B. Potter, a merchant of that place. In 1840 he became a clerk for John Ohlen, and nine years later was admitted as a partner, the business being conducted under the name of John Ohlen & Company. In 1853 this firm was consolidated with that of Barringer & Company, Mr. Barney purchasing the interest of one of the retiring partners. Five years later the form became H.S. Barney & Company, with Mr. Barney as the senior partner. This concern was subsequently incorporated under the name of the H.S. Barney Company, of which Mr. Barney was president at the time of his death. Mr. Barney was for many years a vestryman of St. George's Episcopal Church, and was one of the incorporates of the Schenectady YMCA of which he was also a trustee. He was one of the founders of the Mohawk Club, of which he was a trustee for many years. In 1852 he married Miss Sarah Horsfall, of Schenectady, who died January 31, 1900. Mr. Barney dies Nov 14, 1904.

After his death, John F. Horman took over; the building was enlarged in 1872 and called the Barney block and was completed that year. A new building facing on Liberty Street was built in 1904, directly behind Barney Block and completed in 1908, and all three buildings were joined to give an arcade extending from State Street to Liberty Street. Purchasing offices were opened in London and Paris. During the 1920s the State Street building was enlarged, and polished marble replaced the steel columns at the entrance. Floors were raised to the level of the floors on the Liberty Street buildings, and all three buildings were combined into one gigantic store."

In 1933 the store was celebrating 100 years in Schenectady. It had 35 departments. In 1973 it closed. When it closed it was Schenectady's oldest store.

Barney lived in the mansion on the northeast corner of Union and North Ferry streets, built in the 1850s. In the 1950s it became the Goodrich House for the First Presbyterian Church.

In his will, he left $6,000 to be given to charities and public institutions in Schenectady. St. George's church received $2,000, Ellis hospital, $3,000 and the Schenectady Free Library Association, $1000. Heirs received the remainder of the estate.

His wife Sarah Horsfall was the sister of 1st Lt. William Horsfall of the 18th Regiment of New York Volunteers, who was killed in action in the Civil War and was also buried at Vale.

He was 82 when he died of old age at his home. Today, the famous building that housed his department store on lower State Street is the Barney Square apartments.

A Barney delivery wagon in livery behind the store.

Ernst Julius Berg

January 7/9, 1871 - September 9, 1941
Location: M3 #12 EB

Ernst Julius Berg. (Courtesy of Museum of Innovation and Science, Schenectady.)

Ernst Julius Berg was born in Östersund, Jämtland County in Sweden. After graduating from the Royal Institute of Technology in Stockholm in 1892, with a M.E. degree, he moved to the United States and began working as an assistant to Charles Proteus Steinmetz at General Electric in 1894. Berg and his brother Eskil, along with Charles Steinmetz, all lived together at 53 Washington Avenue. Berg and Steinmetz spent a lot of time in their early years on Washington Avenue getting into mischief, such as shifting downtown business signs so that upon opening, the beer garden would be a dry goods store and vice versa. They were also known to have kept many pets in pens and cages, including alligators. In 1899, he ran Steinmetz's department at G.E., which had responsibility for designing advanced alternating current machines, approving all design changes to AC equipment and developing theories of design.

Berg, along with Steinmetz, made important discoveries in the early history of the General Electric Company and made major contributions to electrical engineering theory. In 1897 they completed the classic <u>Theory and Calculation of Alternating Current Phenomena</u> (1897).

In 1906 he married Gwendoline O'Brien. The "Three Amigos" worked at General Electric until 1909, when Berg left G.E. to head the Electrical Engineering Department at the University of Illinois. He was enticed to go to Illinois when several large Illinois corporations agreed to supplement his university salary by giving him retainer fees as a consulting engineer. Berg remained as head until June 1913, when he resigned and returned to Schenectady, replacing Steinmetz as head of the Electrical Engineering Department at Union College, who moved over to Chair of Electro Physics. He received a salary of $10,000 which, at the time, was the most any college professor made anywhere. He continued his work in the calculation of alternating current circuits. He deviated somewhat from Steinmetz in the late 1880s, and his publication of Operational Calculus in 1929 made him one of the experts in that field. He wrote several textbooks on electrical engineering. He stayed at Union for 28 years, retiring in 1941.

A pioneer of radio, he produced the first two-way radio voice program in the United States. Starting in 1915, he helped the Union College Radio Club, where students learned telegraphy, took courses and listened to weekly talks by Berg. The college started the first college radio station (now WRUC) in the country, and the radio club broadcast the school's basketball scores throughout the country and messages by the students themselves.

On the evening of October 14, 1920, there originated from the Union College campus one of the most historic broadcasts in the annals of American radio. The newspaper headline was "College Students Give Concert by Radio Telephone." The phonograph playing was heard in a 50-mile radius.

The "baby carriage incident" of May 6, 1921 had a group of Union students rigging a wireless receiving set into a wicker baby carriage and, complete with live baby, wheeled the contraption across the campus and through the streets of downtown Schenectady. Projecting from the top was an antenna, between the handles was the tuning device, concealed within the carriage proper was the vacuum tube amplifier and associated components, and strapped underneath were the storage batteries.

His sister, Dr. Tekla Berg, a graduate of Tufts Medical School in 1896, died in 1939 in Massachusetts, but practiced medicine in Schenectady in 1928.

His house at 1336 Lowell Road was broken into on April 11, 1930 and $50 cash stolen. The home of his colleague Oscar Jungren at 1179 Lowell was also broken into by burglars, but they only destroyed some furniture.

Ernest J. Berggren

1863 - September 9, 1943
Location: D #31

Ernest was born in New Jersey but raised in New York City, and in 1880 became Edison's assistant bookkeeper. However, he began working for Edison in a strange start. In a 1939 edition of *The Piper*, a annual publication of the students of Cohasset High School, the following story is told.

As a youth he was employed in a company that sold medicine under Edison's name. It wasn't widely known publicly that Edison was a believer in home-concocted medicines. In his laboratory, which resembled a drug store with its hundreds of bottles of chemicals, drugs and oils, he prepared a straw-colored mixture which seemed to relieve his neuralgia. When anyone came to his laboratory complaining of an ache or pain Edison would give them a dose of his medicine. When asked the ingredients Edison would willingly tell them the formula.

Little did Edison realize that by his kind-heartedness he would be involved in a patent medicine manufacture which was to be marketed with his picture and name on the label. The "cure" was named "Edison's Polyform" and was supposed to relieve almost any ache or pain. The "Edison Polyform" was not widely advertised or distributed before Edison bought out the concern to save his name and reputation. Perhaps that is why the existence of this company has not been recorded in history and is so little known today.

Ernest Berggren did not realize that at sixteen he was entering the employ of persons unauthorized to use the great inventor's name. It was his good luck that the subsequent negotiations to buy out the firm brought him in contact with one of Edison's men whom he favorably impressed. Consequently this gave Mr. Berggren an opportunity to really be a worker under Edison.

Edison's name was used without permission when a drug manufacturer set up a special company called the Menlo Park Manufacturing Co. to handle sales for the product. It appeared in ads in New York in 1879 as a cure for almost any kind of ache or pain. To silence the company he bought it.

Berggren came to Schenectady with Edison in 1886 and three years later when several Edison companies were merged he was named head accountant. Edison consolidated his companies Edison Electric Light Company, Edison Machine Works, Edison Lamp Works, Bergmann and Company, Sprague Electric Railway and Motor Company, United Edison Manufacturing Company, and the Canadian Manufacturing Company, and Berggren he was appointed head accountant of the Schenectady plant. In 1892 Edison and the Thomson-Houston Company consolidated into General Electric. Berggren resigned in 1910 to become secretary treasurer of Thomas A. Edison Inc. in Orange, New Jersey.

In 1893 Berggren purchased a canal liner, "The City of Schenectady," for passenger and friend traffic. It was 80 feet long, with a 15-foot beam and a draught of 5 feet. It plied between Albany and Amsterdam.

He married Olive Furman (1865-1925), daughter of Henry Furman and Catharine Myers. They had two children, Hilda and Linda. Henry was the son of James Furman, who was the brother of Col. Robert Furman, who helped get Edison to Schenectady.

He was active in local politics while in Schenectady and served on the Schenectady City Council as an aldermen in the second ward in 1907.

In March 1916, Berggren, Secretary-Treasurer, and Harry T. Leaming, Assistant General Manager of Thomas A. Edison, Inc., resigned their positions with the company. *The New York Times* reported the incident:

Neither Mr. Leaming nor Mr. Berggren nor Carl H. Wilson, General Manager of Thomas A Edison, Inc., would make any comment on the resignations. It was said at the Edison offices that the two had resigned on their own initiative. However, it is known that an efficiency expert has been looking over the offices of Thomas A Edison Inc. which controls activities ranging from the manufacture of phonographs and storage batteries to moving picture acting, and it is understood that he recommend a tightening up of the organization and perhaps the elimination of several executive positions.

The impression is current here that the plans of the company include the cutting down of the amount paid out for salaries, presumably by the reduction of the force, and the establishment of a closer organization designed to put the various enterprises into a more closely knit relation to one another. Whether the efficiency movement is going down into the mechanical part of the establishment could not be learned.

Both Mr. Learning and Mr. Berggren have been with the firm for a number of years. Mr. Learning was in succession traffic manager, purchasing agent and assistant general manager.

One of the Edison activities, the phenol factory at Silver Lake, is still having trouble with a strike. It has been hoped yesterday that the strikers would agree to enter into negotiations with the company, but this morning they decided not to take this course but instead to attempt the organization of a union. So far all the Edison industries are unorganized and if the organization makes progress it is believed that there may be serious complications.

The strikers also decided to insist on the re-employment of Dominick Laddi, the strike leader, who quit works after the firm had refused to promote him to be a foreman. Eight of the strikers returned to work this morning without interference from the pickets, and work in the yard was assigned them, as the plant is shut down.

Harry F. Miller succeeded Berggren at TAE, Inc. No one knows why he resigned.

He then went into the Schenectady insurance field after his wife died on February 18, 1925, coming back to Schenectady from East Orange, New Jersey, and working as an agent for the Ter Bush and Powell Insurance company (Travelers Insurance Company). She was brought back to Schenectady and buried at Vale.

In 1936 Berggren and Theodore Van Deveneter, both pioneer associates of Edison, and both living in Schenectady, carried on the first successful wireless conversation between a police automobile and the high-flying Goodyear blimp, "Resolute," moving over G.E. in Schenectady. It was a demonstration during the Golden Jubilee anniversary. The broadcast went through the WGY radio station to the public. Berggren was in the blimp as he was interviewed, and it was to demonstrate the progress of wireless telegraphy. He did it again on August 27, 1940. Berggren was in the blimp with 12-year-old Evan Richards as they were interviewed on WGY. The blimp was promoting Canada Dry Ginger Ale.

In June 1940, a special screening of the movie "Edison the Man," starring Spencer Tracy, was shown at Proctors Theater and it was known as General Electric Night. It was to celebrate Edison bringing G.E. to Schenectady. Berggren was one of the invited guests. In addition, Charles Coburn, who as director of the Mohawk Drama Club at the time, had a feature role in the movie.

All during his life he spoke at various events praising the genius of his former employer Thomas Edison. He even attempted to get Erie Boulevard renamed as Edison Boulevard in his honor.

Most his life he lived at 225 Lafayette Street. In his twilight years he lived at the Ingersoll Home on Albany Road (Route 5, Albany Schenectady Turnpike, now State Street). He was injured in an auto accident as a car struck him on State and Jay streets on September 23, 1938, and was in the hospital in serious condition with a fractured jaw and right leg, concussion of the brain and head injures and lacerations on the neck. He was 76 years old, but survived. It forced him to retire completely. He was 80 when he died there and was the last surviving member of the group that worked with Edison at Menlo Park.

Newspaper article on Berggren's mobile call from blimp to ground.

Helen Brown

May 24, 1858 - March 31, 1947
Location: Sec. B; Plot 10

Helen (Nellie) Brown was born in Schenectady to Theodore (1828-1864) and Julia Elizabeth Strong Brown (1833-1911). Albert Brown came to Schenectady in 1829 from Stockbridge Massachusetts and made chairs on lower State Street. His son Theodore (Nellie's father) joined in the 1850s, and it became A. Brown & Son. Theodore died in 1864 and his son Clinton took over. They moved to State and Dock streets, but Albert died in

1880 and Clinton became sole owner. The building was destroyed by a water main break in 1910. A new building was built in 1913, but they went out of business in 1917 and sold the building to the Masonic Temple.

Nellie worked for the family at the furniture store, but in September 1893, at age 40, started a private school on the second floor of her home at 237 Liberty Street, with 11-12 children. The school originally proposed to serve only the children of General Electric personnel, which at the time had 40,000 people working there. At the time Liberty was an exclusive street with many of the city's wealthy citizens as residents. Next to Nellie was a set of row houses called "Pious Row." Lewis Behr, proprietor of Gents Furnishing Goods; Abraham Van Vorst, President of the Schenectady Bank; Dr. Herman Vedder Mynderse, President of the Mohawk Bank; Christopher Van Slyck, owner of Van Slyck & Garnsey Coal; and J.B. Clute from the Clute Brothers Machine Shop all lived there. Next door to the east was the home of John Ellis, founder of Schenectady Locomotive Company. In 1897, famous G.E. Scientist Charles Steinmetz lived in this same house along with his laboratory, the first research laboratory in America, which sat next to Nellie's backyard. His children went to Brown School.

Helen Brown. (Courtesy of Brown School.)

Helen and her pupils on Liberty Street. (Courtesy of Brown School.)

Nellie had many bright students and two in particular made a mark. Robert Brainard Corey (August 19, 1897 - April 23, 1971) is considered the "Father of Molecular Biology," along with Linus Pauling. He became an American biochemist, mostly known for his role in discovery of the α-helix and the β-sheet with Pauling. The α-helix and β-sheet are two structures that are now known to form the backbones of many proteins. Alexander Russell Stevenson Jr. (May 28, 1893 - August 28, 1946) made the first successful commercial refrigerators and leapfrogged over competitors after introducing the G.E. Monitor Top in 1927.

When Nellie made plans to retire in 1920, the Parent's Association of the Brown School organized and the Board of Trustees took over the financial management of the school. Jane Louise Jones was hired to replace Brown. The high school grades were discontinued in 1938, which started in 1928 for girls only, while the lower grades were co-educational. The association then purchased the school in 1924.

The private school moved to Park Avenue in 1900, to 1184 Rugby Road in 1905, and eventually to the former Catholic school off Corlaer Road in 1996, where it still provides excellent education from Kindergarten to 8th grade.

James Seaman Casey

January 28, 1833 - December 24, 1899
Location: Section G, Lot 13 (Thornton Plot)

James Seaman Casey.

James Seaman Casey was born in Philadelphia on January 28, 1833. His wife was Adelia Thornton, who died at Fort Leonard, Kansas on November 20, 1875, is buried at Vale. Adelia was the daughter of Brig. Gen. William A. Thornton (1803-1866) and Helen (Smith) Thornton (1810-1885).

Casey joined the 7th New York Militia, known as the "Silk Stocking" Regiment, in April 1861 in New York City, just after the outbreak of the Civil War, and was commissioned as a second lieutenant of the 5th Infantry Regiment (called the "Bobcats"), the third oldest infantry regiment in the U.S. Army) in August of the same year. On September 25, 1861, Casey was promoted to First Lieutenant. The 5th Infantry spent the Civil War in the New Mexico Territory. He was then promoted to Captain on December 1, 1863, and became Commissary of Musters of the Army of the Potomac. On March 25, 1865, Casey, "5th US Infantry, commissary of musters" was brevetted to Major "for faithful conduct of his department and gallant services in the assault on the enemy's lines before Fort Sedgwick, April 2, 1865," at the recommendation of Maj. Gen. Parke, Commander of IX Corps, who, during the Battle of Fort Stedman, became the acting commander of the Army of the Potomac. In the 1870s the 5th Infantry, under Col. Nelson Miles, moved to Montana, and built a camp that would later become Fort Keogh. Casey commanded Company A 5th Infantry from 1877 to 1884.

Stereo view of interior of Fort Sedgwick. (Courtesy of Library of Congress.)

After the war, Casey, now a Captain, served under Col. Nelson A. Miles in the Black Hills War, later receiving the Medal of Honor for leading his company's (Company A) assault in the Battle of Wolf Mountain, Montana on January 8, 1877. Miles returned to the Tongue River with a force from the 5th and 22nd Infantry to pursue Crazy Horse. They captured several important prisoners in the valley below the Wolf Mountains on January 7, 1877, leading to a confrontation with the main body the following day. The 5th, attacking superior numbers in near-blizzard conditions, drove the Lakota and Cheyenne force off the high ground, forcing them to retreat.

According to the Home of Heroes web site (*http://www.homeofheroes.com*), Col. Nelson Miles' cavalry detachment

> *... engaged 600 Indians in a five-hour battle in a canyon in the Wolf Mountain range. At one point the Indian force surrounded the cavalry from bluffs above the canyon, but were dispersed by two Napoleon guns. One band of warriors attired in battle dress and led by a Medicine Man named Big Crow, were poised in a strategic location on a high bluff to the left and above the column of soldiers. For several minutes Big Crow did a war dance before the astonished cavalrymen who did not fire a shot, for several minutes, then missed repeatedly. Incited by the "magic" of their medicine man, the Indian warriors prepared to destroy the cavalry when a bullet pitched Big Crow into the snow. Captain James Casey, along with Captain Edmond Butler and First Lieutenant Robert McDonald, immediately and valiantly stormed the high bluff, leading their men in scattering the warriors. For this gallant charge, all three officers were awarded the Medal of Honor.*

The 5th continued to pursue and round up bands from the broken confederacy into the summer of 1877.

In 1878 at Fort Keogh, Montana, he was found guilty of drunkenness on duty. Because of his record he was returned to duty by order of the President.

On June 27, 1884, Casey ended twenty-three years of service with the 5th Infantry, when he was promoted to Major and transferred to the 17th Infantry.

He was promoted to Lieutenant Colonel of the 1st Infantry on April 23, 1890. The 1st Infantry Regiment were known for their campaigns against the Sioux in the 1870s and 1890s and against the Apache, led by Geronimo, from 1882 to 1886.

He was promoted to Colonel of the 22nd Infantry, January 21, 1895, and commanded the 22nd Infantry until he retired from the Army on January 28, 1897. Before he joined, in December 1891 the 22nd participated in repressing the feared revolt of the Ghost Dancers, supposedly led by Sitting Bull, and later took part in patrols in Montana through the end of 1892, trying to keep the peace. This was during the time when Sitting Bull was killed by an Army officer.

Medal of Honor Citation
Rank and organization: Captain, Company A, 5th U.S. Infantry. Place and date: At Wolf Mountain, Mont., January 8, 1877. Entered service at: New York City, N.Y. Birth: Philadelphia, Pa. Date of issue: November 27, 1894.
Led his command in a successful charge against superior numbers of the enemy strongly posted.

Awarded for actions during the Indian Campaigns
The President of the United States of America, in the name of Congress, takes pleasure in presenting the Medal of Honor to Captain James Seaman Casey, United States Army, for extraordinary heroism on 8 January 1877, while serving with 5th U.S. Infantry, in action at Wolf Mountain, Montana. Captain Casey led his command in a successful charge against superior numbers of the enemy strongly posted.

General Orders: Date of Issue: November 27, 1894. Action Date: January 8, 1877. Service: Army Rank: Captain. Division: 5th U.S. Infantry

James S. Casey was born in Philadelphia, Pennsylvania. On April 17, 1861 he enlisted as a private in Co H of the 7th Regiment of the New York State Militia. He was discharged from the Militia on June 3, 1861. He was offered a commission as a 2nd Lieutenant in the 5th US infantry on August 5, 1861, a position that he accepted on August 26 of that year. The 5th Infantry spent the Civil War on duty in the New Mexico Territory.

Casey died December 25, 1899 in New York City and was buried at Vale Cemetery. A marker was placed on May 15, 1960.

He was an Original Companion of the Military Order of the Loyal Legion of the United States, a support group formed after the assassination of President Lincoln in 1865.

William Cermak

1856 - October 15, 1907
Location: U 205

William Cermak was born in Kasejovice, Blatna (now the Czech Republic), and came to America in 1886 at age 30. He lived in New York City and found work in the pottery business on the lower East Side with his wife and three sons, Frank, Charles and Edward. He was invited to come to the new porcelain division of the Edison Electric Company, which became General Electric in 1892.

In 1893, Cermak developed a new "petticoated" porcelain insulator that could withhold 10,000 volt transmission lines, since the usual glass ones were too fragile and not able to withstand high voltages.

He lived in the Mont Pleasant area of Schenectady in 1904 on Fourth Avenue, and was appointed Alderman for the Ninth Ward. In 1905, after being ill, he, his wife and son Edward went back to Europe, but he returned and died two years later.

The importance of the clay-made insulators was written by his son Frank, who followed his father in the business and worked at General Electric, and who is also buried at Vale (died August 14, 1964 and located with his father). In writing about the early porcelain history in the U.S., Frank wrote:

Frank Cermak, Superintendent, Porcelain Factory, General Electric Company, Schenectady, N. Y.

August Weber and I have made a thorough investigation of the manufacture of dry-pressed porcelain; we find that the General Electric Company of Seventeenth Street and Avenue A, New York, N.Y., made receptacles and cutouts under the Edison patents. The insulating parts, made of wood, were unsatisfactory owing to their fire hazard. They began an investigation of the possible use of porcelain. John J. Kraus manufactured artistic pottery at East Eighteenth Street, New York, N.Y., and William Cermak, my father, was the foreman. They began experimenting with dry-pressed porcelain in 1887, and they put it into production in 1888. The Bergman Electric Company took the total output. This company was absorbed by the Edison Machine Company, which later became the General Electric Company. Wet-process porcelain used as switchboard work by the General Electric Company was made by the Smith Company of Brooklyn, N.Y., until its production began at Schenectady in 1902.

William himself developed a porcelain holder for the filament and the G.E. light bulb that allowed the possibility of using the advanced filaments being designed by G.E. He headed a group of porcelain workers at G.E. He also brought in his sons, Charles and Frank, and his daughter Ethel, who also worked for G.E.

He turned down an honorary Ph.D. from Alfred University because he would have had to make a speech, embarrassed by his Czech accent.

William Childers

? - 1890 (or 1892)
Location: F 23 grv 19

William Childers was born in Tennessee. In the early 1860s, he was living in Ballston and working as a waiter. He enlisted on December 19, 1863 and served as a private in Company F of the 26th Regiment, U.S. Colored Infantry. The designation was changed to 94th U.S. Colored Troops, on April 4 1864, and mustered out on August 28, 1865.

This regiment, under Col. William Silliman, was organized at Riker's Island, New York harbor, February 27, 1864, to serve three years; it served in the Department of the East to March, 1864; in the District of Beaufort, Department of the South, to April, 1865; at Port Royal, South Carolina, until it was honorably discharged and mustered out, under Col. William B. Guernsey, August 28, 1865.

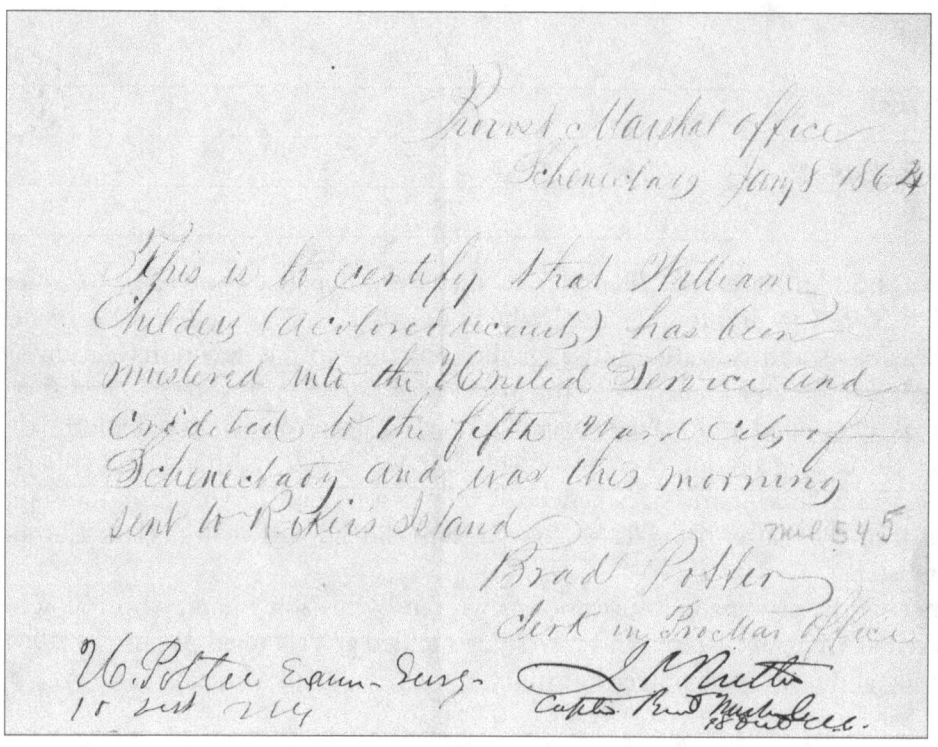

Certification that William Childers, "a colored recruit," mustered into the Union Army and was credited to the 5th Ward of the City of Schenectady.

During its service the regiment lost by death, killed in action, 21 enlisted men; of wounds received in action, 2 officers, 7 enlisted men; of disease, 2 officers, 102 enlisted men; drowned, 1 officer, 4 enlisted men; murdered, 1 enlisted man; of sunstroke, 2 enlisted men; of causes not stated, 3 enlisted men; total, 5 officers, 140 enlisted men; aggregate, 145.

His service record indicates that he served in the action of July 1864 at Bloody Bridge, Johns Island, South Carolina, also known as Burden's Causeway. On July 21,864, Brig. Gen. John Hatch's troops, more than 4,000 of them, landed in the Legareville section of Johns Island. Hatch wanted to cross Johns Island, then cross the Stono River and lay siege to James Island. The Union troops met the Confederate troops where the creek becomes a swamp. Around 2,000 outnumbered South Carolina soldiers held off a Union force of roughly 5,000 men. After three days of fighting, Hatch's troops left the island and retreated.

In total the 26th saw the following actions in 1864:

- Expedition to Johns and James Islands July 2–10
- Operations against Battery Pringle July 4–9
- Actions on John's Island, July 5 and 7. Burden's Causeway July 9
- Battle of Honey Hill November 30
- Demonstration on Charleston & Savannah Railroad December 6–9
- Action at Devaux's Neck December 6
- Tulifinny Station December 9
- McKay's Point December 22.

After the war, William moved to Schenectady, where he worked as a coachman and a hostler until his death in 1890 at the age of 49. He was still listed as living in a house in the rear of 506 Smith Street in 1892.

His name is included on the African American Civil War Memorial in Washington, D.C.

Cadwallader C. Clute (1 of 3 Clute Brothers)

October 18, 1814 - August 16, 1876
Location: Section L, plot 114, lot 816, Gr. 10

Cadwallader Colden Clute, eldest son of Peter I. Clute (1784-1870) and Sarah Fratt Clute (1788-1855), was born in Schenectady. The Clute Brothers Foundry and Machine Shop, also known as the Schenectady Iron Foundry and Machine Shop, was founded in the 1840s by Cadwallader C. Clute, originally from this father's firm Clute & Bailey, stove makers. Cadwallader purchased the shares of Joel C. Bailey in 1842. In 1849, it became Clute Brothers & Company, working with his brothers John B. (1818-1892) and Jethro (1823-1903). (See also their biographies in the following articles.)

Portrait of Cadwallader Clute.

Clute also owned a hardware store at 142 State Street. Later he formed the Clute Brothers Steam Engine and Tool Builders at 49 & 51 Liberty Street, with his brothers John and Jethro.

Clute Brothers also built bridges that spanned the Erie Canal. In an 1862 *Scientific American* article, George Heath, the inventor and patentee of a new iron truss bridge, was featured for his new improved design, which Clute built for him. Clute also built a cast iron bridge for Schenectady inventor Benjamin Severson. Finally, in later years, they built sawmills, complete with boilers and water wheels, of various designs.

Cadwallader was a director of the Mohawk Bank in 1859 and continued until he died. He left $6,000 to the Home of the Friendless. He lived at 52 Union Street.

Clute brothers built the turret rotating gears and donkey engine for the *U.S.S. Monitor*. (See the article on page 70.) They also made farm machinery, precision instruments, caloric engines and boilers, marine and stationary engines, and valve gates for the Erie Canal. They also made the Lay Torpedo (page 73) and were instrumental in the building of the *Spuyten Duyvil* (page 74).

On January 18, 1867, the Clute shops burned. After the Arcade building was erected on the same site, they went back in business in 1870 on a smaller scale, but by 1882 were out of business. The Arcade building burned to the ground in 1909.

John B. Clute (1 of 3 Clute Brothers)

1818 - April 6, 1892
Location: C#2

John B. Clute, son of Peter I. Clute, lived on Albany Street near State Street and was known for being a volunteer fireman. In 1830-32, he served as Treasurer in the Schenectady Legislature. He served as an elder in the First Reformed Protestant Church in Schenectady in 1833 and 1834, 1839, 1840. His father Peter also served there. John Clute probably also taught Sunday school.

In May 1846, John Clute applied for a patent for an improvement on cast iron stoves, showing a combination of two side flues with the vertical flues on the elevated oven. He served as a Director on the Schenectady & Susquehanna Railroad when it began in 1869. In 1870 he, along with his brother Jethro, worked for George Westinghouse and Company, next to the Edison Electric Company. His son John Ericsson Clute 1865-1889) became a Schenectady physician, and who is also buried at Vale.

Jethro Wood Clute (1 of 3 Clute Brothers)

October 19, 1823 - January 21, 1903
Location: H#37

Jethro Clute died at his home at 15 Liberty Street in Schenectady, aged seventy-nine years. For many years he was a member of the firm of Peter I. Clute & Sons. During the Civil War, the engines and boilers for the *U.S.S. Monitor* were built at the company's foundry, of which Mr. Clute was the proprietor. He retired from the business in 1883. He ran for Second Vice President of the Young Men's Association in 1847. He was a city alderman in the Second Ward (1853-1855) and Whig delegate from the Fourth Ward in 1855. In 1870 he worked for George Westinghouse and Company.

He was married to Margaret Jane McCorkell. A Jethro W. Clute married Sarah Jane Mathews, daughter of Andrew Matthews, on July 21, 1848, but she died at age 30 on March 13, 1854, being married for only six years.

He was survived by his wife and four children. His daughter Sarah H. was married to Dr. Hames Lemuel in 1875. His daughter Alice married William Grosvenor Ely in 1897.

The Clute Brothers and the *U.S.S. Monitor*

On March 9, 1862, the most famous naval battle in American history took place almost 600 miles from the Capital District. Yet, this important event had Schenectady and Troy stamped all over it when a small floating "cheese box on a raft" helped turn the War of the Rebellion against the South.

This is the famous storybook battle between the northern ironclad *U.S.S. Monitor* and its southern counterpart the *C.S.S. Virginia* (formerly the *U.S.S. Merrimac*) during the Civil War.

On the afternoon of March 8, the Union Navy was not faring well. The clearly-outnumbered sole Confederate ironclad *Virginia* steamed its way down the Elizabeth River into Hampton Roads in Virginia and attacked the wood-sided Northern blockading fleet anchored there. This was no small blockade. It was comprised of several ships armed with 204 guns, and aided by land batteries. Fortress Monroe, under the command of Troy's General John Wool, was nearby and in sight of the action.

By six o'clock, the lonely *Virginia* had sunk the *Cumberland*, burned the *Congress*, forced the *Minnesota* ashore, and forced the *St. Lawrence* and the *Roanoke* to seek shelter under the guns of Fort Monroe. The Union fleet was in shambles and the *Virginia* planned on returning the next day to finish them off.

However, an unexpected guest—the *Monitor*—greeted the *Virginia* the next morning. It had slipped in the previous night under fog. The *Monitor*, more heavily armored and with a revolving gun turret (a first), was also speedier and more agile in the water, due to the inventive genius of its designer John Ericsson.

While eight foundries were responsible for making the *Monitor*, the primary work for iron plate, castings, and fittings was contracted out to three New York rolling mills. Holdane & Co. (New York City) produced 125 tons of plate, and the Albany Ironworks and Rensselaer Ironworks (of Troy) manufactured hundreds of additional tons of hull plate and castings. H. Abbott & Sons of Baltimore rolled the 1-inch-thick iron plates for the turret that was then shipped to Novelty Ironworks in New York for assembly. Delmater Ironworks (NYC) and Clute Brothers Foundry of Schenectady cast and assembled most of the components of the ship's machinery. Niagara Steam Forge of Buffalo made the Turret's port stoppers and flaps for the cannon's firing openings on the turret. Clute Brothers also made the gun carriages.

The ship was 124 feet long, and 34 feet broad at the top. While in water, all that was visible was the turret, for the most part; only 18 inches of the deck was visible above the water line. The ship was launched on January 30, 1861, 18 days past the 100 days Ericsson promised it would take to deliver it to the government.

The Clute Brothers Foundry, at the corner of Liberty and Wall Streets (now a parking lot), founded in 1840, already had a relationship with Ericsson as one of the builders of his famous patented Ericsson Caloric Steam Engine. They also prided themselves on producing marine engines, boilers, and scientific instruments. It was the donkey engines they fabricated that moved the gears of the turret, and naval historians agree that it was the rotating turret that changed the course of naval warfare forever. If it had not worked, the war may have had a different outcome.

According to the U.S.S. Monitor Center (Mariner's Museum):

Clute Brothers workers who built the equipment for the *U.S.S. Monitor*.

The most innovative feature of the Monitor *and the one that became her distinguishing characteristic was her revolving turret. Though other designers had toyed with the idea of developing turrets for warships, Ericsson's* Monitor *was the first warship to use the invention successfully. The turret rested amidships of the vessel and was furnished with a separate steam engine that propelled the turret in a complete rotation. It measured 20 feet in diameter and 9 feet in height, and its armored walls were made of eight layers of 1-inch armor plate. Two massive 11-inch Dahlgren smoothbore cannon, capable of firing solid shot weighing 180 pounds, were installed inside the turret. Though the* Monitor *would go into battle with only two cannon, she had a distinct advantage even over an opponent with ten cannon. This was because the revolving turret would allow her to fire and aim her guns rapidly in any direction regardless of the direction in which the ironclad might be steaming. All other ships of her time were forced to aim their guns in part by steering the vessel into a position where the guns, mounted in broadside arrangement, could be brought to bear on the enemy.*

The turret bulkhead was opened only where two gun ports for the two 11-inch Dahlgren guns were located. The open ports could be covered from within by huge iron pendulums that were swung in or out of position as needed. The flooring in the turret was four-inch thick wood, supported by an iron ring running around the inside base of the turret.

The turret was rotated by two Clute Brothers-made steam engines operating a crank that rotated four gears. During battle, three officers and 16 sailors composed the gun crews and would have been in the turret, along with the massive Dahlgren guns. Troy's John Griswold (then Congressman) and John F. Winslow, owner of the Albany Iron Works, financed the deal, along with John Ericsson who designed the *Monitor*.

For about five hours the two ironclads battled it out with both ships retreating, each of their captains thinking they had won. In effect, the North did win, since it halted the further destruction of the fleet and sent the *Virginia* running.

In the annual report of the Secretary of the Navy for 1862, the following was written about the epic battle between the *Monitor* and *Virginia* (*Merrimac*):

The fierce conflict between these two ironclads lasted for several hours. It was in appearance an unequal conflict, for the Merrimac *was a large and noble structure, and the* Monitor *was in comparison almost diminutive. But the* Monitor *was strong in her armor, in the ingenious novelty of her construction, in the large caliber of her two guns, and the valor and skill with which she was handled. After several hours' fighting the* Merrimac *found herself overmatched, and, leaving the* Monitor, *sought to renew the attack on the* Minnesota; *but the* Monitor *again placed herself between the two vessels and reopened her fire upon her adversary. At noon the* Merrimac, *seriously damaged, abandoned the contest and, with her companions, retreated toward Norfolk.*

Thus terminated the most remarkable naval combat of modern times, perhaps of any age. The fiercest and most formidable naval assault upon the power of the Union which has ever been made by the insurgents was heroically repelled, and a new era was opened in the history of maritime warfare.

Ironically, it was the forces of nature that sunk the *Monitor*, 20 miles off Cape Hatteras, when it was being towed back on a stormy New Year's Eve in 1862. Several sailors went down with the ship.

The *Monitor* rested in the deep for 111 years before it was relocated in 1973, and then designated the Monitor National Marine Sanctuary. It is managed by the National Oceanic and Atmospheric Administration

Crew on the *U.S.S. Monitor*. (Courtesy of Library of Congress.)

(NOAA). The purpose of the Monitor National Marine Sanctuary is to preserve the historic record of this significant vessel and to interpret her role in shaping U.S. naval history. Over the past several years NOAA has made extensive surveys of the wreck site and recovered over 250 artifacts from the *Monitor*.

A Navy-funded, $6.5 million project was the last major recovery effort of the *Monitor* since surveys in the mid-1990s showed that corrosion of the vessel was accelerating. The eight-inch-thick iron turret still contained the two 11-inch Dahlgren cannons, many smaller artifacts, and the remains of some of the crewmen who went down with the ship—along with Seaman Francis Butts' black cat—the mascot that was stuffed into the barrel of one of the cannons to keep it dry as the ship bounced around the rough sea. Underwater archaeologists and Navy divers recovered the 150-ton turret (the "cheesebox"), along with the remains of two crew members on August 5, 2002.

Today, Museum visitors can stand just feet away from the Monitor's two 11-inch Dahlgren cannons, unique screw propeller, and the construction site for the $30 million U.S.S. Monitor Center, which opened in 2007.

The Clute Brothers assisted in the production of parts for other ships during the war as well. For example, they built the propeller wheel for the *U.S.S. Picket* Boat #3, a screw steamer on March 3, 1865, for which they were paid $47.50.

Ericsson went on to build other Monitor Class warships for the army: *U.S.S. Passaic* (launched Aug. 30, 1862); *U.S.S. Patapsco* (launched Sept. 27, 1862); *U.S.S. Montauk* (launched Oct. 9, 1862); *U.S.S. Sangamon* (launched Oct. 27, 1862); *U.S.S. Catskill* (launched Dec. 16, 1862); *U.S.S. Lehigh* (launched Jun. 17, 1863); *U.S.S. Dictator* (launched Dec. 26, 1863); and the *U.S.S. Puritan* (launched July 2, 1864). The *Montauk* and *Patapsco* were damaged or sunk by Confederate torpedoes.

The Clute Brothers and the Lay Torpedo

The word "torpedo" was first used by American inventor David Bushnell during the 18th century. Torpedo is from the animal family, genus Torpedinidae, the electric ray. The "shock and awe" of a torpedo was aptly named.

Bushnell first used the term for a mine attached to the hull of a ship and detonated. He completed this by using a boat that he designed that was manually pedal-powered and was submerged, perhaps the first submarine. During the 18th and 19th centuries, however, all types of water-bound explosive devices, *i.e.*, floating mines, floating barrels of burning pitch (carried to the target by the water current), and spar torpedoes were all called torpedoes.

Robert Fulton developed Bushnell's submarine into a more workable type, which he named *Nautilus*. With this boat he sank several ships during demonstrations, but was unable to sell his submarine to the American Navy.

Throughout the century, many attempts were made to develop torpedoes and during the Civil War, the "spar" type was popular. This consisted of a steam launch having an explosive 60-pound charge mounted at the end of a 25-foot long pole projecting ahead of the boat, and exploded below the waterline. Unfortunately, the aggressor had to get pretty close to the enemy boat, although the Confederates used it successfully.

After the war, in 1870, a "Torpedo Test Station" was set up at Rhode Island for research on spar torpedoes, but a year later the first "automobile" torpedo was tested. Instead of adopting the successful torpedoes of British inventor Robert Whitehead, the U.S. government set about building under the supervision of J.L. Lay, an officer in the U.S. Navy, a series of unusual and unreliable weapons.

Clute Brothers in Schenectady was contracted to make some of Lay's first torpedoes from designs from M. Hubbe, a marine architect and draughtsman who worked for Lay. They were tested in the Mohawk River between two bridges at the foot of Governors Lane in the present Stockade.

On October 11, 1872, the first successful test was made with 300 onlookers, including several Navy officials, at the Schenectady location. After the event, Rear Admiral A. Ludlow Case made a toast to Lay: "We congratulate him on the perfect success of his Torpedo. It moved with ease and is under perfect control, both of which are the great and essential points." Unfortunately, with Lay's design, most of his weapons floated and could not strike at any depth at an enemy ship. The Lay torpedoes floated with only a few inches of hull showing, and were controlled by an operator using electrical impulses sent down a wire. The power unit was a gas en-

Clute Brothers monument at Vale.

gine driven by compressed carbon dioxide, and the steering impulses transmitted down the wire operated electromagnetic relays on the rudder. The position of the weapon was indicated by two flags or discs. A later form used liquefied carbon dioxide as the power source, with the liquid warmed in pipes external to the weapon.

These weapons were unreliable and vulnerable to destruction by gunfire. In a trial carried out off the British coast for the Royal Navy, the Lay weapon heeled over badly so that the propeller was located only half under the surface.

Two Lay torpedoes were sold to the Peruvian Government for use in their war against Chile. In 1879, a Lay weapon was fired from the Peruvian ironclad *Huascar* at a Chilean ship. When it reached halfway to the target, the weapon turned around and headed back at 15 knots to the mother ship, despite the frantic and much-surprised knob-twiddling of the operator. The ship was saved only by the quick thinking and heroic action of a ship's officer, who dove in the water and swam out to intercept the weapon and deflect it. The captain took the two weapons to a local graveyard where they were buried. (Ironically, they were later exhumed by the Chilean rebels!) The Lay weapon was also exported to Russia for harbor defense work, but only in small quantities. It wasn't until 1896 that the Austrian naval officer Ludwig Obry invented the gyroscope, making the torpedo a reliably stable weapon.

The Clute Brothers and the *Spuyten Duyvil*

The Clute Brothers were also instrumental in building the first torpedo ship for the Navy known as the *Spuyten Duyvil*, which in Dutch means "In Spite of the Devil." It was built in early 1865, just before the fall of Richmond. Naval constructor Samuel H. Pook designed the hull, but the torpedo-laying machinery was designed by Capt. William W.W. Wood, Chief Engineer, U.S. Navy, and constructed by the Clute Brothers of Schenectady. The ship was constructed at Fairhaven, Connecticut, in only three months. It was completed under the name *Stromboli*, in October 1864, but was renamed a month later.

After the ship's arrival at Hampton Roads, Virginia, in early December 1864, the same place as the earlier *Monitor* battle two years previous, *Spuyten Duyvil* was sent to operate on the James River. On January 23-24, 1865, it took part in the battle at Trent's Reach, after Confederate ironclads attempted to attack federal forces on the lower James.

As the Civil War drew to a close in early April 1865, *Spuyten Duyvil* used its unique torpedo-placing mechanism to clear obstructions on the river, which allowed President Abraham Lincoln to go up the James River to visit Richmond, the former Confederate capital city.

The ship continued clearing the river's obstruction even after the fighting ended, and at the end of its career was sent to the New York Navy Yard, where it was decommissioned, later used for experiments, and then sold in 1880.

The vessel was propelled by a single four-bladed screw, and the engines for working the propeller were constructed at Mystic, Connecticut, by Mallory and Co.

For working the vessel and torpedo machinery nine persons were required, the total number of the staff on board.

William David Coolidge

October 23, 1873 - February 3, 1975
Location: F#23

Coolidge was born on a farm near Hudson, Massachusetts. His father, Albert Edward, was a shoemaker and farmer. His mother, Martha Alice, was a dressmaker. After graduating from Hudson High School as valedictorian, from 1891 to 1896 he studied electrical engineering at M.I.T. and, following a year as a lab assistant, went to Germany and received his doctorate from the University of Leipzig. He then became a research assistant to Arthur A. Noyes in the chemistry department at M.I.T. from 1899 to 1905.

At the request of Willis Whitney, director of General Electric's new research laboratory, he accepted a job on September 11, 1905, and was instrumental in discovering ways to use tungsten as filaments in light bulbs, inventing "ductile tungsten," allowing it to be drawn into filaments. By 1911 G.E. was making millions with their new "Mazda" bulbs. While he received a patent for this in 1913, the U.S. Court ruled that it was not valid as an invention later.

He married Ethel Woodward, the daughter of the president of a local bank in Granville, on December 30, 1908. They had a son, Lawrence, and a daughter, Elizabeth. His wife died in 1915 after becoming seriously ill. A year later he married Dorothy Elizabeth MacHaffie, the nurse from Ellis Hospital who worked for his former wife, helping to take care of his children.

That same year he invented the Coolidge tube, an X-ray tube with improved cathode. The "C" tube was used to detect submarines during the war, and a "K" tube and C" tube followed. He also developed a mobile X-ray system that doctors could use in field hospitals. His invention of the self-rectifying tube and small transformer allowed the development of the safe X-ray equipment for the dentist. He used himself as a test subject to see if his X-ray tube worked.

Patent drawing for Coolidge's vacuum tube. (Courtesy of U.S. Patent Office.)

He became Assistant Director of the G.E. research laboratory in 1908, Associate Director in 1928, Director in 1932 and a Vice President of G.E. in 1940, until he retired in 1944. He lived at 1480 Lenox Road and died at the age of 101. He held 83 patents.

The American Academy of Arts and Sciences awarded Coolidge the Rumford Prize in 1914. Coolidge was awarded the American Institute of Electrical Engineers' Edison Medal in 1927 for his contributions to the incandescent electric lighting and the X-rays art. He rejected this prestigious award in 1926 on the basis that his ductile tungsten patent (1913) was ruled by the court as invalid. He was awarded the Howard N. Potts Medal in 1926, the Louis E. Levy Medal in 1927, the Faraday Medal in 1939 and the Franklin Medal in 1944. In 1975 he was elected to the National Inventors Hall of Fame, shortly before his death.

Jonathan Crane

February 5, 1790 - October 9, 1870
Location: M#1

Jonathan Crane was born in North Mansfield, Connecticut, where he passed his boyhood days, receiving his early education in the country schools. At the age of eighteen he left home and relocated at Newburgh, New York. In 1814 he moved to Schenectady as a clock peddler, in which place he afterwards made his home. In 1819 he purchased a large tract of land and erected factories. He may have also been a lawyer by training.

He was an early industrialist who brought the wood screw industry and rope making to the area. His factory called Crane's Mills was at Mohawkville, which started at the end of Broadway (then Centre Street) and ran for a mile along the road into what is now Rotterdam. His area was called Cranesville, and he is credited for bringing the English screws to America. He also he produced oil and brakes, and made flax and cornhusk twine for more than 30 years.

Crane placed his first ad in the *Schenectady Cabinet* newspaper on September 29, 1819, announcing that he would buy 2,000 bushels of flaxseed for which "the highest prices in cash will be paid." On January 5, 1820, it was announced that Jonathan Crane's Oil Mill was in complete operation. On June 3, 1829, he removed his store to "the east side of Canal Bridge in State Street" which would have been opposite the Edison Hotel building. He took on a partner and on May 7, 1834, a notice in the paper that E.L. Freeman & Co was moving to 70 State Street (now 217 State near the entrance to the old H.S. Barney Co.). By August 23, 1834 the partnership dissolved, with Crane, Freeman carrying on.

In 1882 his mill was taken over by the Mohawk Twine Company and lasted until 1884, when the depression killed it, laying off 35 workers.

He was also an inventor.

After Crane saw the Mohawk & Hudson Railroad come through his neighborhood in 1831, he decided to get into the railroad business and had part of the contract to build the Utica & Schenectady Railroad in 1836-39. While watching the excavation of sand for the railroad (it was located in the Pine Bush at the time), he invented the "Circular Receiver"—or, as listed in the patent records, "circular car"—a device that was a sort of turntable later used by railroads. It was patented on October 1, 1830. It was a success and he traveled to other areas where railroads were constructed, acting as a consultant for his product for such railroads as the Boston & Providence, Hartford & New Haven, Providence & Stonington, Boston & Albany, and Boston & Maine. In June of 1831 he received a patent for a stone-drilling machine. There are no images in the patent office of either invention. He and F.H. Hamilton received a patent on January 1, 1850 for improvements in hemp-brakes, a device for braking flax or hemp.

He had his own store on State Street to sell his own products, and was a civic and church leader. He also organized the first temperance society in Schenectady, and formed the first Sunday school in Schenectady County using his own basement kitchen in his house in 1817. It was called the Mohawkville Sunday School.

Crane was a member of the Elders of the Presbytery of Albany and was part of a group that oversaw a trial of two minsters that were accused of slander, Rev. John Chester and Mr. Mark Tucker. on April 8, 1817. Chester made a declaration of falsehood in Schenectady along with Tucker, accusing another Rev. Hooper Cumming of being drunk.

He also served as Alderman for Schenectady in 1828.

Crane may also have been a founding member (along with Archibald Craig, Samuel W. Jones, Archibald L. Linn, Edward Yates, Jabez Ward, Robert Cunningham, Oliver Ostrom and Jonathan Burnham) of "The Schenectady African School Society," on April 18, 1829. The purpose of the organization was "declared to be the encouragement and promotion of the education of the coloured population residing from time to time in the city of Schenectady, and the expenditure of their funds shall be for no other purpose than such as may be reasonably deemed by the said trustees conducive to that object."

He married Orpha Barrows, on May 10, 1810. She was born in Mansfield, Connecticut on December 27, 1788, the daughter of Ethan. She died in 1824. He then married Azubah Hamilton, of Brookfield Massachusetts. He had ten children: Ethan B. (b. July 11, 1811); Jonathan (b. March, 1814); Edward (b. 1816); Cordial S. (b. 1819); Eliza (b. March 24, 1820), who married J.R. Hayward and lived in 1842 at Hannibal, Missouri and whose son David died in infancy; Catharine Hamilton (b. 1825); Lucinda (b. 1827); Henry Martyn (b. 1828); and Martha (b. 1834).

Crane Street is named for him and was next to Chrysler Avenue, which is an old roadbed of the Mohawk & Hudson Railroad.

It is reported after he died that at one time a well-organized band of counterfeiters at Glenville was known to exist, and Crane skillfully connected himself with the bunch, learned the trade, and then exposed the organization. Several of them went to state prison, others fled, and Crane did his deed.

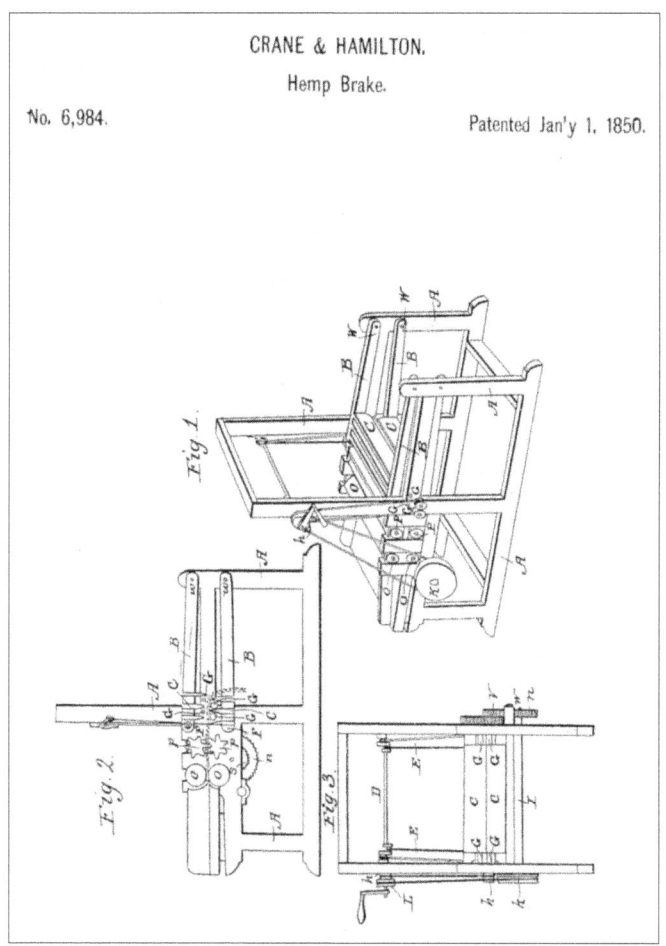

Patent drawing for Crane's hemp brake. (Courtesy of U.S. Patent Office.

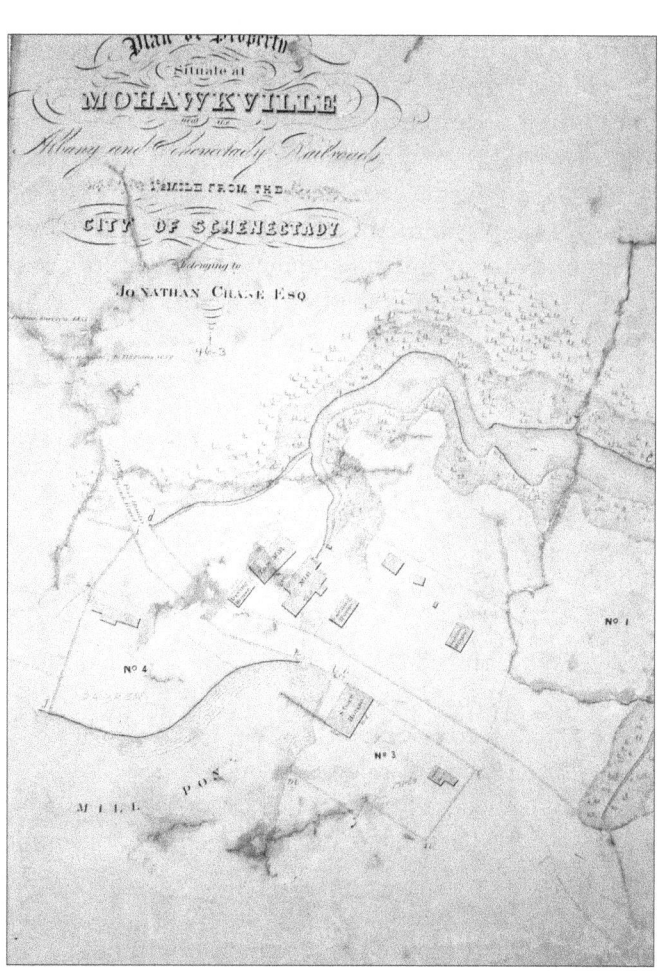

Map of Crane's property at Mohawkville, now part of Schenectady. (Courtesy of Schenectady County Clerk.)

Maxwell W. Day

1865 - September 25, 1950
Location: L2#114

Maxwell Warren Day was born in the old parsonage at Richmond Center in Honeoye, Ontario County, New York. His parents were Rev. S. Mills Day and Lucy Maxwell Day, and he was descended from Ralph Day, who came from England to Massachusetts before 1660. He had three sisters and was graduated from Williams College in 1887 with the degree of A.B. He was salutatorian of his class, and was a member of the Zeta Psi and Phi Beta Kappa college societies. A year later he took a post-graduate course in mathematics at the same college.

In June 1889 he entered the employ of the Thomson-Houston Electric Company, at Lynn, Massachusetts, where he worked in the testing design and worked two years later in the special motor engineering departments.

After the consolidation of the Thomson-Houston and Edison General Electric Companies, he came to Schenectady in June 1894 as a draftsman. In December he transferred to the Industrial Engineering section of the Power and Mining Department.

On June 17, 1891, he married Nellie G. Davis of Honeoye, daughter of Charles G. and Sarah G. (Putney) Davis. Their son, Irving M. Day, was born April 1, 1894. Mrs. Day died August 10, 1900, at age 32. He later married Bertha Case. When she died in 1943, he lived with his son Irving in Chevy Chase, Maryland.

In 1903 he was appointed Assistant Manager of the Power and Mining Department, and later devoted his entire attention to marine and government work. In 1914, when the company formed a separate engineering department for this work, he was appointed Engineer of the Marine Department. He retired in 1925.

He became well known for his application of electricity to marine auxiliaries of U.S. naval craft, including the turning of turrets, operation guns and handling of ammunition and electrical equipment for steering gear, anchor windlass, pumps and ventilation systems. He was granted 13 patents covering control of motors for various applications, the best known relating to control of ammunition hoists and boat cranes.

Mr. Day was a member of the First Reformed Church, and has served at different times as Deacon and as Assistant Superintendent, and Superintendent of the Sunday school.

Due to his inventions, G.E. was able to deliver three-fourths of the propulsion and auxiliary turbine horsepower for the U.S. Navy during WWII. He lived at 1032 Brierwood Boulevard in Schenectady.

16 Patents as Inventor

- Controller for Electric Motors; Pat. 644,666; March 6, 1900
- Controlling Electric Motors; December 2, 1902; November 2, 1899
- Motor Control; May 28, 1907
- Electric Cableway System; June 5, 1906
- Electric Steering Gear; August 23, 1901
- Protective Means for Electric Boosters; July 6, 1903
- Electric Motor Control; June 27, 1904
- Ccontroller for Electric Circuits; June 17, 1901
- Automatic Motor Controller; July 15, 1909
- Motor Control; October 15, 1906
- Elevator Controller; June 12, 1897
- Controller for Electric Motors; September 17, 1898
- Motor Controlling Device; July 16, 1909
- System of Control for Electric Motors; May 15, 1905.

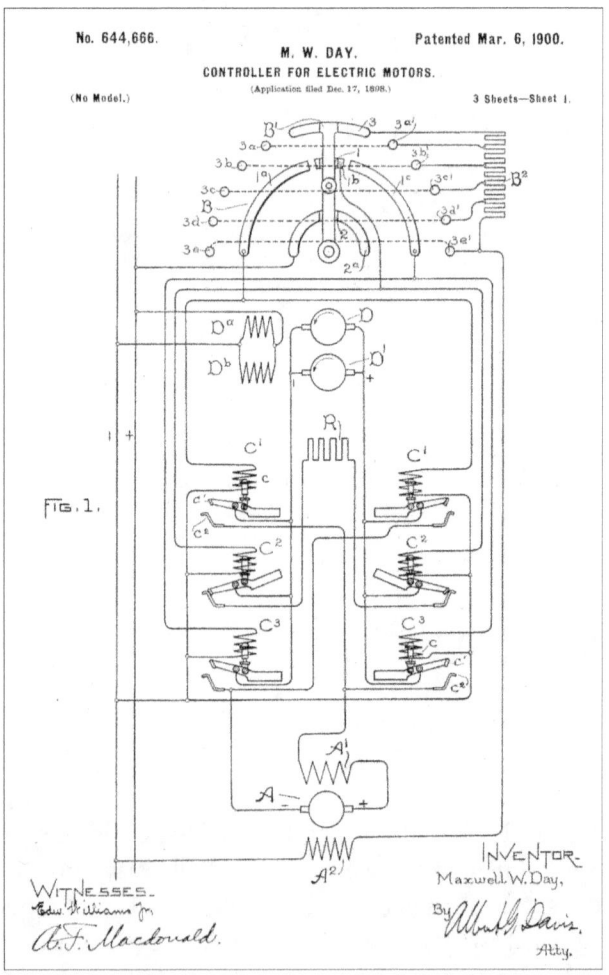

Patent drawing for Day's Controller for Electric Motors. (Courtesy of U.S. Patent Office.)

Ernestus Josephus De Spitzer

1709 - 1789
Location: I-1 58

Ernestus De Spitzer was born in Helibronn, Kingdom of Württemberg, Germany, on April 6, 1709. He married Barbara Wilfelin, who was Dutch. He was a clergyman before coming to this country; the following is a translation of a license given him:

We give to the bearer of this paper, Rev. Ernest Spitzer of the Diocese of Vienna, permission to say mass during four days in all the churches in and outside the city, if he, according to the rules of the church, in honest priestly clothing, will appear before the rectors and trustees of the church. Beben Bratz, the 25th March, 1745. Louis Berthold, Archdeacon.

Ernestus was surgeon to the British garrison at Oswego from October 28, 1753, to May 22, 1755, and perhaps longer during the French & Indian War. A letter to him while he was at Oswego suggests how to get a raise:

Albany ye 29 Aug. 1755
 Mr. Ernestus Spitzer: your wife is now in town & have made up your account with her by which there is coming still to me after your first years salary is taken of b44,0,11 which is pretty considerable so that I cant well send up anything to you before I have a certificate for your second years salary ... Don't delay but send the certificate Directly other wise you may run grate risq ever to gite it—you would do well to gite from severall officers a certificate that you ought to have more salary as you now tend severall companies, and send it Down to me that I may lay it before the Assembly ... I am sir Your Humb Servt. Jno DePeyster.

After the French & Indian War, he settled in Schenectady and practiced medicine. He had a farm in Glenville, about seven miles above the city, where there was a family burying ground.
He died on October 8, 1789 in Schenectady, and originally was buried in the Old Dutch Cemetery.
In 1901 the monument of Ernestus was restored by some of his descendants, and the names of his sons, Garret (Garrit) and Aaron were added because they served in the Revolutionary War.

Ernestus' Children

1. Aaron. Aaron served as a medical officer during the Revolution.

Camp Windsor, March 7, 1783
 This may certify that Mr. Aaron Spitzer served in the 2nd New Hampshire Regt as a surgeon's mate from the 1st day of November 1782 till the 1st day of March instant, and was discharged, at the reduction of the Regt.
 A Morrell, Major
 Commanding 2d N.H. Regt.

In June, 1780, as a Corporal under Capt. Jesse Van Slyck, 2d Albany County Militia, he went in command of a detail to Beaverdam and Harpersfield. He served also in the Levies under Colonel Morris Graham. He is buried in Vale.

2. Elisabeth. Born May 18, 1755 (or April 23, 1754), married Aaron Potman (Putman) on February 21, 1772. She died on May 18, 1797 (or May 18, 1796) at age 42.

3. Gerrit. Born July 2 (or June 28), 1758; died June 2, 1801 in Woestina Amsterdam (now Rotterdam Junction, Schenectady County). He married Annatje Sixbury on June 25, 1780, daughter of Nicholas Sixbury and Susanna Clement. They had eight children; Aaron, Nicholas, Jeremiah, Susanna, Peter, John, Barbara and Joseph. Annetje died on November 20, 1806 at Woestina.

On September 24, 1776, he enlisted in Capt. John A. Bradt's company of State Rangers. In 1778 he was serving as a Sergeant under Capt. Jesse Van Slyck, 2d Albany County Militia. In May he commanded a detail to Sacandaga and in April, 1779, a detail to Ballston and Glens Falls. In November he commanded at the Upper Fort, Schoharie, and went in charge of a detail for scout duty to the Norman's Kill and Beaverdam. In April, 1780, he went on scout duty to Glens Falls and Lake George, and in June, 1781, was in command of a detail sent to Sacandaga to watch the movements of the Sacandaga Indians. In September he went to Beaverdam and Harpersfield on scout duty, and in July, 1782, commanded a party sent by the Schenectady Committee to Harpersfield to reconnoiter and spy on the enemy. In September he was in command of a scout at Sacandaga and Mayfield.

He is also buried in Vale.

4. Ernestus. Born September 27, 1761. No other information.

Ernestus' future descendants would become movers and shakers of Toledo, Ohio. Gen. Celian Milo Spitzer and Adelbert Lorenzo Spitzer founded Toledo's first prominent investment bank in the 1880s, Spitzer & Co. It was the first investment house west of New York City to engage exclusively in bond sales and was considered the "father of the municipal bond business of the middle west."

Other Spitzer's in the 1890s built the first steel skyscraper in Toledo—the Spitzer Building at the corner of Madison Avenue and Hudson Street. In 1905 they erected the 16-story Nicolas Building on the opposite side. Lyman P. Spitzer founded the Spitzer Paper Box Company in Toledo. Lyman F. Spitzer was a successful Toledo lawyer who died in 2011. His uncle Lyman Spitzer, Jr. became one of the youngest-ever chairmen of the Astronomy Department at Princeton, at the age of 32. He was regarded as the father of the Hubble Space Telescope and led early studies of nuclear fusion.

Philip Tell Dodge

1851 - August 9, 1931
Location: P#32

Philip Tell Dodge was a lawyer, inventor and financier, and an important part of the development of modern printing. He was born in Fond du Lac, Wisconsin in July, 1851, the son of a patent attorney. He moved to Washington with his family when a boy, after having lived for a time in Schenectady, where he studied mechanical design. His family was originally from Schenectady but moved west to improve the health of his mother. His father published a newspaper in Minnesota, but the plant burned down and they returned to Schenectady when he was ten. He went to night school and worked in a machine shop. In 1873 he received his law degree from what was then Columbian College, now George Washington University, and began practice as a patent lawyer. He began his career pleading cases before the U.S. Supreme Court as a patent lawyer.

Becoming head of the Mergenthaler Company in 1891, when it was heavily in debt, his interest in mechanics and his ability as an organizer were largely responsible for the development of the modern linotype machine.

As a patent attorney for the Remington Arms Company, he filed the papers for patents on the newly invented typewriter, and he recalled later, the application, written on the typewriter, was returned by the Patent Office to comply with rules that all applications be in handwriting!

He combined several of the features of the typewriter with the typesetting machine as it existed then and through his inventive genius the device was soon developed sufficiently to displace typesetting by hand. There was

Philip T. Dodge.

worldwide protest when the machine was made public by those that thought thousands of typesetters would be out of a job. In 1922 he ended his improvements with the ability to print Chinese language by reducing the number of Chinese characters from 40,000 to 40+ symbols. He is credited with more than 100 inventions.

In an interview about leaving law to go to the linotype he said, "I was fascinated from the first and accordingly gave up my good law practice as patent attorney to devote myself to improving the machine. Eleven years passed before any money began to come back from the capital I and those whom I interested put in. I had had to borrow money to pay grocery bills and keep my children in school, but went ahead with the machine."

His reputation was one to bring success to everything he was involved in. When he was elected to the head of the International Paper Company, the company was in financial difficulties, but he was able to bring it to the modern age, including building at the time the largest mill in the world.

He headed the Royal Typewriter Company and the Columbia Phonograph Company, and was also director of the Bank of New York & Trust Company, the American Surety Company, American Paper Exports, the Atlantic Coast Steamships Company, the Continental Paper Bag Company, 5th Avenue Coach Company, and the St. Maurice Lumber Company. He was Vice-President and Director of the Domill Construction Company.

He retired in 1928 and divided his attention between his home at 944 Park Avenue and one in Rye, New York.

He was the founder and President of the Boys Club, and was active in other civic and philanthropic undertakings. He belonged to the Union League, Lotos Engineers, New York Republicans, St. Andrews Golf, Rockaway Hunting, New York Yacht, Larchmont Yacht and Metropolitan of Washington.

He headed the Mergenthaler Linotype Company for 37 years, and 11 as President and Chairman of the Board of the International Paper Company. He died from an attack of bronchial pneumonia after an illness of ten days. He was 80 when he died.

He married Lilias Sutherland Dodge in Seattle in 1928, and had a son, Norman, and a daughter, Olive, by a former marriage in 1876 to Margaret A. Ball of Ohio, which ended in divorce. Norman succeeded his father as head of the Linotype in 1927.

He was one of the first to ride a bicycle in the country, and he also talked on the first telephone.

In Shortsville, New York in 1888, a lawsuit between Brown & Sheldon, and George H. Preston, seeding machine manufactures, was in progress. Philip Dodge was hired for Brown & Sheldon. As the case went forward Preston hired a second attorney, and when the attorney came to Shortsville he had to get a room at the Cottage Hotel. He was advised that he would have to share a room with another man. Surprisingly, the other man was Philip Doge, his brother, attorney for the other side. Since they considered it unethical he looked for other hotels.

When he died in Rye, New York at his summer home, his value after his death was $3,422,507, which went to his wife and two children.

James Chatham Duane

1824 - 1897
Chief of Engineers, Civil War (October 11, 1886 - June 30, 1888)
Location M*3 7

James Duane was born June 30, 1824, in Schenectady, New York. His grandfather, also named James, was a member of the Continental Congress, signer of the Articles of Confederation, and Mayor of New York City. He later founded the town of Duanesburg, hoping it would become the capital of New York State.

James C. Duane graduated from Schenectady's Union College in 1844 and from the U.S. Military Academy (West Point) in 1848. He ranked third in his class.

Duane taught practical military engineering there (1848-54) during the superintendency of Robert E. Lee. He was then employed in the construction of fortifications until 1856, and was lighthouse inspector at New York in 1856-58. Serving with the Army's company of sappers, miners, and pontoniers for nine years before the Civil War, he led its celebrated 1,100-mile march to Utah in 1858. He was afterward instructor of engineering at the military academy until the beginning of the Civil War. He was stationed at Fort Pickens, Florida, in 1861, and commanded select engineer troops to guard President Lincoln at his inauguration in 1861. During the winter following he organized engineer equipage for the Army of the Potomac, went to Harper's Ferry in February 1862, to bridge the Potomac, and commanded the engineer battalion at the siege of Yorktown, constructed bridges across Chickahominy and White Oak swamps, was engaged at Gaines's Mill on June 27, 1862, and in the subsequent operations of the Peninsular campaign made roads, fieldworks and bridges, notably one 2,000 feet long across the Chickahominy. Duane built the first military pontoon bridge over the Potomac at Harpers Ferry in 1862, and served as Chief Engineer of the Army of the Potomac (1863-65), and in seven hours in 1864 built the longest pontoon bridge of the Civil War (2,170 feet) across the James River.

In the Maryland campaign he served as Chief Engineer of the Army of the Potomac, and was engaged at South Mountain and Antietam. In 1863, as Chief Engineer of the Department of the South, he took part in the attack on Fort McAllister, Georgia, and in operations against Charleston. From July 15, 1863, he was again attached to the Army of the Potomac, and was engaged at Manassas Gap, Rappahannock Station, the Wilderness, and Cold Harbor, and distinguished himself at the siege of Petersburg. He became Captain of Engineers on August 6, 1861, Major on March 3, 1863, was brevetted Colonel on July 6, 1864, and Brigadier General at the close of the war.

From 1865 to 1868 he superintended the construction of the fort at Willet's Point, New York, receiving promotion as Lieutenant Colonel on March 7, 1867. He served subsequently as Superintendent of Fortifications on the coast of Maine and New Hampshire, as Lighthouse Engineer of the northeast coast, as a member of various engineer boards, and as President of the Board of Engineers in New York City (1884-86). He was promoted to Colonel on January 10, 1883, and in the autumn of 1886 was appointed Chief of Engineers, with the rank of Brigadier General. He retired in 1888. He then became Commissioner of Croton Aqueduct, New York. He published books titled, <u>History of Bridge Equipage in the United States Army</u> (1868) and <u>Duane's Manual for Engineer Troops</u> (1862), and a paper on the "Organization of the bridge equipage of the United States Army with directions for the construction of military bridges" (1870).

General Duane died December 8, 1897, in New York City.

Sketch of General Hunt and Major Duane, Chief of Artillery, September, 1864.

Isaac Groot Duryee

(July 29, 1810 - February 6, 1866)
Location: P38

Duryee (sometimes spelled Duryea) was born in Glenville to William Duryea (1784-1871). He married Lydia Augur Budington (1821-1910) and had nine children: Isaac, Sarah Julia (1845-1917), George E. (1852-1920), Charles C. (1858-1920), Harry Budington (1864-1930), Helen (1843-1914), William Budington (1847-1917), Jeanette (1855-1864) and Anne (1861-1917).

He received his undergraduate degree from Union College in 1838 and graduated from the Andover Theological Seminary in 1841. Duryee was a co-founder in 1836 of the Anti-Slavery Society at Union College and of the Anti-Slavery Society of the City of Schenectady in 1838. He also helped to create the first African-American church in Schenectady, known as the African Church (now the Duryee Memorial AME Zion Church), in 1837 on Jay Street. He served as the first Pastor of the Second Reformed Dutch Church, from 1852 to 1858. He then went on to serve a congregation in Montgomery County. From 1862 to 1865, he served as a chaplain to the 81st New York State Volunteers during the Civil War. According to the Underground Railroad Project, his granddaughter, Ruth M. Duryee, wrote in 1937 for a Union College alumni record that Duryee "helped with underground railways and drove many an escaping Negro from Schenectady to the next stop, with the Negro lying flat under hay in the back of the wagon."

In 1855, the General Synod of the Dutch Church had, without warning, to deal with the question of slavery. Discussion of a resolution to bring in the southern classis in North Carolina marked the commencement of a long debate, focused on the fact that among the North Carolina Classis' eight ministers were three slaveholders, owning a total of five slaves.

When confronted with the possible acceptance of southern classis as the debate developed, three distinct factions emerged. One favored acceptance of the southern classis without qualification. The second faction, represented primarily by Reverend H.D. Ganse and Duryea, feared that acceptance would be understood by their congregations and the public as an implicit sanction of slavery by the Synod; it thus sought outright rejection of the application. The third faction, led by the Rev. George Bethune, an active member of the New York Colonization Society, feared internal disruption of the Church and tried to keep the whole subject of slavery out the Synods deliberations.

Duryea posited an argument of a radical abolitionist as he attacked the Committee on Correspondences' resolution. Duryea declared:

> *I have conscientious scruples against the formation of such a relation. I am a Northern man. I have been reared under the principles of Liberty and Freedom. I am in conscience opposed to the system of slavery. I can say that my inmost soul shrinks from the idea of extending the fellowship of our Church to slaveholding Churches as I shrink from the touch of the torpedo.*

Frederick F. Eisenmenger

March 21,1849-1912
Location: M1 238

Frederick Eisenmenger was born in Schenectady and was the son of Ferdinand and Wilhelmina (Laman) Eisenmenger, both of whom were born in Germany, the father about the year 1827.

His father Ferdinand came to America in 1846, having received a good education and mastered the machinist's trade and intending to engage in business, but instead went to work for the Schenectady & Utica Railway Company for about sixteen years. In 1862 he enlisted as a private in Company K, 134th Regiment, New York Volunteers, with which he served in the Civil War until he died of wounds in June 1864. Mrs. Wilhelmina Eisen-

Frederick F. Eisenmenger.

menger, his wife, was left with two children: Pauline, who died in 1865, aged five years, and Frederick. The mother died in 1886, at the age of sixty-eight.

On August 11, 1862, thirteen-year-old Frederick Eisenmenger joined the same regiment in which his father enlisted, and was enrolled in the ranks of Company B, being one of the youngest volunteers to enter the service. He was detailed to serve at division headquarters under Maj. Gen. John W. Geary, commander of the Second Division, 20th Army Corps, and later Governor of Pennsylvania. He was with Sherman on the famous march to Atlanta to the sea. While in front of Atlanta he received a severe wound in the jaw, and he was mustered out with his regiment in June 1865.

In 1868 he began a four years' apprenticeship at the machinist's trade in the Schenectady Locomotive Works. He continued his education at nights, and while still employed at the works, he began to read law under the direction of Judge Austin Yates. He practiced law until May 2, 1882, when he was appointed Police Justice, which he performed from May 1882 to December 31, 1903.

In September 1874, he married Louisa Pepper, daughter of Louis A. Pepper. They had two children; Frederick, who was graduated from the high school in 1895, and worked in the experimental department of the General Electrical Works; and Clara, who married W.C. Fagal. Louisa died on October 12, 1930 at her home at 1226 Wendell Avenue, after three months illness. She is also buried at Vale.

Eisenmenger belonged to St. George Lodge, No. 6, F. & A.M.; was Past Commander of Horsfall Post, No. 90, G.A.R.; and was president of the 134th Regimental Association. He was a member and was an official of the Methodist Episcopal church. He built his residence at 105 Union Avenue in 1887, and he purchased for his mother the house in which she spent her last years. Politically he was a Democrat.

Frederick F. Eisenmenger was also Mayor of Schenectady, elected 1904, serving for two years, retiring due to failing health. In 1908 he was appointed Schenectady County Supervisor of the Poor.

In 1910, he found the burial of his father at Chattanooga while at a dedication of a monument of the New York State Troops at Lookout Mountain.

Charles F. Evans

October 15, 1889 - September 2, 1916
Location: Unknown

Charles Franklin Evans was born in Arlington, Vermont on October 15, 1889. He had a short life and a brief major league career of just 17 games and 52.2 innings pitched. But he did leave a major mark in baseball. He threw a perfect game in which not a single batter hit a ball out of the infield. He died just eight years later.

Evans grew up in North Bennington and attended Burr & Burton Seminary in Manchester, where he was the captain and star pitcher of the baseball team. He was nicknamed "Chick."

After graduating from Burr & Burton in 1907, Evans joined a semi-pro team in Hoosick Falls, New York, where he was scouted by "Buttermilk" Tommy Dowd. a ten-year big league veteran who last appeared in the majors with the Boston Americans in 1901 and who after the big leagues played and managed in several minor and independent leagues and coached the college teams at Amherst and Williams.

As manager of the Hartford Connecticut League he signed Evans to a contract for the 1908 season. Evans won 13 games as an 18-year-old rookie, but his outing against Bridgeport on July 21, 1908 is what really made major league teams take notice.

The following account appeared in the *Hartford Times*:

There was not a fly or a ground ball handled by the Hartford outfielders during the entire game. Only twenty-seven men faced Evans in the nine innings. Ten of these struck out. He fanned at least one man in eight of the nine innings, and in the sixth and ninth had two in each to his credit. Nearly all of the crowd of 1,500 stayed until the end, hoping that Chick would turn the trick. He fanned the last two in the ninth inning. After the game the crowd gathered around Evans and congratulated him on his great pitching feat.

He was sold to the Boston Nationals after winning ten games halfway through the 1909 season, but was basically benched, pitching in only four games, with a record of 0-3.

In 1910 he started the season pitching one-hit ball during the last three innings to beat the New York Giants 3-2 in 11 innings. However, there appears to be some controversy as to it being his only major league win, with some writers giving him a 3-0 record instead of a 1-1 record.

Following the 1910 season, he pitched on October 12 for the Hoosick Falls Council of the Knights of Columbus in an all-star aggregation of minor leaguers in a game against the Bennington council. They lost 11-1 as Bennington had hired the Boston Red Sox as the opposing team. Evans gave up nine runs in four innings.

After 1910 his career started to dwindle, pitching for a the Syracuse team in 1911-12 with arm trouble, then moving to Schenectady in 1916 where he worked for General Electric in the munitions department and played outfield for the company team. He also became sick later in the year and was hospitalized in Schenectady's Ellis Hospital from the end of July until his death on September 2, 1916. His death was listed due to "general septicemia and acute gonorrheal endocarditis," with a "cerebral embolism" listed as contributory. His funeral was held at his brother's home in North Bennington and his body brought to Vale on September 4, 1916.

His obituary reads:

Charles (Chick) Evans, who had pitched for both Pittsfield independent and league club is dead. He died in a hospital in Schenectady on Saturday night of heart trouble. Evans first went to Pittsfield as a pitcher when Cy Ferry ran an independent team on the common and did fine work. He went to the Hartford club of the Connecticut league and became famous by pitching a game in which no hits nor runs were made off his delivery, no player reached first base and no ball was batted to the outfield. Evans later went to the Boston Nationals where he remained for two seasons, a lameness bringing about his release. In 1913 he joined the Pittsfield Eastern association club at the start of the season, but only remained a short time. Evans has played with various New York state clubs.

Silas Watson Ford

1848 - June 25, 1895
Location: K-102

Silas Watson Ford is a name that doesn't come up often in the annals of American Geology but he made a major contribution to the field. Ford, a Troy telegrapher, was an amateur paleontologist who made some of the most important discoveries regarding Cambrian paleontology in the 19th century. He found the first early Cambrian period fossils in North America, helping to resolve a geological controversy that was going on for 30 years. In his short life span, Ford published more than 23 scientific papers. His seven-part series of geological processes in the New York Tribune in 1879 was so popular that Union College awarded him an honorary master's degree.

The Ford family was originally from Glenville. Silas and his family moved to Schenectady after the death of his parents, and then to Troy. His brother, Stephen Van Rensselaer Ford, went from station agent for the Rensselaer and Saratoga Railroad in 1854, to a joint partnership with George P. Ide in 1865 to make collars and cuffs. Ide & Ford located their business at 506 Fulton Street.

Silas appears to have moved to Troy the following year, boarding at 208 North Second Street, and was listed as a telegraph operator. His brother, Isaac, was a telegraph operator at the Union Railroad depot and probably trained his younger brother. Later, he is listed as a bookkeeper and may have worked at Stephen's collar company. The partnership dissolved between Ford and Ide, and George Ide went on to become one of Troy's largest collar companies. Silas went back as a telegraph operator, but his keen interest in geology finally led him to James Hall, the State Geologist in Albany.

Hall and fellow geologist Ebenezer Emmons were in an intellectual battle. Emmons had proposed the Taconic System to describe the formation of the Taconic Mountains and rocks of easternmost New York and western Massachusetts. Emmons had given an older Cambrian age (540 to 505 million years ago) to these rocks, while Hall said they were younger, of Ordovician age (500 to 438 million years ago). The Taconic Orogeny or mountain-building period happened about 450 million years ago when a volcanic island arc collided with proto-North America (around the Connecticut Valley region). This event ran from Newfoundland to Alabama. The rocks, which had originally been deposited in a deep-water area were stacked together by these plate collisions and formed the Taconic Mountain range. Originally this mountain range was as high as the Himalayas, but quickly eroded and the sediments were deposited into a shallow sea that covered most of the middle half of proto-North America.

In Troy you can see this overthrust where older rocks are sitting on top of younger rocks (especially in the Mt. Ida Gorge) and geologists attempted to explain this anomaly (now called the Emmons Thrust, earlier Logan's Fault). Ford had found fossils in parts of these rocks in Beman Park, which helped explain the older age of the rocks and in the long run helped support Emmons theories. Eventually Emmons was proven correct (he is buried close to Hall in Albany Rural Cemetery and it's reported he is facing Hall in his grave—poetic justice?).

Ford jumped into the fray. His discoveries of fossils of Cambrian age proved that portions of the Taconic were older than what Hall had proposed. While not formally trained in geology, early on he wrote to Hall, at the urging of William Gurley, in an attempt to get help and guidance in training in geology, his real passion. Ford had offered loans of his fossils to Hall and Hall visited Ford in Troy. In 1871, Ford published an important article in the American Journal of Science that correlated the Troy rocks to the older Cambrian period and described the first ever fossil, *Hyolithes opercula*, found in North America. At 23, this established Ford as a leading authority on Cambrian fauna east of the Hudson. He even had one of his fossils named after him by a leading paleontologist, in 1881. *Fordilla troyensis* is one of the oldest know bivalves in the world. Throughout all of this he was still a telegraph operator now working for the American Telegraph Company, then absorbed into Western Union at 249 River Street, where the City Hall was recently torn down. He was given an honorary M.A. in Geology in 1877 and was a member of the Psi Upsilon fraternity in 1875, Union College in Schenectady.

What appeared to be a promising career however came to an early end. He temporarily worked with the U.S. Geological Survey, got married, and was prolific in his writings. However, Ford had either an alcohol or opium addiction and always seemed to be in debt, needing to borrow money. Eventually most of the geologists he had been corresponding with or working with wrote him off. Ford had a $72.20 debt that he couldn't afford to pay off.

Separated from his wife, she tried to sell off his fossil collection of 419 specimens and 170-volume personal library to repay the debt. Ford himself had been declared legally incompetent, so Mrs. Ford assumed all liability for the debt. Her second husband sued her on the grounds that she told him that Ford was already dead.

James Hall tried to get the State Regents to buy the fossil collection, but problems arose and continued to occur as they agreed to buy it, then reneged on the deal. While the state

---

HUSBAND NOT DEAD BUT INSANE.

The Woman's Second Husband Therefore Wants His Marriage Annulled.

John J. Powell, an ice dealer of 368 Gold Street, Brooklyn, has brought suit in the Supreme Court of Kings County to annul his marriage with Caroline Powell, on the ground that when she became his wife she had a lawful husband living. He alleges that when he married her on July 3, 1889, he was aware that she had been the wife of one Silas W. Ford, but she had alleged that Ford, who was insane, had died in the Middletown Insane Asylum. Relying on the truth of this statement, plaintiff married her.

The defendant, in her answer, denied that she had said her husband was dead. She said Powell understood that he was alive, although incarcerated in an insane asylum. She also testified that plaintiff led her to believe the insanity of her husband released her from the bonds of wedlock, and that a marriage in another State would be lawful.

Justice Bartlett yesterday handed down a decision that the papers in the case had not been properly served on the defendant.

DEADLY ELECTRICAL SHOCK.

Philip Pearson Fatally Injured by an Electric-Light Current.

Philip Pearson, twenty-seven years old, of 1,396 St. Mark's Avenue, Brooklyn, a lineman in the employ of the Western Union Telegraph Company, while repairing a wire on a pole at the foot of Broadway, Williamsburg, yesterday morning, accidentally came in contact with a live electric-light wire. He received a severe shock and was badly burned.

Pearson hung for several minutes on a mass of telegraph wires with his head hanging over, while his body swayed and threatened to slip and fall head first to the pavement, forty feet below. A crowd gathered, ladders were procured, and the man was lowered to the ground in an unconscious condition.

An ambulance from the Eastern District Hospital was summoned. Ambulance Surgeon McCleary pronounced the man fatally injured. He was removed to the hospital and his friends were notified.

Article from the *New York Times*, August 27, 1893.

bickered back and forth, Mrs. Ford died on February 24, 1895. The collection was finally purchased (no one knows who the seller was) in 1900 for $70.70 and is now in the state paleontology collections. No one knows what happened to Ford's personal library, but it may have been lost in the great Capitol fire of 1911, in which almost half a million of the state's library's collections were lost.

Four months after Mrs. Ford died, Silas died at the home of his cousin, William F Hodges, in Wilton on June 25, 1895, and was buried in Schenectady's Vale Cemetery. He was 47. His death was caused by "General Debility."

Regardless of his personal problems and short life, the 20-year contributions of Troy's Silas Watson Ford to American Paleontology are well documented and finally given the recognition they deserved.

Richard Hansen Franchot

June 2, 1816 - November 23, 1875
Location: M2#9

Richard was born in the Town of Morris in Otsego County, New York, and was the son of French immigrant Judge Stanislas Paschal Franchot (1774-1855) and Catherine Hansen (1783-1818).

Richard Franchot attended the public schools and the Hartwick and Cherry Valley Academies, and then studied civil engineering at Rensselaer Polytechnic Institute, in Troy, New York. He served for several years as President of the Albany & Susquehanna Railroad.

Franchot was elected as a Republican to the Thirty-seventh Congress (March 4, 1861 - March 3, 1863). He was not a candidate for renomination in 1862.

He moved to Schenectady, New York, and raised the 121st Regiment, New York Volunteer Infantry. Franchot was commissioned as a Colonel on August 23, 1862, and was brevetted as a Brigadier General of U.S. Volunteers, dating from March 13, 1865. At Antietam, his regiment occupied Crampton's Gap after the fighting there was over, gathering stragglers and burying the dead. They did not see combat at Antietam, arriving on the battlefield on September 18th. Franchot resigned his commission on September 25 in favor of Emory Upton as his replacement. While successful as an organizer, with no previous military experience or training he felt unequal to the task of combat leadership. He returned to Congress for the duration of his term. He was brevetted Brigadier General of Volunteers in March 1865 in honor of his service.

After the war, he was associated with the Central Pacific Railroad part of the Transcontinental Railroad as a paid lobbyist, around 1864.

He married Anna Van Vranken (September 10, 1822 - January 10, 1881) and they had several children: Janet McClelland Franchot; Gertrude; Mary; Anna; Katherine; and Richard Huntington Franchot. New York Superintendent of Public Works Nicholas Van Vranken Franchot (1855-1943) and State Senator Stanislaus P. Franchot (1851-1908) were also his sons, and Assemblyman Nicholas V.V. Franchot II (1884-1938) was his grandson.

Richard died in Schenectady, New York on November 23, 1875.

Robert M. Fuller

1845 - 1919
Location: M-128

Robert Fuller was born in Schenectady to John Irwn and Louisa (Gardner) Fuller. His father was a merchant and banker, and later a maker of pianos in New York City. Robert went to Union School, graduating in 1863, and received his M.D. degree from Albany Medical College in 1865. He started his practice in Albany, but in 1866 moved to New York City. He never married. Fuller is credited for inventing the tablet for the taking of medicine. Basically every pill you take can be attributed to his invention.

The Albany Medical Annals, Volume 41 1920, published the following bio:

Dr. Robert M Fuller died at his home in Schenectady N.Y., on Saturday morning, December 27, 1919.

Dr. Fuller was one of the most successful and most distinguished of the alumni of the Albany Medical College, particularly from his researches in microscopy and pharmacology. For many years after his graduation he went quietly ahead with his investigations and avoided publicity, but he had quietly and unostentatiously studied out the now universal method of dispensing drugs in tablet form. Few physicians are acquainted with the fact that the small tablets, which form so prominent a part of their equipment, originated with Dr. Fuller. In 1900 he retired from work and took up his residence in Schenectady, the city of his birth, and in 1915 he joined the three other surviving members of his medical class in a semi-centennial anniversary of their celebration, which was held in Albany on May 25th. The occasion was a notable one, because rarely have the class reunions been marked by such a gathering of a remote class. Since his return to Schenectady Dr. Fuller had renewed the interest of his youth in Union College and in the Albany Medical College, and has been a free contributor to the activities of these institutions, more particular in the establishment of a library for the Chemical Depart at Schenectady. His enthusiasm, for his Alma Mater has been revealed by the bequests, and he has given for the Medical Department Thirty Thousand dollars, the income of which is to be used to assist needy medical students in obtaining their education.

But apart from all these personal and processional activities of Dr. Fuller, there have been incidents in his life of great moment and interest. These were described in a biographical sketch provided for the history of the Class of 1863 of Union College, published at Schenectady in June, 1913, as follows:

He is another one of the Class of '63 who has brought great credit to Union College. He was born in Schenectady New York October 27, 1845. He attended the Union School Schenectady, studied pharmacy in New York City, then took a chemistry course of five terms at Union College under Dr. Charles F. Chandler, being entered in the Class of 1863. He received a certificate from Dr. Chandler, dated August 12, 1863, of the work done. He graduated at the Albany Medical College in December, 1865. While there he took a special course in toxicology, and invented the method of using the photographic camera to aid chemical analysis. He made photographs of the octahedral crystals of arsenious acid, which were afterwards used with effect in a notable trial for murder by poisoning. Dr. Fuller developed this use of the microscope and camera and applied it to the study of bacteria and other microorganisms. He was a pioneer in this field and gained a national reputation. While a student in Dr. James H Armsby's office in Albany, he was Dr. Armsby's assistant in surgery in the Ira Harris United States Hospital at Albany. Many of the photographs, which he took of wounds, have been used as illustrations in the official Medical and Surgical History of the War. While thus employed he was sent to City Point, VA, to bring home a wounded officer [Lt. John Dempsey]. On his way there he stopped a day in Washington, and, as it happened, he attended Fords' Theater the night President Lincoln was shot. He had seen Lincoln enter the box, followed by Major Rathbone and Miss Harris of Albany. The audience cheered the President. Soon a puff of smoke, a man jumping from Lincoln's box to the stage, tripping and falling to the stage floor, rising and shouting "Sic Semper Tyrannis, Revenge for the South," then turning to the stage entrance, which was filled by actors and actresses coming on the stage, he waved his knife in the air and literally cut a passage for himself and was gone. Meanwhile cries of "the President's shot": rang out, and from the audience cries of "Kill him! Kill him! Great confusion ensued, with fears of other murders and through the night exaggerated reports on every side. Fuller slept none that night. It was a tragic experience, and there are few living who saw it. His pass to City Point is dated April 15th, 1865. There he found the officer he sought, too sick to be moved, so he was detailed in the 6th Army Corps Hospital at City Point for nearly a month and had some insight into surgical methods at the front.

In October, 1866, Dr. Fuller settled in New York City, and later on 42nd street, where he practiced for forty years. In 1878 he had invented a new system of preparing drugs in the form of tablet triturates to secure accuracy of measurement. On February 21, 1878, he gave the results of his investigation in a paper read before the New York Academy of Medicine, entitled, "An Easy, Economical and Accurate Method of Dispensing Medicine in a Compact and Palatable Form." This paper was published in the Medical Record of March 9, 1878. This invention has been adopted by all the leading pharmaceutics of today, Dr. Fuller's work was recognized by his appointment as a delegate to aid in revising the United States Pharmacopoeia.

In an editorial New Remedies, March 1878, the editors say:

Dr. Fuller's method of subdividing remedies so as to enable them to be administered in an agreeable form, and in uniform and adjustable strength, with the least expenditure of labor, appears to be a step in advance of previously known pharmaceutical methods, and like some other inventions of practical utility, surprises us by its simplicity and makes us wonder why it was not suggest long ago.

The American Druggist in January 1887, quotes Dr. Fuller in the Medical Record of March 9, 1878 and March 25, 1882, and says

The method of making tablet triturates was original by Dr. Fuller, who has very generously given it to the public and voluntarily denied himself the very considerable income which would have resulted from a patent right.

In a communication from Sharpe and Dohme, Dr. Fuller is called "The Father of Tablet Triturates." In fact his work has been recognized and adopted by many pharmaceutical associations and manufacturers both here and abroad.

In regard to his foundation work and study in the Union College Laboratory, Dr. Fuller said recently: "If I live fifty years more, what I learned there would give me plenty to do." In 1862, he was Treasurer and Librarian and in 1863 Vice President of the Chemical Society of Union College. A few years ago he returned to Schenectady where he resided in the old homestead at 12 North Ferry Street. He attended the 50th reunion of the class of 1863.

The 1921 volume of the Albany Medical Annals, the Journal of the Alumni Association of the Albany Medical College added the following:

Robert M. Fuller of Schenectady bequeathed a fund to Union College, the income of which is divided into ten scholarships, awarded to students in the Albany Medical College who have taken their premedical courses in Union College. By the terms of the bequest, the committee of award consists of the President and the Dean of the Faculty of Union College, and the Dean of the Albany Medical College. These scholarships will be given only to those students who have shown, while in Union College, general mental and physical fitness for the work of the medical profession, and who have excelled in the premedical courses in chemistry. Five of the scholarships are reserved for those students who, at the time of entering the medical college, have received or are candidates for a bachelor's degree from Union College. The other five may be awarded to students who have completed the two years premedical course.

Thirty thousand dollars was given to the college for the scholarships and they are still available to Union College students.

Dr. Fuller developed a method of used medicated milk sugar to fill pill molds with medicine and proposed the concept in a paper read at the American Medical Society on February 21, 1878. He and Horatio N. Frasier, a New York pharmacist, went into business in 1893 to make them and with the public statement that the process will not and should not be patented so that all pharmacists could make them.

When he died at his house on 14 North Ferry Street, the *New York Times* said he was a millionaire.

Fuller's house at 14 North Ferry Street, restored in 2015. (Courtesy of Richard Vang.)

William Kendall Fuller

November 24, 1792 - November 11, 1883
Location: P#29

William Fuller was born in Schenectady, New York, to Jeremiah Fuller (1766-1839) and Mary Kendall (1775-1860).

Fuller attended the common schools and graduated from Union College in 1810.

He studied law in the office of Henry and John B Yates. He was admitted to the bar in 1814 and commenced practice in Schenectady. He went into a partnership with John B. Yates.

In 1814, during the summer, they moved to Utica, New York and practiced until 1816, then moved to Chittenango, in Madison County. William became very popular there and in 1823 Governor Joseph C. Yates (also from Schenectady) appointed him Adjutant General of New York State, serving through his administration and several months in Governor Clinton's, declining to continue on political grounds. After serving his post, he became interested in management of real estate and became commissioner to drain the Canaseraga marsh, and was a Director and Secretary/Treasurer of the "Side Cut" of the Chittenango to the Erie Canal, completed under his supervision.

He served as District Attorney of Madison County (1821-1829) and as a Member of the State Assembly in 1829 and 1830. He also served as postmaster, judge advocate, judge of the common pleas, supervisor, town clerk, school trustee and justice of the peace.

Fuller was elected as a Jacksonian to the Twenty-third and Twenty-fourth Congresses (March 4, 1833 - March 3, 1837).

He resumed the practice of law back in Schenectady for twenty years before he died. He donated $10,000 to the city of Schenectady towards the erection of a city hall in 1881. He never married and died in Schenectady, almost 91 years old.

Robert Furman

1819-January 5, 1894
Location: M#178

Furman arrived in Schenectady in 1843 from Herkimer, New York, at age 17. His brother Rensselaer Furman, a merchant, requested that he come and work for him. While working there he got a job for Myndert Van Guysling who occupied the State and Ferry Street building, and on December 2, 1857, he married Catherine Van Guysling. He eventually owned it. He did well and was very civic-minded. He donated land to make Crescent Park on the top of State Street (now Veteran's Park) in 1860

Furman was a lawyer and a merchant but promoted the development of railroads, parks, business and public buildings. He helped organize the Schenectady & Ogdensburgh Railroad, the Schenectady & Athens Railroad, and convinced New York City's A.R. Chisholm to build a street railroad in the city, laying the groundwork for the Schenectady Street Railway Company in 1886. The horse car line went from Washington Avenue up to Brandywine Avenue.

When Walter McQueen and Charles Stanford formed the McQueen Locomotive Works in 1886 they built two large buildings, but Stanford died suddenly and McQueen resigned so the buildings sat empty. It was Robert Furman and others who decided to intervene and purchase the buildings so that Thomas Edison would move his electric works to Schenectady. Furman rushed to Albany to let Edison's people know that the buildings were available. Edison would not pay more than $37,500 of the $45,000 asked for, so the citizens came up with the other $7,500 to secure the deal. Furman led the fundraising, and Schenectady would become General Electric's home.

His home, which he built in 1857 and died in at the corner of Lafayette and Smith Streets, has served as the Rectory for St. Josephs Roman Catholic Church since 1928. His daughter Catherine etched her name on the second floor window, which is still there. His business establishment was located at the northeast corner of State and Ferry streets, now owned by the Schenectady County Community College. George Westinghouse Jr. also rented office space in the building.

He was a trustee of the YMCA, and as assemblyman helped get $30,000 to build an armory, $30,000 to survey for a railroad to run to Canada, and a $100,000 appropriation for an observatory for Union College that got vetoed. He also helped raise money for the Home of the Sisters of Charity and the Old Ladies Home. He also helped get Vale Cemetery started.

During the draft riots in 1863, he raised a regiment called the Washington Continentals at the request of the governor, and his buffalo regiment went to the front against General Lee. He got his Colonel designation from this regiment, the 83rd New York.

He also represented Schenectady in the New York State Assembly in 1868.

Carroll A. "Pink" Gardner

1894 - September 28, 1969
Location: 1 F N

Carroll "Pink" Gardner was born in Poughkeepsie and moved to Schenectady with his family when he was 13 years old.

He was the owner of the Chas. N. Gardner & Sons monument company that specialized in building memorial headstones, and was and located at 918-920 State Street. His father started the company in 1900. Carroll was President of the New York State Retail Monument Builders Association and built his own elaborate headstone in 1951. It shows two ancient Roman wrestlers from 300 B.C., and a statement about wrestling. He also owned the Gardner School of Physical Culture.

A former world-class wrestler, he started wrestling with the Schenectady YMCA in 1911. While only 5 feet, 8 inches tall and weighing 162 pounds, he had a neck of 16 inches, a chest of 41 inches, 14-1/2-inch biceps, forearms of 12-1/2 inches, thighs of 22 inches and a calf of 14-1/2 inches. His titles included World Middleweight Champion in 1921 and 1922 and World Heavyweight Champion in 1932. He made the carnival circuit and traveled the country. He stopped fighting at age 42 but was still in great physical shape throughout his life. He taught wresting and jujitsu during WWII at the Marine barracks in Scotia.

Gardner in 1924 and 1949. (Courtesy of *The Rotarian*.)

He became County Sheriff in 1930-31, the first Democrat in 30 years. He was a controversial official to say the least. When he became County Clerk in 1936, it took him three months to decide to use photostat machines instead of typewriting public records. The Motor Vehicle Bureau of which he was in charge was late in submitting records to the state DMV. He also had 17 extra employees on his payroll that were unexplained.

Gardner, undefeated as County Clerk, held the position for 11 terms from 1936 to 1969. He was the leading vote-getter in the county's history, but lost bids for Congress three times, the last in 1934 to Mayor Sam Stratton in a primary, and Stratton had every Democratic leader against him. Stratton won heavily anyway by 68% of the vote.

Pink was the son-in-law to four-term Schenectady Mayor George R. Lunn, a socialist and later Democrat. He married his daughter Eleanor Lunn and had three children; Carroll A. Jr., George R.L., and Mrs. James H. Jewell. His son George graduated from the University of Rochester with a B.A. in Political Science in 1961 and was later Mayor of St. Petersburg, Florida.

Gardner was a member of the Rotary Club of Schenectady. In 1966, he was awarded the Mason's "Man of the Year" award. He was a member of New Hope Lodge No. 730, F. & A.M.

He and his wife Eleanor lived at 1248 Waverly Place in Schenectady. Gardner died at his summer home in Newfane, Vermont at age 75. He collapsed while entertaining the annual outing of the Schenectady Oldtime Football Players, Inc. When he died his Schenectady address was 116 Governors Lane.

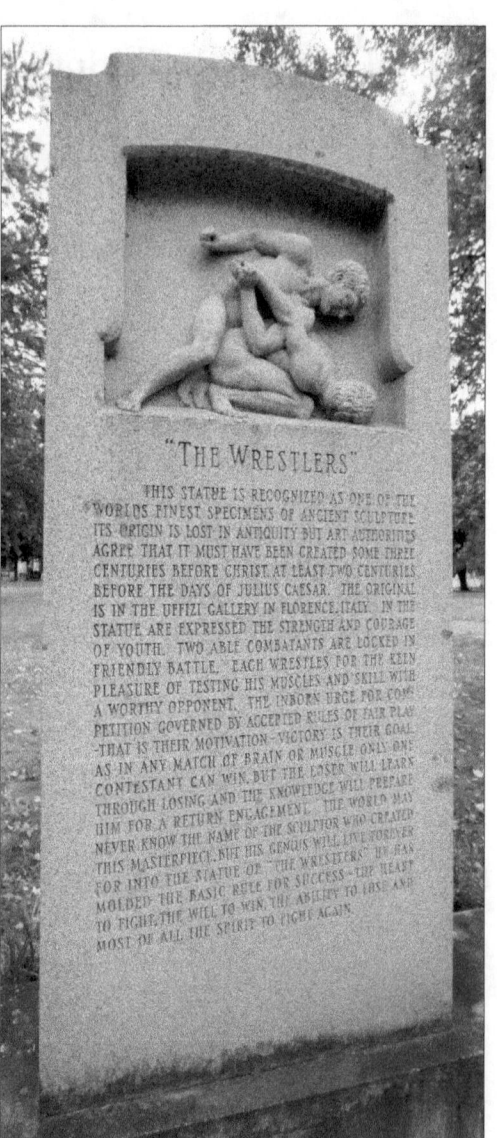

Gardner's monument at Vale, and a political ad from 1942 (left).

Stephen Gates

November 15, 1750 - July 21, 1837
Location: H2

Stephen Gates was born in Huntington, Suffolk County, New York. He married Eve Young after his first wife, Eunice, died. He served as a private in Captain Woodworth's Company of Colonel Morris Graham's Regiment in 1775.

He took part in breaking up a band of Tories that was under the command of a Mr. Jones. Jones escaped and took part in raids in the Mohawk Valley.

He was ordered to cut off the advance of Sir William Johnson in 1780, but failed to find Johnson near Lake George. He later served as scout and guide in the Burgoyne Campaign, until the British surrendered.

He served in the Albany County Militia, 13th Regiment, and served under other officers. He lived only three miles west of Bemis Heights in Saratoga and served as a volunteer guide to the scouting portion of the Continental Army under General Horatio Gates.

He later lived in Dutchess County. His remains were removed to Vale Cemetery after 1857.

He had a son, also named Stephen Gates (1785-1850), who married Hannah Gates (1788-1850).

Gravestones in Vale of Stephen Gates and his wife Eva Young.

Henry Jacob Glen

July 13, 1739 - January 6, 1814
Location: L2#19

Henry, also known as Hendrick, was born in Albany, the son of Jacob Glen and Elizabeth Cuyler, and grew up in the Dutch culture of the region. While early on in his career he was successful in Indian trade and land speculation, he operated a company with his brother, John Glen, and Jacob Teller. Glens Falls was named after his brother John (Johannes)

As an early settler of Schenectady, he was appointed Town Clerk on February 27, 1767, and served until March 11, 1809.

He was the commander of the 2nd Company of the Schenectady Militia at the beginning of the Revolution and was ranked a Captain. He also served on the Schenectady Committee of Safety. He accompanied George Washington on his tour of the Mohawk valley in 1783.

Henry was also Deputy Quartermaster General in the Revolutionary War, rising to Colonel. He was a member of the First, Second and Third Provincial Congresses (1774-1776), and served as a Member of the State Assembly in 1786 and 1787. He was elected to the Third and to three succeeding Congresses, March 4, 1793 to March 3 1801. In 1810 he was a Member of the State Assembly for one more term. He was one of three Commissioners of Indian Affairs.

His house at the south corner of Washington and Union streets in the Stockade burned in the great fire of 1819. Glen had sold that house to James Murdoch to pay off his debts. Henry moved to 5 Front Street, still standing, where he lived until he died.

He owned property in both Albany and Schenectady, and in 1790 his Albany residence included seven slaves.

He was buried in the First Dutch churchyard, but removed to Vale.

His sister Janet was the wife of Abraham Cuyler, Mayor of Albany from 1770 to 1776, who was banished to Canada for having Tory leanings, and who founded the town of Yorkfield.

Henry married Elisabeth Vischer on December 9, 1762 ,and had several children: Elisabeth, Catarina, Jannetje, Jacob, Johannes and Cornelius.

His papers consisting of fifteen letters are in the William L. Clements Library at the University of Michigan.

William Elliot Griffis

September 17, 1843 - February 5, 1928
Location: I2

William Griffis was an author, traveler, historian, lecturer and minster. Much of the following information is from his biographical article on *Wikipedia*.

Griffis was born in Philadelphia, Pennsylvania, the son of Captain John Limeburner Griffis, a sea captain and later a coal trader. During the American Civil War, he served three months in the 44th Pennsylvania Volunteers Regiment, after Lee invaded Pennsylvania in 1863. After the war, he attended Rutgers University at New Brunswick, New Jersey, graduating in 1869. At Rutgers, Griffis was an English and Latin language tutor for Taro Kusakabe, a young samurai from the province of Echizen (part of modern Fukui).

After a year of travel in Europe, he studied at the seminary of the Dutch Reformed Church in New Brunswick (known today as the New Brunswick Theological Seminary).

In September 1870, Griffis was invited to Japan by Matsudaira Shungaku, for the purpose of organizing schools along modern lines. In 1871, he was Superintendent of Education in the province of Echizen. In recompense, he was provided with a salary of $2,400, a house in Fukui and a horse.

In 1872-74, Griffis taught chemistry and physics at Kaisei Gakkō (the forerunner of Tokyo Imperial University). He prepared the five-volume "New Japan Series" of reading and spelling books (1872). He also published primers for Japanese students of the English language, and he contributed to the Japanese press, and to newspapers and magazines in the United States, numerous papers of importance on Japanese affairs.

Griffis was joined by his sister, Margaret Clark Griffis, who became a teacher at the Tokyo Government Girls' School (later to become the Peeresses' School). By the time they left Japan in 1874, Griffis had befriended many of Japan's future leaders. Griffis was a member of the Asiatic Society of Japan, the Asiatic Society of Korea, the Historical Society of the Imperial University of Tokyo, and the Meirokusha.

Griffis came to Schenectady in 1877 to become pastor of the First Reformed Church, and left in 1886. Griffis taught at Union College for a short time while in Schenectady. He was called to the pastorate of the Shawmut Congregational Church in Boston, and served there for seven years. In 1893 he accepted a call to the First Congregational Church of Ithaca until 1904,

William E. Griffis.

when he resigned to give his time entirely to his special work. While in Ithaca he was a professor at Cornell and was named Historian of the Finger Lakes Association in 1919. He was also chairman of the Congress of Religions in St Louis. He received his D.D. degree at Union College in 1884 and a L.H.D. at Rutgers at 1899.

While in Schenectady he married Katherine L. Stanton on June 17, 1879, daughter of Professor Stanton, Principal of the Classical Department of Union School. They had a daughter, Lillian, and two sons, Stanton and John. His second marriage was to Frances King at Pulaski, New York in 1900.

In 1903 he resigned from the active ministry to devote himself exclusively to writing and lecturing. His books on Japan and Japanese culture were complemented with extensive college and university lecture circuit itineraries. In addition to his own books and articles during this period, he also joined Inazo Nitobe in crafting what became his most well-known book, Bushido: The Soul of Japan.

In 1907, the Japanese government conferred the Order of the Rising Sun, Gold Rays with Rosette, which represents the fourth highest of eight classes associated with the award. Griffis and Dr. Guido F. Verbeck are credited with doing more for the progress and education of Japan than any others.

The prolific writer was also a prolific traveler, making eleven trips to Europe—primarily to visit the Netherlands. In 1898, he was present at the enthronement of Queen Wilhelmina; and he attended the Congress of Diplomatic History. He was among the group of Bostonians who wanted to commemorate the Pilgrims' roots in Holland; and the work was rewarded with the dedication of a memorial at Delfshaven and the placement of five other bronze historical tablets in 1909. He was one of four Americans elected to the Netherlands Society of Letters in Leiden.

In 1923 Griffis published The Story of the Walloons: At Home in Lands of Exile and in America. In this work he reveals the long history and contributions of these Belgians. The last half of the book relates the story of New Belgium (Nova Belgica) in America, the first settlers of Manhattan being a group of Protestant Walloons who petitioned the Dutch West India Company to be sent to establish a colony in the New World. These Walloons were sent to Manhattan as well as to other smaller locations on the Delaware, Hudson and Connecticut Rivers. They sailed out of Leiden, Netherlands in 1624. Griffis draws parallels to the thoughts of government and freedom of the Walloons and the US Constitution of 1787, and how their ideas made a lasting contribution to this country, though at the time (1923) the Walloons were generally unknown and overshadowed by the Dutch and later, English. This remains true to a great degree even today. In 1914 he tried to get Schenectady interested in celebrating the burning of Schenectady in 1690.

In 1926, Griffis was invited to return to Japan and got a hero's welcome; on this trip, the Japanese government conferred a second decoration. He was presented with the Order of the Rising Sun, Gold Rays with Neck Ribbon, which represents the third highest of eight classes. A private rail car was provided by the Japanese government, and he visited several cities in the course of this return trip. He visited Fukui where he established the first technical school in 1872, and dignitaries and 10,000 school children turned out to welcome him.

Griffis was a founding member of the National Institute of Arts and Letters (later to become the American Academy of Arts and Letters), the American Historical Association, and the U.S. Naval Institute. His papers are in the Rutgers University archives. Many of his books can be downloaded for free at *http://www.archive.org*. A full list of Griffis' accomplishments, honors and publications appears in the *Wikipedia* article.

His sister Martha died in 1923 in Philadelphia, but was also buried in Vale with her two other sisters.

His daughter Lillian, who died at age 45 in 1934, gained some attention when she predicted the inundation of Manhattan Island by a tidal wave under her professional name of Kevvoh Deo Griffis. She was off by a few years. She had a national reputation as an astrologer and writer on the subject. While a Vassar graduate she married a well-known artist in New York City, but it only lasted a few years.

One of Griffis' two sons, Stanton Griffis, would become U.S. Ambassador to Poland, Egypt, Spain and Argentina under President Truman. Stanton Griffis was ambassador to Argentina while Juan and Eva Peron were in power, and wrote of his experiences in a book titled Lying In State. Stanton was called the "Genius of Wall Street." He was Chairman of the Executive Committee of Paramount Pictures, Chairman of the Board of the Madison Square Garden Corporation and a partner in the Hemphill, Noyes and Company brokerage firm. Stanton also made headlines in 1939 when he, age 52, married 26-year-old Helen Bourne, granddaughter of millionaire Commodore Frederick G. Bourne, co-founder of the Singer Sewing Machine Company. She also began a career in theater and movies in 1932.

The other son, John, became a composer.

In 1928, Griffis died at his winter home in Winter Park, Florida, of heart disease. His body was flown back to Schenectady with his wife, who was with him at the time.

Willis T. Hanson

1858 - 1933
Location M 3 26

During the 19th and early 20th century there were few laws governing patent medicines and there were hundreds of different remedies that could be purchased without any real knowledge if they were beneficial at all. One Schenectady man, Willis T. Hanson, became wealthy selling Dr. William's Pink Pills for Pale People in the late 1800s, a very popular cure-all pill at the time.

The pills originated with a Dr. William Jackson in Brockville, Ontario, Canada, who patented his pill in 1886 and sold the rights for $100 in 1891 to Canadian Senator George Fulford in Brockville. He formed the G.T. Fulford & Company in 1887 to manufacture and distribute patent medicines. He formed the Dr. Williams Medicine Company and sold Pink Pills for Pale People (the trading arm of Fulford). He did so well he was expanded through North America, Europe and the British Empire. The pills were advertised in 82 countries. The claims ranged from curing digestive problems for Civil War vets to curing all disease resulting from the "vitiated humors in the blood." The publication of testimonials from satisfied users of Pink Pills was his principal advertising technique employed. Designed to appeal to the average person's trust in other human beings, they provided a gripping, first-hand account of a "miraculous" cure. An early one claimed that Pink Pills had cured him of *locomotor ataxia*, a disorder affecting coordination. Testimonials were customized to fit the locality of business. One produced for the American market in the mid-1890s, for example, drew notice to the health problems of Civil War veterans. When Fulford expanded his enterprise to England, he attracted attention to Pink Pills by offering bicycles as prizes in different areas to those who collected the best testimonials.

Ads for the pills were cleverly made. They often read like a newspaper article or feature only for the reader at the end to see that the person was cured when they took Dr. Williams' Pink Pills for Pale People. The person cured was usually a local person and would sometimes have local or regional connections to it.

In Kansas, "Hobo Day" at Kansas University would tout the pills. From the beginning, Hobo Day combined pep rallies with street theater. In 1919, two students founded Doc Yak's Medicine Show, which soon became a Hobo Day staple. Doc Yak imitated the medical hucksters of so-called Patent Medicines (which were usually neither patented nor medicinal) by combining the instincts of the carnival barker with the latest in medical quackery. He advertised himself as a "Purveyor of Pink Pills for Pale People" and held massive on-campus rallies. Taking Doc Yak's medicine was said to ensure a KU victory.

Fulford became very wealthy and built a Beaux Arts style mansion called Fulford Place, designed by Albany architect Albert W. Fuller.

After Fulford's death in 1905, the company was run by his partner William T. Hanson of Schenectady until 1929, when George Taylor Fulford Jr. took over.

Hanson acquired the rights in 1892 to market the pills in the U.S. His company, the Dr. Williams' Medicine Company was at 147 Centre Street (Broadway). It was also listed as 195 State Street in 1887, where he is listed as an agent for the American Pharmaceutical Association. It was the location of his pharmacy.

Hanson lived at 821 Union and had a summer house at The Knolls where the General Electric Global Research Center now sits. He was the first President of the Union National Bank, President of the Board of Managers of Ellis Hospital, the Board of Trade, and a Trustee of Union College.

The tax laws of 1863 until 1883, and from 1898 to 1902, were passed to help pay for the Civil War and later, the Spanish American War. Companies that were taxed were allowed to make a special tax stamp that

Hanson's mansion at 821 Union Street.

they could put on their product. The products included medicine, perfumes and cosmetics, chewing gum and sparkling wines. A few companies such as Hanson's used the stamps. He had his own private die stamp beginning in 1899. 480,000 of them were printed. Hanson's tax was for the Spanish American War.

Most companies used general issue stamps bearing the picture of a battleship, but a handful chose to have their own made to give them some additional advertising and to set them apart from competitors. These private die stamps were approved by the IRS before they could be used, so they are considered to be federal revenue stamps.

Hanson did well until the passage of the Pure Food and Drug Act in 1906 and articles began to be published about the fraudulence of these claims from patented medicines. A scientific analysis of his product revealed they were mostly iron sulphate, starch and sugar, but also had some strychnine in it (in Australia the pills had arsenic in it). The company was sued and found guilty of mislabeling. By the 1930s the boon was over. Hanson died in 1933.

The label on this package shown of Dr. Williams' Pink Pills for Pale People reads:

Safe and Effective Tonic for the Blood and Nerves.

Anemic conditions, diseases caused by or dependent thin, impoverished blood and for nervous disorders resulting from malnutrition. Useful wherever a nervine or digestive tonic is required. These pills are guaranteed to contain no opiates or narcotics. Contents 40 pills.

Price 50 cents. 6 boxes for $2.50.

The Dr. Williams Medical Company. Schenectady, N.Y. and Brockville, Ontario.

W.T. Hanson Company, Schenectady, N.Y. U.S. distributors.

Directions inside in English, French, German, Spanish, Italian.

Dr. William's Medicine Company continued as a business until 1989. Hanson's monument is pink.

George Cochrane Hazelton

January 3, 1832 - September 4, 1922
Location: U#5

George was born in Chester, New Hampshire, the son of William and Mercy Jane Hazelton, and attended public schools there and then went to Pinkerton Academy in New Hampshire and Dummer Academy in Massachusetts. He then moved to Schenectady and attended Union College in 1858, where he studied law when admitted to the bar in Malone, New York. He practiced law in Amsterdam and Schenectady until 1863.

He married Ellen Van Antwerp of Schenectady in November 1863. They had four children, Harry and Alice, who died young, and two sons, George Jr. and John Hampden.

He moved to Boscobel, Wisconsin and became prosecuting attorney for Grant County from 1864 to 1868, was elected to the Wisconsin State Senate in 1867, and again in 1869. As a Republican he was elected to the House of Representatives in the 45th, 46th, and 47th Congresses, representing the state's 3rd congressional district, serving from March 4, 1877 to March 3, 1883. He was unsuccessful for a fourth term and practiced law in Washington, D.C. during the Harrison administration.

He died in Chester, New Hampshire at age 90 and was buried in Vale at Schenectady, the home of his wife. There is a bio of him while at Boscobel at: *http://www.rootsweb.ancestry.com/~wigrant/Hazelton_GeorgeCochrane.htm*.

George C. Hazelton.

Oswald D. Heck

February 13, 1902 - May 21, 1959
Location: M 3 61

Oswald was born in Schenectady to Oswald E. Heck and Magdalena Wurster, and became prominent as a New York politician as a liberal Republican and longest-termed Speaker in New York State history.

He graduated from Union College in 1924, but left Albany Law School where he was called "too liberal." He married Beulah W. Slocum in 1933.

He was a member of the New York State Assembly from 1932 to 1959 (Schenectady County 1st District 1932-44, Schenectady County 1945-59), was Majority Leader in 1936, and Speaker from 1937 until his death in 1959.

He was a delegate to the Republican National Convention in 1944, 1948, 1952, and 1956. Using his wit and influence he became the state's most influential legislator of the 20th century.

According to an *Albany Times Union* article, written by Bruce W. Dearstyne on October 22, 2011:

> *In 1937, Heck rallied fellow Assembly Republicans to oust the incumbent speaker who had blocked legislation needed to qualify the state for federal funding of programs passed through Social Security. As the new speaker, Heck quickly enacted the legislation.*
>
> *Heck's actions over the years redefined the Republicans as moderate liberals and progressives, in line with Republican governors Thomas Dewey and Nelson Rockefeller. Heck described his philosophy in 1954 as "a hard and conservative attitude in economics and a gentle, understanding attitude in human relations."*
>
> *Be steadfast: Heck had a reputation for dogged persistence on issues that rallied allies and wore down opponents. He passed a compulsory auto insurance law in 1954 and 1955, only to see Senate Republicans defeat it both times. Undaunted, he reintroduced it in 1956, patiently citing an increase in the numbers of cars registered and accidents. The bill passed.*
>
> *Balance fiscal conservatism with support for valid programs: New programs meant new taxes and had to prove their worth to win Heck's support. He battled Democratic Governor Herbert Lehman's burgeoning budgets, but supported much of his reformist legislation. He negotiated with Dewey, corralling votes to pass the governor's school aid increase in 1948, but convincing him to rein in a proposed spending increase in 1949. When Rockefeller sought a dramatic increase in state spending a decade later, he had to persuade a skeptical Heck.*
>
> *Resist the incentive of partisanship: Heck was a proud Republican leader who kept his party moving and reached across the political aisle whenever possible. But his statesman-like approach was much more tempered with Democratic Governor Averill Harriman. He regarded Harriman as a big spender and poor administrator who was using the governorship as a stepping-stone to the presidency.*
>
> *Harriman, politically inept, was defeated by Rockefeller in 1958. Heck dreamed of running for governor himself that year and was driven at least in part by less-than-noble partisan motives.*
>
> *But his sharp attacks on Harriman highlight his statesman-like approach to just about everything else during his long tenure, which ended in 1959 with his sudden death. The principles he espoused—cost efficient but responsive government, avoiding impasse and moving legislation along, and partisanship aligned behind public good—are valid and timely today.*

He was a member of the Freemasons and the American Bar Association. He died of a heart attack at age 57. Four governors attended his funeral. A center where people of disabilities lived bearing his name stood for years along Balltown Road in Niskayuna.

Nicholas Hill

December 22, 1766 - June 14, 1857
Location: G54

Nicholas Hill was the eldest son of Henry and Martha (Forse or Foresen) Hill and was born in Schenectady.

When he was eight years old he enlisted in the Continental Army with his brother Harry because his father was whipped by British military officers who construed something he said was disrespectful to them. He was beaten in front of his wife and the two children.

The two boys vowed to get revenge. In the winter of 1776-7 Nicholas, ten years old, and his brother joined Capt. Hick's Company, 2nd New York Regiment, as drummer boys, and continued to the end of the war. He did not get mustered the first two years because of his young age.

He was discharged on June 8, 1783 and signed by Gen. Washington, stating "Nicholas Hill, Sergeant, in the 1st NY regiment, having faithfully served the United States five years, and being enlisted for the war only, is hereby discharged from the American army."

At the bottom a memo signed by Lieut. Col. Cornelius Van Dyck, "The above Sergeant Nicholas Hill, has been honored with the badge of merit for five years faithful service."

For his first service he was sent by Col. Gansevoort to convey a message to headquarters at Albany of a possible attack by the Natives on Fort Stanwix in the winter of 1777. After traveling halfway, his companion, named Snook, had an accident and dropped out. Hill, being pursued by Hostile natives, ran all night over the crusted snow and finally delivered his message to headquarters. He described the scene as he was getting close to Albany writing "The smoke from the forts and houses stood up through the still morning air like a forest of ghostly white tree tops."

Hill also accompanied Sullivan's expedition against the natives, was with the army at Morristown in 1779-80, and witnessed the surrender of Cornwallis at Yorktown. In his writings about his sufferings at Morristown, when the army was on the verge of starvation, rations of whiskey were distributed among the troops. A large Irishman gave him a spoonful and he dropped almost dead. The Irishman carried him for miles before they reached a place where he could receive treatment. Baron Steuben became interested in him and took him to his own tent and offered to adopt him and his younger brother.

In the summer of 1779 his regiment, under Col. Van Schaick, was sent to cooperate with Gen. Sullivan along the Chemung Valley, where he took part in that campaign. He wrote about the surrender of Cornwallis.

After the war he returned to Schenectady and found out that his mother and father had died shortly after he enlisted, all that was left was his sister Martha and brother Henry. His father never recovered from his beating. His father and mother were removed and reburied at Vale, but in unmarked graves.

Hill moved to Florida in Montgomery County, called Shalletbush (Scotch Bush), and entered the ministry of the Methodist denomination, and in 1803, at age 35, was ordained at a Methodist conference in Ash Grove near the Vermont line.

He lived to be 90 and died as a result of a fall and a broken limb.

He married four times: May 30, 1785 to Anna Newkirk, who died July 6 1810; to Catherine Rowe (September 21, 1784 - March 9, 1815) on March 12, 1811; Sarah Mosier (Mar 19, 1792 - ?) on February 23, 1816; and Sarah Hegeman in 1834.

Hill's monument at Vale.

With his first wife, Anna, he had Martha (May 6, 1786), Petreshe (June 3, 1783), Henry (August 13, 1791), Eleanor (March 17, 1794), Nancy (April 19, 1800), William M. (September 21, 1802) and Nicholas Jr. (1805).

With his second wife, Catherine, he had Catharine Anne (Nov 29, 1813).

With his third wife, Sarah, he had Stephen M. (November 20, 1816) and Francis Asbury (January 27, 1820).

With his fourth wife, Sarah, he had Adrian Hegeman (April 4, 1835) and John Lindsay (October 31, 1840).

Alexander Holland

February 7, 1817 - March 12 1885
Location: Q3

Alexander Holland was born in the house that his father Capt. James (Jonas) Holland, of the War of 1812, built on the north side of Union Street between Ferry and Church Streets in 1817.

He was Registrar and Treasurer of Union College from 1839 to 1854, a post his father also held for years. He left to assume that of Treasurer to the American Express Company when it was founded in 1850. American Express was the consolidation of Wells & Co, Livingston & Fargo, and Butterfield, Wasson & Co. His father-in-law, John Butterfield of Butterfield, Wasson & Co., became President of the new company.

Alexander was also Treasurer of the Overland Mail Company, owned by Butterfield, but then appointed Secretary to the company on November 10, 1859. It was Butterfield that hired the famous Jack Slade to rid the Rocky Mountains of outlaws that tried to rob the Overland. He hanged them.

Alexander was appointed New York agent to the new American Express Company. He directed the building of their offices in July 1858 at the corner of Hudson and Jay Streets in New York City. Holland held the position for more than 25 years. Alexander was also was one of the originators of the American Safe Deposit Company.

He died at his home on 52 East 25th Street in NYC, at age 68. Several years before he was injured in a carriage accident near his summer home at West Park and he never fully recovered. He developed meningitis.

Alexander married Sophia Parker Butterfield (August 3, 1824 - November 17, 1887). Sophia was Daniel Butterfield's sister; he was the creator of "Taps," the famous bugle tune played at military funerals and at night before soldiers went to sleep. She is buried with Alexander in the family plot.

He left behind his widow and four adult children, Joseph and John B., and two married daughters. The oldest was Margaret, known as Lady Allchin, who married Sir William H. Allchin, a royal physician, on August 19, 1880. The other was Leila Holland Palmer, married on December 30, 1882 to Pedro Nolasco Palmer of Havana, Cuba. His son Joseph (June 26, 1846 - February 11, 1924) was also born in the same house in which his father was born. Joseph was a Colonel in the New York National Guard, 7th regiment, and is also buried at Vale in the family vault.

William Horsfall

April 7, 1816 - September 14, 1862
Location: T31

The call to arms of President Lincoln on April 15, 1861 for 75,000 volunteers was quickly responded to by the citizens of Schenectady, who held a meeting on the evening of the 19th. 47 men enrolled and organized into a company with William Seward Gridley as Captain and Daniel Daley as First Lieutenant. It was attached to the 18th Regiment upon its organization, May 11th, and designated as Company A. It numbered 74 besides the officers, 60 of them were from the city. The regiment was commanded by Col. William A. Jackson. The company was in the first battle of Bull Run, and in several other engagements remaining in the service two years.

On the May 2nd another company as organized and led by Capt. Stephen Truax and 1st Lt. William Horsfall. It numbered 78 men and was attached to the 18th regiment as Company E. Capt. Truax resigned soon after on account of ill heath, and Lt. Horsefall was promoted to the command on December 27, 1861. He led the company in the various battles fought by the Army of the Potomac, and was killed on September 14, 1862 at South Mountain, Crampton's Pass, Maryland, while cheering his men on to the conflict.

Lt. Colonel George R. Myers described Horsfall's final moments:

On rising the hill to the road, which ran along its side, we received a terrific volley from the enemy. It was here that I met my heaviest loss, the fire of the enemy being well directed and fatal. At this point, the lamented Captain William Horsfall was killed while gallantly leading his men to the charge.

Companies A and E were one of the first regiments enrolled in the Civil War.

The Schenectady City Council passed a resolution acknowledging his sacrifice on September 24th, 1862. When his body was returned, his funeral was "one of the largest and most impressive ever seen in Schenectady." He was killed

… while cheering them forward, and in obedience to an order to take on of the ten rebel batteries. This battery was taken by his company. He fell, when within a few feet of the battery, after witnessing the success of his brave act.

Capt. William Horsfall. (Courtesy of New York State Military Museum.)

He was 46 years old.

The *Schenectady Evening Star & Times* published the following regarding his funeral on the 23rd of September.

Seldom have we seen a larger concourse of citizens together than that which assembled at the funeral obsequies of the lamented Captain William Horsfall, yesterday afternoon. Although hundreds had left the city to witness the departure of the 134th Regiment, the streets were crowded with pedestrians and vehicles. At three o'clock the military and firemen were drawn into line on State-street, and, preceded by the Schenectady Cornet Band, marched to the residence of Joseph Horsfall, Esq, on Union Street, where the funeral was to take place. At the house, the Rev. Dr. Seeley made some timely and affecting allusions to the character of the deceased, the cause in which he had been engaged, and the manner of his untimely death. He introduced to the vast assemblage, the Rev. Mr. Farr, formerly Chaplain of the 18th Regiment. Chaplain Farr paid a handsome and merited tribute to the bravery, moral courage and manly patriotism of the dead solider. Speaking as he did, from personal experience, of the character and disposition of Captain Horsfall, he was enabled to say how deeply he had loved his country, to what trials and hardships he had been subjected in her behalf, and with what sincere resignation he had laid down his life, a sacrifice upon the altar of the Nation. The remarks were worthy the memory of so brave a soldier, and fitting testimonial to his characteristic heroism and loyalty.

After a prayer of the Rev. Mr. Seeley, the procession again formed in line in the following order: Washington continentals, Captain Truax, of which the deceased was formerly a devoted member; Neptune Engine Company No 4, of which he was also a member; Protection No 1; Deluge No 2; Niagara No 3; Hook and Ladder Company; Hearse containing the remains of Captain Horsfall; Mayor and Common council, and delegation of citizens. The procession marched down Union-street to Church, thro' Church to State, and up State to the Cemetery.

After a prayer at the grave by Chaplain Farr, the body was lowered to its last resting place. And thus closed the existence of one who bravely met death in the performance of his duty, and in a cause, at once the noblest and best man, ever engaged in.

Throughout the day, half hour guns were fired by a squad of the City Artillery, which company, although unable to appear at the funeral for the excessive thinning of its ranks caused by the war, took this manner of showing their respect to one who, while living, was a devoted friend and common brother. Business throughout the city was generally suspended, the stores all closed, flags at half-mast, and a universal indication of sorrow and gloom.

To an abler pen than ours, must fall the task of writing the obituary of the lamented dead. Schenectady has reason to be proud of such a son, and she will not easily forget the self-sacrifice, devotion and courage of which he was so worthy an example.

At a meeting of the Schenectady City Artillery, the following resolutions were unanimously adopted:

Resolved, That in the death of Capt. Wm Horsfall, of the 18th New York Volunteers, on the battle-field, the country and flag lost a warm, sincere, indefatigable, and faithful defender.

Resolved, That in his death we feel the loss of a warm friend, an upright citizen, and a man whose worth was only exceeded by his extreme modesty.

Resolved, That identified as he has been with the militia of this State for more than twenty years, and ever ready to be useful and give us the aid of his counsel and practical knowledge whenever called on, we feel his loss as that of one who place it will be hard to fill.

Resolved, That as few of our company are left us, most of them being actively engaged in the field, we will in lieu of accompanying his honored remains to their last resting place, fire a salute from our field pieces half hourly from 10AM till sunset.

Resolved, That the thanks of this company are due, and are cordially tendered to Nicholas Vanderbogart, Esq, for the teams furnished by him for the use of our field pieces.

After the close of the war a company composed of army and navy veterans called the Soldiers' and Sailors' Union was formed of which Major Ralfe Van Brunt was commander. Some time after the company disbanded and formed the Schenectady Zouaves Cadet. Major Ralfe Van Brunt was its first Captain. He was succeeded by Captain Austin A Yates. This company existed for a number of years when its name was changed to William Horsfall Post No 14. A.A. Yates, GW Marlette and William G. Caw were commanders of this company at different periods. The name was changed to Edwin Forest Post No 90. G.W. Tompkins, James F White, Frederick Eisenminger and James R. Reagles were at various times commander of this post. A few years later the name was again changed back to Post Horsfall No 9.

His monument was described in the *Evening Star and Times* on May 14, 1863 newspaper:

MONUMENT TO CAPT. WILLIAM HORSEFALL.
The Albany Express *says: A beautiful Italian monument, to be placed over the remains of the late Captain William Horsfall, who fell at the battle of South Mountain, Maryland, has just been completed by our fellow townsman, William Manson, will be forwarded to Shenectady* [sic] *to adorn the Cemetery at that place.*

The monument is made of the finest Italian marble, and is beautifully and artistically cut and engraved. The front represents a projecting shield, with three stars upon it, backed by a sword and spear, and entwined together with a wreath of evergreens.

Beneath this in projecting letters, is the following:

"Captain William Horsefall,18th Regiment, N. Y. S. Volunteers.Born April 7th, 1816;Died September 14th 1862.On the base is the following:-- "He died in the defence of his country."

On the opposite side, engraved upon the stone, is the following:-- "He fell cheering his men in the gallant and successful charge made by Gen. Slocum in the Battle of South Mountain, near Burkettsville, Frederick Co., Maryland, Sept. 14th, 1862."

The monument is surrounded with a fatigue cap, hewn from the stone, on the foot of which is a shield, with initials, in old English letters, N. Y.

It is certainly a monument choice and beautiful in design and reflects great credit upon the maker as a work of art.

Allan Heyer Jackson

1836 - August 1911
Location: C#6

The fourth company formed at Schenectady during the Civil War was organized by Allan H. Jackson, a Schenectady attorney, Schenectady County Board of Supervisor's Clerk and Union College graduate (one source says Harvard Law), who received a Captain's commission on October 1, 1861. The company consisted of 87 members, including officers, and was enrolled as Company G in the 91st Regiment for a term of three years, being mustered out of service July 3, 1865. The officers who were commissioned at the same time as Jackson were George W. Shaffer, First Lieutenant, and William Harty, Second Lieutenant.

Jackson was given an honorable discharge from this company on February 23, 1863, and promoted to the rank of Major in the 134th Regiment. On March 4, 1863, he became Lieutenant Colonel, and December 10th of the same year, Colonel of this regiment, but was mustered out of service June 10, 1865, as Lt. Colonel. He was married to Mary C. Jackson.

Lt. Col. Allan H. Jackson.

Jackson commanded the 134th at Gettysburg during the time that Charles Coster was temporarily promoted command of the brigade. After Coster's resignation, Jackson assumed permanent command of the 134th until the regiment was mustered out on June 10 1865, near Bladensburg, Maryland.

Jackson led the 134th at the Battle of Gettysburg, which also served as a member of Coster's Brigade in Von Steinwehr's Division of the Eleventh Corps, Army of the Potomac (which in December marched to Fredericksburg in support of Burnside, but the 134th was not in the battle). The regiment was heavily engaged at Gettysburg (July 1-3), in the battle of the first day, and in the "gallant defense" of Cemetery Hill on the second day, meeting with a loss of 42 killed, 151 wounded and 59 missing, a total of 252 out of 400 in action.

Lt. Col. Jackson commanded the 400 men of the regiment while Col. Coster took command of the brigade from Brig. Gen. Buschbeck. Originally held in reserve on Cemetery Hill on July 1, the regiment and its brigade were marched through town and formed on the north side of Gettysburg to help in the collapse of the rest of the 11th Corps. The 134th held the right flank of the brigade, losing over half its strength in a few minutes when assaulted by Hoke's and Hays' Confederate Brigades, and forced to retreat through town back to Cemetery Hill. The regiment defended Cemetery Hill during the attack of the Louisiana Brigade on the evening of the 2nd and during the artillery barrage that preceded Pickett's Charge. Lieutenants Henry Palmer and Lucius Mead and 57 enlisted men were killed or mortally wounded, Captains Otis Guffin and William Mickle and 130 enlisted men were wounded, and Lieutenant John Kennedy and 57 enlisted men captured.

The *Schenectady Republican* published the following report.

OUR BOYS AT GETTYSBURG.—*Lieut. Ben. F. Sheldon, of the One Hundred and Thirty-fourth, who commanded his company during the late battle, writes home a very interesting letter from which we are permitted to make extracts:*

Against three regiments out of our brigade, the 73d Pa., 154th N.Y.S.V., and our own regiment, the 134th, there were two whole brigades of rebel infantry designated as the "Louisiana Tigers." Evidently they deemed themselves sufficiently strong for us as they advanced upon us in splendid style; but, if this was the idea they embraced, they were a little mistaken in their notion, as our boys certainly gave them to understand that free soil was no place for traitors to the time honored flag of our fathers. Among those who are worthy of mention as the heroes of that day, we may mention one well known to our Schenectady friends in the person of Sergeant Henry P. Glen. He fought with determined resistance until unable to fight longer from a wound which he received in the hottest of the fight, and even then he did not leave the field until I ordered him to the rear. As he was passing to the rear in obedience to my order, another ball from the foe passed through the upper portion of his body and he fell with his face to the ground, a corpse.

We may also mention another instance which occurred during the raging of the storm. Our Lieutenant Colonel, Allan H. Jackson, being in command of the regiment in consequence of our loved Col. Costar acting as Brigadier General of our brigade, in the absence of its commander, Gen. Bushbeck, displayed great coolness and determination, not leaving the field until he saw the last of his boys making for a more secure position. Then when making for the same place, finding himself surrounded by the "grey jackets" of the South, he ventured to secure himself in one of the houses of the town where he was fortunate enough to obtain a hiding place for two days and nights from the "rebs." Not feeling at home, however, in his place of security, and desiring to be with his gallant boys as soon as possible, he determined upon making his escape without further delay. Feeling thus, he, together with a private in Co. C, by the name of Levi More, who had also secreted himself in the same place, set to work upon their perilous resolve—passing through the streets of the place in disguise and braving a shower of bullets from our men until they had passed safely into the ranks of the Union hosts. I myself was slightly wounded in the arm and taken prisoner by them, but managed to make my escape.

On the second day of the fight commenced one of the grandest artillery conflicts perhaps ever witnessed on the Continent. For hours the heavens were dim with smoke, and naught could be seen above us but the smoky billows coursing their way beneath the blue arched canopy, save when the misiles from the booming guns carried on the outset of their journey the propelling fire. Flash after flash was to be seen in all directions as the maddened cannoniers applied the fire to their well aimed pieces and sent the heralds of death on their way to the opposite ranks.

Another newspaper gave the following account.

COL. JACKSON, *of the 134th regiment, writes to his friends on Sunday the 5th of July:—*

My poor regiment was horribly cut to pieces on the 1st. Every officer in it was wounded except myself and four others. Young Palmer, acting Adjutant, was killed. Capt. Olcott is reported so likewise, and over fifty of the men. A much larger number were wounded and taken prisoners on the field. Out of four hundred whom I carried into the engagement I can now muster but one hundred; of the balance, many are stragglers. I never imagined such a rain of bullets.

Jackson came close to getting killed when he visited fellow Schenectadian Charles Lewis after some heavy drinking. Dressed in buckskin he rode his black mare to a tree where Lewis was resting and the rebels began firing at the two, hitting Jackson in the boot but inflicting no harm. He remarked "By God that was damned close," and rode away.

Jackson was wounded at the Battle of Resaca on May 14-15 1864.

The following is from correspondence to the *Schenectady Daily Union.*

134TH REGIMENT. HEAD QUARTERS. *134th Regt., N.Y. Vols. in the Field near Marietta, Georgia June 9, 1864.*

Mr. Editor:

Sir.—Though personally unacquainted with you, I thought I would through your invaluable paper, give you a description of what the boys of the 134th Regt. N.Y. Vols. are accomplishing, and their welfare. We left Lookout Valley on the fourth of May last, after being snugly housed in a good camp, for four months and a half. We left buoyant in spirits, earnestly desiring to make some strike which would result in much good towards restoring the Union and maintaining the honor and integrity of our country.

On the second day's march we joined our new Division where we had lately been assigned. Our place is now in the twentieth Army Corps Second Division, and Second Brigade. Our Corps Commander is Gen. Hooker, our Division Commander is Brigadier Gen. J.W. Geary. We marched all the week and on Saturday near dark encamped in a woods, stacked our guns, and quietly laid down behind them, supposing we would rest here in peace at least over Sunday. But on Sunday, an order to march came near noon. Headed by our noble and brave Colonel A.H. Jackson we were up and soon marching along with our brigade. After marching along about three miles, we came to a clearing, where we had a fair view of a mountain ridge, which we were ordered to scale, and if possible, drive the rebels away from the mountain which they were occupying. Soon two strong lines of battle were formed, the 134th N.Y. regiment forming part of the front line of battle. Then skirmishers were thrown into the front and calmly and deliberately we marched up the mountain to assault the rebel positions. Our pathway was obstructed by massive piles of stone and large rocks projecting from the ground. Those were serious difficulties to us, also the ascent of the mountain was very steep. We made three distinct charges up this mountain. At the first charge we got nearly up to the rebel works, but being unsupported, and our regiment alone, and few in numbers, we could not withstand the volleys of the rebels, so we were forced to fall back.—We tried a second time, but did not go far, a third time we tried it, being supported by two companies of the 33d N.J. Vols., but then the rebels got reinforced and came on us in such force that we were compelled to give up the attempt of taking the mountain. The total loss of the regiment was eleven killed and twenty-four wounded. We were obliged to leave our dead on the mountain side. Together with the fighting we were annoyed by rebel sharpshooters, who unperceived in trees on top of the mountain, kept firing continually on us. So passed the eight day of May.

We did picket duty chiefly the remainder of the week and towards the latter part marched towards Ressacca, where our Regiment played a part, just one week after the mountain fight on Sunday, May the fifteenth. Our regiment then assisted in taking two forts, where the rebels had held our forces at bay for some days previous. Our regiment was marched over several lines of battle to occupy a position, which we reached, and fortunately for us, were permitted to occupy, we being protected by a little rise of ground in our front. The rebels poured volleys of grape and cannister at us, but without effect.—The rebel sharpshooters were very busy also. So we passed this day, none of our regiment was killed, and only a few wounded.

In the night the rebels left the place, rendering it so that we could record another great victory for our army. Our army commenced following up the rebels the next day, fighting them step by step, but our regiment has not engaged the rebels since, except once in the night while we were lying in a breastwork, nearly two weeks after. On the 20th, 21st and 22nd our regiment rested.—Then we marched till we found them in force, strongly fortified at a place near Dallas. Instead of charging the works we entrenched ourselves around them and so forcing the rebels back, by getting strategic positions around them, and battering down their fortifications with solid shot.

This is the business of our army now, but we know not the hour when we will be called to do sterner work. The 134th N.Y. regiment is now only a small regiment, but we feel strong and courageous yet. We are sorry to learn there are such things as Copperheads at home, and though we personally wish them no hurt, yet we wish they would amend their manners, and heartily sustain us in serving our common country, and preserving its institutions from downfall.

Very respectfully,
C. W. TAYLOR, 1st. Lieut.134th Regt. N.Y.S. Vols.

At the battle of Peach Tree Creek, Lt. Col. Jackson, while commanding the regiment, was severely wounded, during the furious onslaught made by Hood on the 20th of July, 1864, immediately after taking command of the Rebel forces, but assumed command again shortly afterwards. The loss of the rank and file was about fifty men.

After the battle the 134th accompanied the army on its return to Virginia, and in August was on detached service at Alexandria. In September, 1863, they were ordered to Tennessee with the 11th and 12th corps, and the following month was in reserve at the midnight battle of Wauhatchie, Tennessee. During the Chattanooga-Ringgold campaign they were slightly engaged at Missionary ridge, losing 8 wounded and missing. It was then ordered to the relief of Knoxville, and in April, 1864, was attached to the 2nd brigade, 2nd (Geary's) division, of the newly formed 20th corps, with which it served in the Atlanta campaign. It fought its first battle of the campaign at Rocky Face ridge, where its casualties were 36 in killed and wounded. It was then in the battles of Resaca, Dallas, Kennesaw Mountain, Pine Mountain, Golgotha, Kolb's farm, Marietta, Chattahoochee River, Peach Tree Creek and Atlanta. At Peach Tree Creek the regiment lost 44 killed, wounded and missing. After the fall of Atlanta, it remained there until November, 1864, when it started on the march to the sea, fighting at Sandersville and Greensboro, and sharing with a loss of 13 in the siege of Savannah, Geary's division being the first to enter the city on its evacuation by Hardee. Early in 1865, it moved on its final campaign—through the Carolinas—which ended with Johnston's surrender, then marched with the corps to Washington, where it took part in the grand review, and was mustered out at Bladensburg, Maryland, under Col. Jackson, June 10, 1865. The regiment lost during service, 5 officers and 84 men killed and mortally wounded; 3 officers and 91 men died of disease and other causes, a total of 183.

Another newspaper reported the return of the regiment and Jackson.

THE ONE HUNDRED AND THIRTY-FOURTH REGIMENT N.Y.S.V. reached this city this morning on the Vanderbilt, about five o'clock. A salute was fired by Captain Bowden, and a lunch was furnished them by the Common Council Committee, after which they proceeded to the barracks on the Troy road. The regiment was raised in Schenectady and Schoharie counties, and was mustered into the United States service on the 22d of September, 1862, at Schoharie C.H. It joined Gen. Sigel's corps (the 11th) at Fairfax C.H., about the 2d of October following, and served with that corps through the battles of Chancellorsville and Gettysburg. In September, 1863, the 11th and 12th Corps left for Tennessee, under Gen. Hooker. On the 28th of October, this command opened "the cracker line" through Lookout Valley, to Rosecrans' army, who were heartily glad to have free communication once more with the outer world. They lay in that Valley until the battle of Lookout Mountain, and Missionary Ridge, in which latter engagement the Regiment participated in the charge and drove the Rebels from their works. Immediately after those battles the Eleventh Corps started for Knoxville, Tenn., to the relief of Gen. Burnside. About the time they reached there, the siege was raised and Longstreet retreated. Without entering the place, the Corps turned about, marched back and encamped in Lookout Valley. During this march the regiment suffered terribly, living entirely on the country, having nothing to eat but flour captured from the enemy, with a little pork. It took no supply trains, and marched on a "dog trot" all the way. It came back fatigued and in rags. It lay in Lookout Valley until the 4th of May, 1864, suffering terribly from privations of tents and rations, when it broke camp and started on the memorable Atlanta campaign. The regiment was engaged in every battle on the march, the principal of which were Rocky Faced Ridge, where it suffered severely, losing 50 men killed and wounded; Resaca, Dalles, Pine Knob, East Mountain, Peach Tree Creek, and innumerable skirmishes, culminating in the entrance of Atlanta, triumphantly, on the 3d of September 1864. It garrisoned Atlanta while Hood was being driven north, and on the 15th of November started on the Savannah campaign. The only trouble experienced on the march was to force their way through the swamps and forests, and to procure sufficient subsistance off the country.

In December it arrived in front of Savannah, and besieged it for a week, during which it suffered for want of rations, having nothing but captured rice and beef, the latter of which was more bones than meat. The entry into Savannah took place on the 21st, when the One Hundred and Thirty-fourth pitched its tents near the jail, in which members of its own regiment had once been confined as prisoners of war. It remained there until the 27th of January, 1865, when it started on the famous march through South Carolina, in which, it had a large number of skirmishes, crossed almost impassable swamps, and experienced many privations and hardships. The incidents of this march are very interesting, but we have not space now to recount them.

In the month of March, the regiment arrived at Goldsboro, N.C., and shortly afterwards marched to Raleigh and remained in that section until the surrender of Gen. Johnston, when they took up their line of march for Washington, where they participated in the grand review of Sherman's army. It was mustered out last Saturday, the 10th, and on the following Monday left on its homeward march. It will be paid off in this city.

The following is a list of the field, staff and line officers:—Lieutenant-Colonel—Allan H. Jackson, commanding. Major—William H. Hoyt. Surgeon—George C. Douglas. Assistant Surgeon—Peter M. Murphy. Chaplain—Rev. F. Fletcher. Adjutant—Henry Palmer. Quartermaster—Henry Ramsay, Jr. Company—Captain, B. F. Sheldon, commanding; First Lieutenant, James T. Joslin. Company B—Lieutenant John W. ____, commanding. Company C—First Lieutenant James ____, commanding. Company D—First Lieutenant M. Jones, commanding. Company E—First Lieutenant John R. Boughton, commanding. Company F—Captain Charles F. Griffin, commanding; First Lieutenant H.P. Dillion. Company G—Captain C.W. Taylor, commanding; First Lieutenant N.M. Van Antwerp. Company H—Captain Delos W. Olcott, commanding.Company I—Captain B.S. Smith, commanding. Company K—Captain Perry E. McMaster, commanding.

The regiment went out with about nine hundred men, and returns with two hundred and seventy-five tried and veteran soldiers, with tattered colors, thoroughly riddled, evincing, together with the history and losses of the Regiment, the indomitable bravery and heroism of the true sons of Schenectady and Schoharie.

Jackson remained in the regular army after the war, serving with the 7th US Infantry and being decorated for his service during the Indian Wars. During the War in 1877 at Fort Shaw Montana, with the Nez Perce, he saw heavy fire while serving as Regimental Quartermaster. Colonel John Gibbon was commanding the 7th Infantry and recommended a brevet to each officer.

Jared A. Jackson

May 20, 1849 - November 21, 1888
Location: F 13

After Jared Jackson's parents George and Jane Ann moved from New York City to Bethlehem to become farmers, their son Jared was born on the farm on May 20, 1849. When Jared joined the U.S. Colored Troops on December 14, 1863 in Albany, he became a member of the 20th Regiment, Company N. He entered service as a Private and was appointed a Corporal in August 1864. There were three Colored Troops from New York State: the 20th, 26th, and 31st.

The United States Colored Troops (U.S.C.T.) were regiments of the United States Army during the Civil War comprised of African-American soldiers. African-Americans were first authorized to be employed as combat soldiers right in the beginning of the issuance of the Emancipation Proclamation on January 1, 1863, and the formation of African-American soldiers into regiments under state designations was officially begun later that year. By the end of the Civil War, the U.S.C.T.'s 175 regiments supplied about one-tenth of the Union Army's manpower.

But instead of facing combat, the 20th Regiment was destined for more menial tasks as laborers, cooks and guards in areas with inhospitable working conditions. Jackson was among a 200-soldier contingent sent to Elmira to guard a hastily constructed prison camp, formerly a military training camp, for Confederate soldiers.

The conditions at the camp were the worst, with more than 10,000 captured grey coats living among 35 buildings and many tents. Tensions among the Confederate inmates were further aggravated by the contingent of black soldiers stationed to guard them. The camp became known as "Hellmira."

The black solders guarding the camp were unfairly accused of allowing the escape of ten confederate prisoners, even though it was proven the escape occurred during the watch of white soldiers. Jackson and fellow black soldiers were assigned to labor duty in South Carolina and Louisiana as a result. It seems that bigotry had not yet left even in the Northern ranks.

26th U.S. Colored Troops on parade at Rikers Island.

Jackson was transferred to Company H of the 26th Regiment in Beaufort, South Carolina, where he unloaded a navel vessel and sustained a back injury. He was discharged, and after a brief stint back at the farm in Bethlehem, he moved to Schenectady and married Hannah E. Wendell, eventually owning a home at 523 Schenectady Street. He continued to work as a laborer. He had difficulty getting his pension from the military disability, but in September 1888 began receiving $12 per month. He died ten weeks later, at the age of 48, of "Consumption and Chronic Liver Disease." His wife Hannah died on December 5, 1809, at age 65.

His name is listed on the African-American Civil War Memorial.

Cpl. Jared Jackson's headstone at Vale.

William Ayrault Jackson

**March 29, 1832 - November 11, 1861
Location: Sec. X Union College Plot 10**

William Jackson was born in Schenectady on March 29, 1832, the son of Isaac W. Jackson, then Professor of Mathematics at Union College. William was the eldest son and entered Union at the age of 15 in 1847.

He became an experienced debater in college and graduated with honors in 1851. While studying law he spent a few months with his uncle I.C. Chesbrough, a civil engineer, and surveyed for the Albany & Susquehanna Railroad. In December 1852 he moved to Albany and began working with attorney Marcus T. Reynolds and attended Albany Law School, getting admitted to the bar on April 10, 1853. He later formed a partnership with his cousin Frederick Townsend, who was the Adjutant General of New York State, and who was a Colonel of the 3rd Regiment of the New York Volunteers who distinguished himself at the battle of Big Bethel. Now a Major in the U.S. Infantry, he and Jackson, along with Alfred Conkling, formerly the U.S. District Judge of the Northern District of New York State, worked under the firm of Conkling, Townsend & Jackson for a short time during 1857. Conkling left in 1858, and they took on Richard M. Strong as a partner and continued until the Civil War broke out.

Jackson had been appointed Inspector General of New York State in 1861 but had to give it up to fight for the North.

He raised a regiment and took the title of Lieutenant Colonel, but ended up Colonel instead due to his inexperience, receiving the commission on June 18, 1861 with the 18th Regiment of the New York Volunteers.

The regiment left for Washington, D.C. in June, a regiment of mostly inexperienced officers and soldiers. On July 12 his regiment was ordered across the Potomac and encamped near Alexandria. The regiment joined with the 16th, 31st and 32nd N.Y. Volunteers, forming the 2nd Brigade under the command of Col. Davies of the 16th Regiment.

On July 16, they advanced with Jackson's regiment from Alexandria in the afternoon and took part in the battle and skirmishes on the 18th. During the battle of Manassas on July 21 they did not fight while the rest of the brigade did, and started to retreat from unauthorized orders. Capt. Green gave the following report of the incident.

At this point an unauthorized person gave orders to retreat: I refused the order, but all my supporting regiments but one (Col Jackson's 18th NYV), moved off to the rear. Col Jackson most gallantly offered his Regiment as a support, say-

ing "that it should remain by me as long as there should be any fighting to be done there." The above mentioned person again made his appearance at this time and again ordered me to retreat, and ordered Col Jackson to form column of division on my right and retreat with me as all was lost. The order was of course disregarded and in about two minutes the head of a column of the enemy's Calvary came up at a run, opening out of the woods in beautiful order. I was prepared for it, and the column had not gone more than a hundred yards out of the wood before shells were burst at their head and directly in their midst. They broke in every direction, and no more Calvary came out of the woods.

They continued to Alexandria. Jackson wrote to a friend on July 23, "From half past two Sunday morning until Monday at midday, we neither slept nor rested. I was in my saddle nearly all the time."

Even though the battle had disastrous results, Jackson's regiment remained near Alexandria shifting places, and helped build Fort Ward to protect Washington. The 18th Regiment was then placed in Gen. Newton's Brigade and Gen. Franklin's Division.

Jackson's health was deteriorating while on the field, even though he had been healthy all his life. He was moved to a hospital in Washington on October 30, but it was too late. He died on November 11, just before six o'clock. He whispered before his death, "I do believe in the Lord Jesus Christ, I trust in Him."

He was brought to Schenectady and buried on November 14, 1861. Many local celebrities spoke at his funeral. Ironically, a resolution by the 18th Regiment honoring the fall of Jackson was signed and witnessed by Lt. William Horsfall, acting Adjutant, a fellow Schenectadian and resident of Vale.

Walter A. Jones

1846 - 1923
Location: L2 299

In 1872 the Schenectady Car Company was created on the old farm of N.I. Schermerhorn in Rotterdam, and was only in operation for about four months when the J.M. Jones & Company from West Troy purchased the company. J.M Jones & Company succeed Jones & Company in 1874 and was composed of John H. and Walter A. Jones, taking over from their father. In 1879 they discontinued in West Troy; in 1882 they resumed making street cars.

Thousands of street cars were made at these works for railway companies in the U.S., South America, Australia, England, Germany, India and other countries. In 1870, 200 were made for the Bombay Tramway Company. They made about 300 street cars per year. The Schenectady plant operated for a short time building street cars with some 400 men, but the works was transferred to the Troy works.

In 1884, the sum of $300,000 was subscribed to establish a new locomotive works in Schenectady, known as the McQueen Locomotive Works. Ex-Senator Sanford, Walter McQueen, formerly Superintendent of the old Schenectady works, Walter A. Jones, President of the Jones car works, and F.W. McCamus, President of City Bank, were the principal owners. This deal fell through when Sanford died suddenly and McQueen quit, but two buildings had been built.

On January 30, 1885, the Schenectady car works was leased to Walter A. Jones, of the Jones Car Manufacturing Company for 18 months, at a rent of $3,700 per year, and they began repairing and manufacturing Wagner's Palace and Sleep Cars for the New York Central Sleeping Car Company. They added five new buildings to the Schenectady plant, but went into receivership with $200,000 in liabilities and judgments against them for $128,000. They were sued over a mortgage non-payment. Jones also lost his house that was being built in the General Electric Realty Plot, called Brookside. It was purchased instead by Frederick Eisenmenger.

On February 4, 1885 the Jones Car Works Company was reorganized and incorporated with Walter A. Jones President. However, in June the New York Central Sleeping Car Company purchased the lease of the Jones Company. In July they turned over the works to the NY Central, but at the same time were delivering four elegant cars to the Brooklyn City Railway from their West Troy plant.

Walter was a founding member of the American Street Railway Association in 1882. He was on the board of the New Williamsburgh & Flatbush Railroad in 1881and 1885, although the railroad was based in Brooklyn.

Oscar Jungren

1863 - 1935
Location: M3 #64

Oscar Jungren (also spelled Junggren) came to America from Sweden in 1889 to work for Edison Electric as an engineer and draftsman. In 1902-03 he was Chief Design Engineer and collaborated with W.I.R. Emmet in the construction of the huge Curtis Turbine that had a generation capacity of 5000kw, and about which was said it could not be built.

The turbine was ten times more powerful than any previously built. When it was installed in Chicago in 1903 it was hailed "as the greatest single step forward in power plant progress since James Watt invented the steam engine." It was so important that General Electric stock rose when it ran, and dropped when it didn't. The Curtis-Emmett turbine is on display at the G.E. Schenectady works.

From 1924-32, thirty new turbines, each separately designed and more powerful than the last, were designed by him, an average of one every four months. He held 130 patents. He is credited with single-handedly developing the large turbines which generated nine-tenths of the nations' electric power.

He was married to Grace Jungreen and they had a son and two daughters. His house at 1179 Lowell was broken into on April 11, 1930. Burglars destroyed some furniture, while $50.00 cash was stolen from his colleague Ernest Berg at 1336 Lowell Road.

Gilbert D. Kennedy

1827 - 1863
Location: P 40

Gilbert D. (also listed as H. in some sources) Kennedy was a member of the 134th Regiment, along with fellow Schenectadian Allan H. Jackson. At age 35, he was mustered in on August 29, 1862 as a Private in Company F. He organized and enrolled most of the soldiers into Company F in August of 1862. He was promoted to Captain on August 30, 1862 and was promoted and Commissioned Major on June 23 (also one source listing August 30), 1862. He died in a hospital of disease at Philadelphia, September 22, 1863.

According to a pension request, his wife's name was Sarah, and they had two boys, Gilbert D. (b. January 10, 1858) and Edward S. (b. July 3, 18?3).

The following appears in *The Union Army: A History of Military Affairs in the Loyal States, 1861-65* (Federal Pub. Co., 1908, vol. II).

> *This regiment, recruited in the counties of Schoharie, Schenectady and Delaware, was organized at Schoharie and there mustered into the U.S. service for three years on Sept. 22-23, 1862. It left the state on the 25th and was at once attached to the 2nd brigade, 2nd (Von Steinwehr's) division, 11th corps, which in December marched to Fredericksburg in support of Burnside, but the 134th was not in the battle. It then went into winter quarters at Stafford, Va. As part of the 1st brigade, same division and corps, it lost 8 wounded and missing at Chancellorsville. The regiment was heavily engaged at Gettysburg, in the battle of the first day, and in the gallant defense of Cemetery hill on the second day, meeting with a loss of 42 killed, 151 wounded and 59 missing, a total of 252 out of 400 in action. After the battle it accompanied the army on its return to Virginia and in August was on detached service at Alexandria, Va. In Sept., 1863, it was ordered to Tennessee with the 11th and 12th corps, and the following month was in reserve at the midnight battle of Wauhatchie, Tenn. During the Chattanooga-Ringgold campaign it was slightly engaged at Missionary ridge, losing 8 wounded and missing. It was then ordered to the relief of Knoxville, and in April, 1864, was attached to the 2nd brigade, 2nd (Geary's) division, of the newly formed 20th corps, with which it served in the Atlanta campaign. It fought its first battle of the campaign at Rocky Face ridge, where its casualties were 36 in killed and wounded. It was then in the battles of Resaca, Dallas, Kennesaw mountain, Pine mountain, Golgotha, Kolb's farm, Marietta, Chattahoochee river, Peachtree creek and Atlanta. At Peach-tree creek the regiment lost 44 killed, wounded and missing. After the fall of Atlanta it remained there*

until Nov., 1864, when it started on the march to the sea, fighting at Sandersville and Greensboro, and sharing with a loss of 13 in the siege of Savannah, Geary's division being the first to enter the city on its evacuation by Hardee. Early in 1865, it moved on its final campaign—through the Carolinas—which ended with Johnston's surrender, then marched with the corps to Washington, where it took part in the grand review, and was mustered out at Bladensburg, Md., under Col. Jackson, June 10, 1865. The regiment lost during service, 5 officers and 84 men killed and mortally wounded; 3 officers and 91 men died of disease and other causes, a total of 183.

William Colgrove Kenyon

October 14, 1812 - June 7, 1867
Location: SI Plot 1

William Kenyon was born in Richmond, Rhode Island and his name was William Collins or Colgrove. Because his family was so poor he was "bound" out to a guardian at age 5. He bought his freedom from the guardian when he was 19 and worked in Westerly, R.I., and New York City at the Novelty Iron Works (1836-37), and then Schenectady, learning the machinist trade until he was 24. The President of Union College, Eliphanet Nott got him the job at the iron works (he was part owner) and helped him secure some funding for school from the Hopkinton Sewing Society and others. He was a volunteer fireman and by 1836, with really not much formal training, he entered Union College in 1836. He left Union for Alfred, New York in 1839, his junior year, but eventually received an M.A. from Union later in 1844.

He was hired by his Union College schoolmate James Read Irish to become principal of the Alfred Select School in Alfred, N.Y. in 1839. The school, a one story building, was created by the Seventh Day Baptists. It was incorporated on March 28, 1857 as the Alfred Academy. When Melissa Ward joined the school as an assistant in the primary department, the two fell in love and married on August 5, 1840. Her nickname became "Mother" Kenyon on campus, and she devoted her life caring for the welfare of her students. Her death in June 27, 1863 was attributed to her overdoing it with a sick student. William was a strong supporter of women's education and was one of the first to hire women teachers as well as make the school coed and nonsectarian. Melissa was born in Schenectady on October 14, 1823 and became a student of Alfred at in 1839.

William C. Kenyon.

Kenyon became co-superintendent of the common schools of Allegheny County and was responsible for sponsoring new methods of teaching, better teacher training and organizing a county teachers' association. He went back to Alfred and became known as the "Boss." Alfred became an academy under Kenyon in 1843. With this new designation duties were assigned to a Board of Trustees. The Boss was not a Trustee but listed as Register and Treasurer. The school began to grow and add departments, faculty and students. Kenyon and the group bought more land and built more buildings. On March 28, 1857 the academy became Alfred University and he its first president. Melissa died on June 28, 1863 at age 42, and he remarried a German speaking woman named Ida Sallan Long on September 4, 1864.

Kenyon had founded the institute with 74 students, and when he died it was at 478. He started with one building and left five. Alumni Hall is the oldest structure still standing on campus. The "Brick" residence hall was built then as well. He started it as a select school and left it a university. In began worth a few hundred dollars in 1839 and when he died it was worth $50,000.

He continued to lead the university until his health failed, and in 1865 he resigned. During a trip with his new wife, he died in England on June 7, 1867 at the age of 54, and was buried on the 11th at Abney Park Center near London. He was later moved to Schenectady to be next to his first wife Melissa.

Melissa Ward Kenyon.

One story describes his understanding of poverty very well. A young man from New England wrote to him and asked if there was any way a boy not afraid of working hard, had ambition for education, but was almost penniless, could take a course. Kenyon wrote back "Come on, young man. There is room here for lots of just such boys as you." The boy was Darwin E. Maxson, who later became a part of the faculty in 1849.

The various positions Kenyon held at the school were:

- First Secretary, 1839-1845
- Second Treasurer, 1841-1857
- Trustee, 1843-1867
- First President of the Faculty, 1857-1865
- Principal, 1839-1857
- Language, Nature Science and Mathematics, 1843-1844
- Natural and Moral Sciences, 1844-1849
- Mathematics and English Language and Literature, 1855-1857
- English Literature and Belles Lettres, 1857-1860
- Latin and English Languages and Literature, 1860-1867.

Not only did he teach five days a week, but Kenyon was an ordained Seventh Day Baptist minister who preached at the church in Hartsville. He was ordained on February 1861.

Kenyon Memorial Hall was built in his honor in 1875 but torn down in 1958 to build the Rogers Campus Center.

Arthur Franklin Knight

1868 - May 2, 1936
Location: L#12

Most people know that the Dutch introduced golf, hockey, and other games into North America during the 17th century. The game of golf has evolved into one of the more popular past times in America and it was a Schenectadian who almost a century ago created a putter that still is in demand.

In 1903, a General Electric engineer named Arthur F. Knight, known as "Biklly" to his friends, and originally from Rutland, Vermont, patented his "Schenectady Putter," named after his hometown. He was a member of Schenectady's Mohawk Golf Club, and it was first introduced there. They have one on display in their clubhouse. The putter was designed with a hickory shaft and centrally connected to an aluminum mallet-head that looked similar to a croquet mallet. It was the first with a shaft protruding from the center of the head. He invented it to improve his own game. He also invented the steel shaft club.

The putter received world attention the following year when Walter Travis became the first American to win the British Amateur Championship (he won the U.S. Amateur the year before with the putter). Travis had the habit of being usually 30 to 60 yards shorter off the tee than his opponents, and used his superb putting ability to win his matches. Sports writers, not happy about the foreigner winning, blamed it on the putter claiming it was illegal. However President William Taft endorsed it by sending Travis a letter telling him how much he enjoyed using it.

In 1908, the Rules of Golf Committee of the Royal & Ancient Golf Club of St. Andrews stated that it would not accept what it called "a substantial departure from the traditional and accepted form of golf clubs," meaning a plain shaft and a head that contained no mechanical contrivance. Two years later, they amended this ruling, stating that "the lower part of the shaft shall meet the heel of the club, or a point opposite the heel, either to right or left, when in the ordinary position for play." This banned the Schenectady putter, and at that time it was a popular putter in America. The United States Golf Association however did not ban the putter, and this difference of opinion lasted until 1952. The ban was finally lifted in 1959.

Unfortunately for Knight, while he patented the putter (March 24, 1903), most golf club makers reproduced it. He produced his own with a local company called the Schenectady Putter Company. He reportedly made about $750,000 in royalties. Spalding began selling an identical club in 1903, followed by the Standard Golf Company and Macgregor. Waverly Horton made a copy with the name "Pay Me" in the 1920s, and in Europe, F.H. Ayers, Lilywhite and the British Golf Company sold Schenectady putters. In addition, they were made from material other than aluminum, such as wood and pyralin, an early form of plastic.

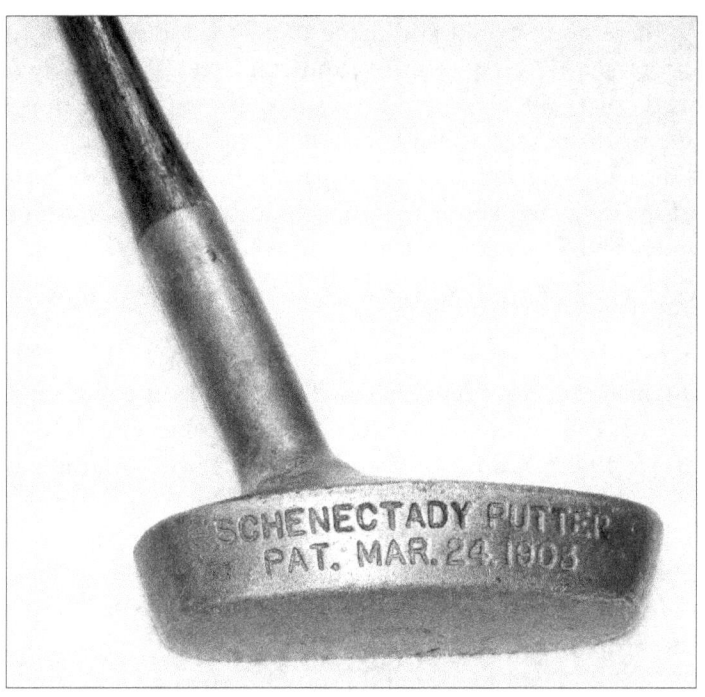

A Schenectady putter, designed by Arthur Knight in 1903.

Knight designed Schenectady's Municipal Golf Course in 1935. With partner E.W. Allen, Chairman of the Emergency Relief Bureau, he was one of the first to play on the course when it officially opened to the public on July 17, 1935 at 2 p.m. He was a member of the first commission overseeing the course. He died the following year.

In 1944, Arthur C. Parker, New York State Archeologist made a hole in one in the "punch bowl," the 15th hole at Mohawk Golf Club, which was named and dedicated in Knight's honor. The hole is only 125 yards long.

Today, you can find Schenectady Putters on eBay going for a tidy sum. Golf collectors prize them and the ones with the patent number on the back of the club are the most desired.

John Heinrich Kruesi

May 15, 1843 - February 22, 1899
Location: M3#9

John Kruesi was born in Spercher, Canton Appenzell, Switzerland, and began working in a machine shop at an early age. Kruesi was a clock maker in Switzerland, moved to Paris in 1867, then to London, finally making it to the U.S. in 1870. He found his first job at the Singer Sewing Machine company in Elizabeth, New York, thanks to his friend August Weber. He moved to Newark, New Jersey. There he met Thomas Edison and began working for him in 1872, making stock exchange tickers and telegraph instruments. After the panic of 1872, Edison opened a second shop for purely experimental work, and as a mechanical engineer Kruesi was in charge of making things that Edison drew up on paper. During the period 1876-1881 he made many working products, including the carbon microphone, incandescent light bulb, quadruplex telegraph and electric wiring systems.

John H. Kreusi.

John Kruesi was one of the founding members of the Edison Machine Works in Schenectady, later to become the General Electric company, in 1887. He was Assistant General Manager under Charles Batchelor. He made the first record player when Edison gave him a sketch, and in 1877 lost a $2.00 bet with Edison that it wouldn't work.

Kruesi ran the Edison Electric Tube Works in Brooklyn where he was Treasurer. Edison was President and Samuel Insull was Secretary. There he invented and made underground conduits for electricity. He invented a two wire conduit where the conductors were separated and insulated. The first two early conduits for lighting anywhere in the world were laid down in lower New York City. His name is on most of the patents.

When the Edison Machine works moved to Schenectady, with Insull as General Manager, it was Kruesi that designed and constructed all the shops while he was Manager, from 1886 to 1892. He became the General Manager of the Schenectady works in 1892, and later Chief Mechanical Engineer for the company in 1896.

When Thomas Edison moved to Schenectady it was to make his bi-polar generators. They were needed to supply electricity for lighting his incandescent lamps. These Edison generators were called "Long Legged Mary Anns."

When he came to Schenectady in 1887 with his wife Emily Zwinger (1853-1897), they lived in a house on the corner of Union and Church streets, now demolished. They had eight children: August H. (March 28, 1876 - May 7, 1925); Olga A. (March 13, 1887 - May 26, 1946); John (October 15, 1891 - March 25, 1930); Emily M. (November 1890 - October 17, 1941); Walter E. (September 3, 1881- ?); Frank E. (June 19, 1885 - April 8, 1948); Paul J. (February 3, 1878 - November 1965); Claire L. (July 1888 - ?).

When John died of "grip" at his home on February 25, 1899, 4,000 employees of G.E. and Thomas Edison attended the funeral. Also attending was Charles A Coffin, President of G.E.; Samuel Insull, President of the Chicago Edison Company; and Charles A. Batchelor, his former boss. Pall bearers included Batchelor; A.J. Pitkins, Vice President of the Schenectady Locomotive Works; G.E. Emmons, General Manager of G.E. in Schenectady; E.W. Rice Jr., Vice President of G.E.; and John D. Remer of Schenectady.

Kruesi Avenue is named for him.

Judson Stuart Landon

January 28, 1888 - February 14, 1955
Location: T#30

Judson Stuart Landon was the owner of Jud's at 711 State Street and was found dead at his store and home in 1955. He was active in the early conservation movement in the Schenectady area and was President of the Schenectady Conservation Council when it was organized around 1925.

He was a fisherman and expert on the subject, especially trout fishing in the Adirondacks and Canada. On May 9, 1927 he was one of the first to broadcast on radio a weekly show on WGY, and by 1928 the 7 p.m. slot was sponsored by the Shakespeare Company. He had his own fishing equipment store on lower State Street, just above Nott Terrace.

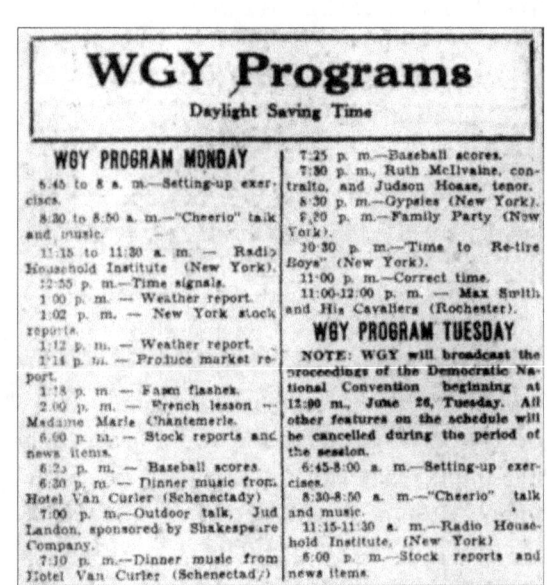

He graduated from Yale, attended Harvard Law, and graduate from Albany Law School. He came from a family of judges. His grandfather was the well-known Judge Judson Stuart Landon who died at his home on September 8, 1905. He was operated upon for an aggravate form of hernia on the Monday previous and never recovered.

The elder Landon was born in Salisbury, Connecticut on December 16, 1832. He went to Yale for law, came to Schenectady in 1856 and practiced, in which year he was elected District Attorney of the county, and held the office until 1865, when he was elected to filled the vacancy as county judge. In 1867 he served as member of the State Constitutional Convention. In 1873 he was elected a Justice of the Supreme Court, and on November 28, 1891, named a member of the Second Division of the Court of Appeals by Governor Roosevelt. When that court was dissolved, he went back to the Supreme Court, and later to the Court of Appeals. He was an author of several law books and a constitutional history of the U.S. He was interim president of Union when E. Nott Potter resigned.

He married Emily Augusta Pierce (b. November 20, 1835), who was an instructor at Princetown Academy, on April 26, 1856. Judson was Principal of the academy at the time. They had five children, two sons and three daughters. Their son Robert Judson Landon also became a judge and was the father of Judson Stuart Landon, of this bio. The father was, at the time of his death in 1941, the oldest practicing attorney in Schenectady city. Both are also buried at Vale.

A Judson Stuart Landon invented and patented a wind motor in 1899. If it was this Judson, he was 11 years old. If it was his grandfather, he would have been 67 years old.

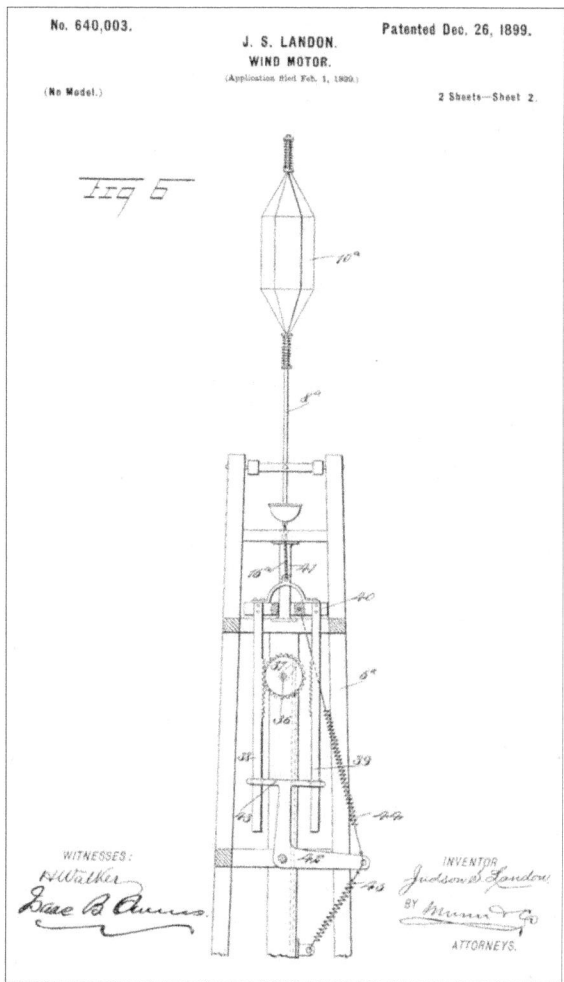

The Judson wind motor. (Courtesy of U.S. Patent Office.)

Charles Frederick Lewis

1844 - 1905
Location: X20:20 (Union Plot)

Charles was the son of Union College professor Tayler Lewis (1802-1977) and Jayne Keziah Payne Lewis (1810-1888). He was a graduate of Union College. On August 8, 1862, at age 18, he became a Private in the 119th New York Volunteers, moving up the ranks to 2nd Lieutenant on August 23, 1862 and 1st Lieutenant on January 1, 1863. He was discharged on February 23, 1863, but reenlisted in the regiment on April 19, 1863 at 1st Lieutenant. He was wounded on May 2, 1863, but made Captain on August 9, 1863, and later Major on July 21, 1864, being discharged for disability on July 21, 1864.

He married Katherine Rosa Smith Lewis (1844-1933) and had two children, Edward Smith Lewis (1868-1905) and Jane Keziah Lewis Seede (1874-1955). Charles had a brother and sister, Tayler Lewis (1847-1879) and Margaret Lewis Peissner (1836-1904).

The late historian Larry Hart wrote a book about him, <u>Through the Darkest Hour: A Romantic Story of a Union College Man's Adventures and Tribulations During the Civil War, 1862-1865</u> (Old Dorp Books, 1990).

Lewis has the distinction of being at the Ford Theater when Abraham Lincoln was shot. He kept a diary and the following entries describe the few days of the event.

> *Thursday, April 13, 1865* – Met Lincoln this morning in Lafayette Square – the old man looked very happy and well this night; what a grand homely face he has, and how nobly and unselfishly has he carried himself during these terrible four years. Posterity will appreciate his services to the country, more even than we can.
>
> *Friday, April 14, 1865* – (a friend) and I were at the theatre, and sat in the Dress Circle only a few feet from the box; saw the assassin enter it, oh and saw him leap from the box on to the stage and dart behind the scenes. What an awful end to all the talk and hopes of re-union, peace and good-will between the two sections of our unhappy country.
>
> *Saturday, April 15, 1865* – Yesterday was a scene of universal rejoicing over the return of peace, is today immersed in gloom and clothed in mourning.
>
> *Saturday, April 15, 1865* – I cannot feel that the death of Lincoln, is an immeasurable loss to the country at this time and to no portion will his death be more serious than to the South. It will almost certainly change the temper of the North from kindliness to sternness if not vindictiveness. (Many a day will pass before we will again see in the White House, the peer of Lincoln.) In every sense he was a noble man, and in his life and conduct – well exemplified the remarkable words of his late Inaugural.

The following from <u>The Union Army: A History of Military Affairs in the Loyal States, 1861-65</u> (Federal Pub. Co., 1908, vol. II) describes the 119th Regiment.

> *One Hundred and Nineteenth Infantry.* — *Cols., Elias Peissner, John T. Lockman; Lieut-Cols., John T. Lockman, Edward F. Lloyd, Isaac P. Lockman; Majs., Harvey Baldwin, Jr., Benjamin A. Willis, Isaac P. Lockman, Charles F. Lewis, Chester H. Southworth. This regiment was recruited and organized at New York City in the summer of 1862, and was mustered into the U. S. service on September 4-5, for three years. On the 6th the regiment left for Washington, where it was attached to the 2nd brigade, 3d (Schurz') division, 11th corps (Howard), and went into winter quarters at Stafford, Va. At the battle of Chancellorsville, Howard's corps was surprised and suffered severely, the 118th losing 21 killed, 67-wounded and 32 missing, Col. Peissner being killed while rallying his men. The regiment was commanded at Gettysburg by Col. Lockman, and was heavily engaged on the first two days of the battle, losing 140 in killed, wounded and missing. After returning with the army to Virginia, it was ordered with its corps on September 24, to Tennessee. It was present but not active at the midnight battle of Wauhatchie, fought valiantly at Missionary ridge, and was then ordered with the corps to the relief of Knoxville, en-during severe hardships and privations during the campaign. In April, 1864, when the 11th corps was broken up, the regiment was assigned to the 2nd brigade, 2nd division, of the newly formed 20th corps, commanded by Gen. Hooker, the veteran Gen. Geary being in command of the division. It moved on the Atlanta campaign and took part in numerous battles in the next four months, including Rocky Face ridge, Resaca, where the*

brave Lieut.-Col. Lloyd was killed, New Hope Church, Kennesaw mountain, Peachtree-creek, and the siege of Atlanta. After the fall of Atlanta, it remained with the corps to hold the city, while the rest of the army went in pursuit of Hood. On Nov. 15, the regiment moved with Sherman's army on the grand march through Georgia to the sea and took part in the siege of Savannah, Geary's division being the first to enter the city upon Hardee's evacuation. Early in the year 1865, it moved on the campaign of the Carolinas, fighting at Averasboro, Bentonville, Raleigh and Bennett's house, but sustaining a loss of only 4 missing. After Gen. Johnston's surrender, it marched on to Washington with the 20th corps, where it participated in the grand review, and was mustered out at Bladenburg, Md., June 7, 1865, commanded by Col. Lockman. The total enrollment of the regiment was 69 officers, 981 men. It lost by death during service, 6 officers and 71 men, killed and mortally wounded; 2 officers and 92 men by disease and other causes, a total of 171.

Charles was related by marriage to Col. Elias Peissure of the 119th New York Volunteers, who died at Chancellorsville after being held prisoner. Peissure was a professor of German Language and Literature at Union college and married the daughter of Professor Taylor Lewis, Charles' sister.

Tayler Lewis

Mar 27 1802-May 11, 1877
Location: X4:4.3 (Union College Plot)

Tayler Lewis was born in Northumberland, Saratoga County. His biography was published in *Notable Americans* (1904).

LEWIS, Tayler, educator, was born in Northumberland, N.Y., March 27, 1802; son of Samuel and Sarah (Van Valkenburg) Lewis. His father was an officer in the Revolutionary army and his mother was a niece of John Tayler, lieutenant governor of New York, and a descendant of Johannas Van Valkenberg, a native of Holland and an early settler of Albany.

Tayler Lewis was graduated from Union college in 1820, studied law in Albany, N.Y., and practiced at Fort Miller, N.Y., 1823-33. He devoted his leisure to the study of Biblical literature and to the Greek and Latin languages. He conducted a classical school at Waterford, N.Y., 1833-35, and one at Ogdensburg, N.Y., 1835-38. In 1838 he delivered the Phi Beta Kappa address at Union, taking as his subject "Faith, the Life of Science." This address, which was published, attracted wide attention. He was professor of Greek and Latin languages at the University of the City of New York, 1838-40, and of Greek language and literature, 1840-44. He was professor of ancient Oriental languages and literature at Union college, 1849-63, and of ancient languages, 1863-77. He received the honorary degree of LL.D. from Union college in 1844.

In the selection of names for a place in the Hall of Fame for Great Americans, New York University, made in October, 1900, his was one of the fifteen names submitted in "Class C, Educators" and received two votes. His published writings include: Believing Spirit (1841); State, Family and Church (1843); Plato contra Atheos (1844); Penalty of Death, in George B. Cheerer's "Defense of Capital Punishment" (1846); Six Days of Creation (1855); The Bible and Science, or the World Problem (1856); The Divine Human in the Scripture (1860); The Heroic Periods in a Nation's History (1866); The Light by which we see Light, Vedder Lectures (1875); Memoir's of Eliphalet Nott, with Van Santvoord and Lewis (1875); Bible Psalmody, the Imprecatory Psalms (1880); Wine Drinking and the Scriptures (1881); and contributions to Lange's Commentary, and to Harper's Magazine and other periodicals. He died in Schenectady, N.Y., May 11, 1877.

Lewis was more of a recluse but made up for his lack of social discourse with his writings. While not famous locally he was well known worldwide. His obituary was also published in the New York Times on

Prof. Tayler Lewis.

May 13. He had conservative views towards slavery but became a supporter of the Union effort during the Civil War. He produced editorials, letters, addresses and several books including The Heroic Periods in a Nation's History that was a testimony to returning veterans. When his son-in-law Col. Elias Peissner was killed at Chancellorsville, Lewis continued to speak out and constantly pushed the editor of the *Schenectady Union* to editorialize. His most popular book was his Six Days of Creation, published in 1855.

On the dome of Memorial Hall at Union College, in Hebrew and Latin letters, Lewis himself, using slate, placed the motto:

The time is short,
The work is vast,
The reward is great
The Master is pressing.

You can download digital versions of some of his books at: *http://onlinebooks.library.upenn.edu/webbin/book/lookupname?key=Lewis%2C%20Tayler%2C%201802-1877*.

His "Discourses commemorative of Professor Tayler Lewis, delivered at commencement, 1877; and of Professor Isaac W Jackson, delivered at commencement, 1878" can be downloaded at: *https://archive.org/details/discoursescommem00pott*.

Austin N. Liecty

October 11, 1866 - February 26, 1955
Location: M1 90a

Austin Liecty, a native of Albany, was the son of John L. and Jane Spellman Liecty and an 1884 graduate of Albany High School. He was an accountant before he became publisher of the *Syracuse Courier* from 1894 to 1897. Liecty became the Business Manager of the *Schenectady Gazette* on March 20, 1899 and, while not part of the family, took over as President, Treasurer and General Manager in 1920 until 1945, when he retired on February 7, due to poor health. He was replaced by Eleanor Smith, daughter of Gerardus Smith. While under the presidency of Liecty the paper purchased property on State Street that it had been renting.

The *Schenectady Gazette* began in 1894 after the Schenectady Printing Association took over a weekly called the *Schenectady Gazette* and turned it into a daily, renaming it *The Daily Gazette* in 1895. Gerardus Smith was the first President in 1899, and ownership of the paper stayed in the family, eventually changing the name to the *Schenectady Gazette* in 1902.

Liecty died at his home at 3 Douglass Road in Schenectady at age 88.

He was also on the Board of Directors of the Schenectady Trust Co., a charter Member of the Associated Press, on the Board of Managers at Ellis Hospital, Trustee of the Children's Home Society and the Ingersoll Memorial Home for Aged Men, a charter Member of the Schenectady Rotary Club, and a Member of the Mohawk Golf Club, Mohawk Club and First Reformed Church. His pastimes were golf and color photography.

Thomas M. Linville

March 3, 1904 - February 27, 1992
Location: FN 76a 5

Thomas was born in Washington, D.C. and was the son of Thomas Linville (1874-1937) and Clara E. Merriam (1872-1954), both from D.C.

He joined General Electric in 1926 and became Manager of the research operation in 1953 and Manager of Research Applications in 1964. He retired in 1966 and served as a consultant to G.E. Was a member of the National Research Council and President of the National Society of Professional Engineers.

During WWII he worked with the Bureau of Ships (U.S. Navy) on the development of submarine propulsion and control, on a technical mission to Pearl Harbor in 1942 and as a technical investigator in Germany in 1945. From 1934 to 1950 he was engaged in engineering development in energy conversion apparatus and control and was Chairman of the Development Committee at G.E. He was in charge of patent operations for G.E. Research from 1953 to 1960. In 1960 he was named Engineer of the Year by the Edison Club. It was cited that he "has toiled for many years on behalf of the engineering profession. He has been in the forefront of the battle to unify the aims and objectives of more than 28 professional engineering societies."

Locally he was Chairman of the Education Committee of the Chamber of Commerce, was Vice President of the Schenectady Museum, and chair of the building fund campaign. Also he was on the boards of the Schenectady United Fund, Mohawk-Hudson Council on Educational Television, Sunnyview Hospital and Schenectady Industrial Development Corporation.

He lived at 1131 Waverly Place, and later at 1147 Wendell Avenue.

The University of Virginia has a Thomas M. Linville Professorship that was established by Thomas and family in 1990. He was a 1926 E.E. degree graduate of the college. He also graduated from Harvard's Advanced Management Program in 1950. He was Chairman of the Development Council for the School of Science at Rensselaer Polytechnic Inistitue, with an interest in the role of patents in research at universities.

Thomas himself was a holder of seven patents and winner of G.E.'s highest honor, the Charles A. Coffin Award. He was Past President of the Schenectady Torch Club in 1946.

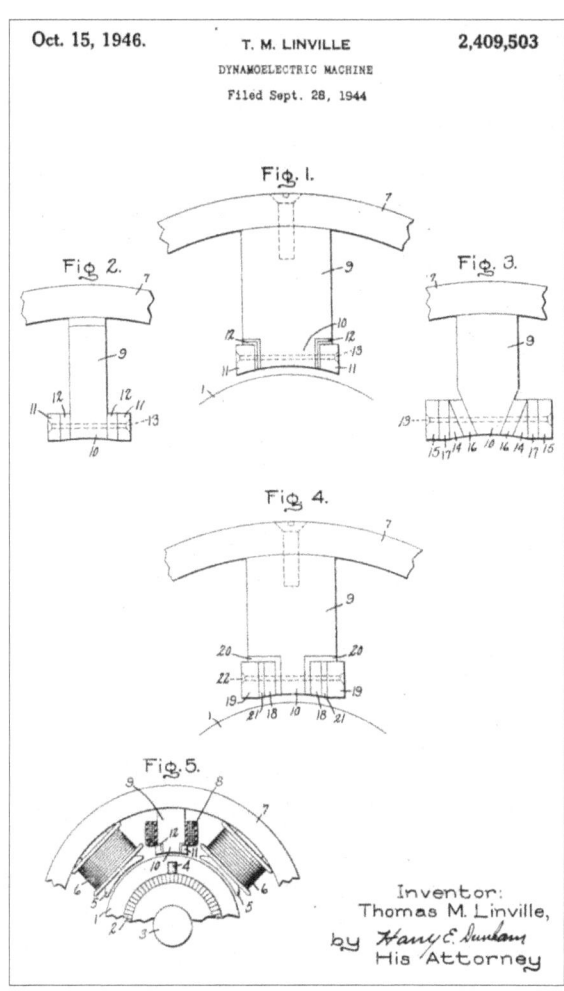

Patent drawing for Linville's dynamoelectric machine. (Courtesy of U.S. Patent Office.)

Simeon Butler Marsh

June 1, 1798 - July 14, 1875
Location: B-32

Simeon was born in Shelburne, New York, one of five children of Eli and Azubah (Butler) Marsh, and began singing in a choir at age 7. At 16 he began studying music, and by the age of 19, he was teaching in local singing schools. In 1837 Marsh was the publisher of *The Intelligencer* (later *The Record*), a newspaper in Amsterdam, New York for seven years, but returned to Shelburne where he began the *Shelburne News*. While there he was the superintendent of the Sunday school for six years. He wrote two compositions there, "The Saviour" for mixed voices, and "The King of the Forest" for boy's voices mostly.

He eventually taught choirs and children for 30 years around Schenectady, Albany and Amsterdam. He took the train to Schenectady once a week to teach kids for free for 13 years. He spent much time with congregations within the Albany Presbytery. Because of his publishing knowledge, he set his own type to three original juvenile books.

In the summer of 1834, while on his way to Amsterdam, he took shade under a tree to rest his horse and penned the melody of a tune, "Martyn." A few weeks later he met his friend Dr. Thomas Hastings, another teacher, and played it for him. Hastings was impressed and asked to have the harmony written, and Marsh obliged.

While the tune was originally set to the John Newton hymn "Mary to the Saviour's Tomb," he instead used the Charles Wesley lyric, "Jesus, Lover of my Soul," with which it has been forever joined.

He married at age 21 to Eliza Carrier (1800-1873) from Hamilton, New York and had two children; John Butler Marsh was a professor of vocal culture and organ instruction in the Elmira Female College.

After his wife died in 1873, he moved to Albany to live with his son and died there. While Marsh wrote many other pieces of music, it is for "Martyn" that he is most remembered.

Marsh's gravestone exhibits the rural nature of Vale Cemetery.

Walter McQueen

October 8, 1817- June 16, 1893
Location: P#41

Walter McQueen was born in Sterlingshire, Scotland and came to America in 1830 with his parents, five sisters and two brothers. They lived in Perth in Fulton County. His first job in the area was as a feeder in a horseshoe machine for the Burden Iron Works in Troy, around 1835. He apprenticed for William B. Many of Albany, who made steam engines and mill work, and in 1838 he erected the first stationary engine in Gloversville for the glove industry. He also began working that year for the Eaton and Gilbert car company in Troy. He went back to Scotland in 1839 and worked in the Napier shops in Glasgow, and on the first Cunard steamship.

He came back to America and worked as a machinist between 1840-1845. He was a machinist and locomotive engineer for the Hudson & Berkshire in Hudson until 1843, where he was in charge of the shops at the foot of West 13th Street in New York City. He then moved to Schenectady and worked on the Utica & Schenectady Railroad. In 1840 he built a small 7-ton, 4-2-0 locomotive at Albany for the Ithaca & Oswego Railroad.

In 1845 he was appointed Master Mechanic of the Mohawk & Hudson Railroad, newly reorganized as the Albany & Schenectady Railroad. He rebuilt several old engines and constructed a new machine called The Mechanic. He was hired as master mechanic for the Hudson River Railroad in 1848.

The Schenectady Locomotive Works formed in 1851 with John Ellis as the lead. McQueen acquired an interest in the company and joined the company. He left the Albany & Schenectady in 1852 to become Superintendent of the Schenectady Locomotive Works. While there the company produced 1,000 different locomotives. He retired in 1876 but remained Vice President until he died.

He was the first to use the cylinder saddle and first to apply the air dome to feed pumps. He was one of the best known mechanics in the country and knew everything about locomotive building.

His reputation was so great that a group of citizens talked him into forming a new locomotive company called McQueen Locomotive Works. Charles Stanford, then State Senator, and brother of famed Leland of the Transcontinental Railroad, was chief promoter and stockholder. Eight acres of land were purchased on the east side of Mill Lane and two buildings were built in 1882 by John McDermott. Stanford died, the buildings were left and McQueen resigned and the company never formed, only to be purchased by Thomas Edison and the beginning of General Electric was initiated.

It was a McQueen locomotive that took part in the building of the Transcontinental Railroad and when the Union Pacific's No. 119 and Central Pacific's No. 60 (known as the Jupiter) met at Promontory Summit on May 10, 1869, it was the Jupiter that was built by the Schenectady works. Both were scrapped, the No. 119 in 1903 and the Jupiter in 1906. Three other McQueen locomotives were shipped to the Central Pacific in 1868 along with the Jupiter; the Numbers 61 (Storm), 62 (Whirlwind), and 63 (Leviathan).

The Jupiter (left), designed by Walter McQueen and built in Schenectady, meets the Union Pacific's No. 119 at the driving of the Last Spike of the Transcontinental Railroad, May 10, 1869.

McQueen's tenure at Schenectady Locomotive, while brief, produced locomotives with high reputations and were called "McQueen" engines because of their popularity, especially on western railroads. Schenectady Locomotive was second largest in the county between 1851 and 1861, producing and average of 190 locomotives per year. The works eventually became part of the American Locomotive Company (ALCO) in 1901, which continued to be innovative, and a leading engine maker into the 1960s.

He married Charlotte Augusta Cole in 1842. She died in 1879. They had five children: Hon. D.P. McQueen; Mrs. Joshua Barker; Mr. Henry B. McQueen of Schenectady; Mrs. F.A. Beckwith of Cleveland; and Mr. Robert F. McQueen of New York. His home at 613 Union Street where he died now serves as a restaurant and bar.

William H. Milton, Jr.

1900 - June 12, 1984
Location: C#6

Originally a native of Roanoke, Virginia, he moved to Schenectady and was Vice President and atomic power engineer for General Electric. As General Manager of Knolls Atomic Power Laboratory, he worked for G.E. for 32 years, but resigned in 1952 to take over the Virginia Military Institute, where he had graduated from in 1920. He was the 8th Superintendent of VMI. Milton was the first VMI Superintendent to come to the job from an exclusively non-military background. Upon his appointment as Superintendent in August 1952, he was appointed a Major General in the Virginia Militia (Unorganized). He served until June 30, 1960.

He set out five objectives at VMI before he retired. First, the firming up and establishment of a sound academic program; Second, reestablishment of the discipline and performance in the corps of cadets to at least a pre-WWII level; Third, putting the VMI physical plant into proper condition; Fourth, placement of extracurricular activities such as major sports, with football number one; and Fifth, to attain a proper balance among the academic military and athletic activities of the cadets.

His son William H. Milton III, who died in 2009 in Galway, was the former Executive Vice President of TRUSTCO.

Superintendent Milton.

George Church Moon

Mar 4, 1861 - Nov 6, 1917
Location: M1#222

Moon was born in Schenectady to George W. Moon (1814-1880) and wife Catherine Rosa (1818-1883). She was the daughter of James Rosa, Superintendent of the Schenectady & Albany Railroad. George attended public schools and graduated from the Union Classical Institute (now the Stockade Inn). In 1881 at the age of 20 he worked as a cashier in the dry goods store of F.H. Reeves & Company on State Street. In 1891 he went into the newspaper business as a reporter for the *Daily Union* where he eventually became the City Editor.

He left the paper to work in the County Clerk's office as a Recording Clerk and on July 3, 1902 he was appointed Deputy Clerk and worked under two clerks, James B. Alexander and George M. Bostwick. In 1910 he ran as a Republican for the position of County Clerk and won by over 2,500 votes, the largest vote-getter of any county politicians up to that time. He was reelected in 1913 and in 1916, again getting the most votes of any county politicians.

On August 9, 1905 he married May Carolyn Hanbridge (1879-1949) and had one daughter Sarah Merrita E. Moon. They lived at 2 Rugby Road. He became ill on June 7 and died of lung trouble at 11:25 a.m. on November 6, 1917.

He attended the First Reformed Church, was a member of Schenectady lodge. No. 480, B. P. O. E., St. George's Lodge. No. 6, F. & A.M., the Schenectady County Republican club, the Republican Club of Glenville. the Schenectady Board of Trade, the Schenectady County Historical society, and several others. He was one of the organizers of Colonel Cornelius Van Dyck chapter of the Sons of the American Revolution in Schenectady, and on June 30, 1915, was elected its first President. He was fond of music and literature and he possessed a large library.

Janet Murray

July 22, 1856 - February 20, 1940
Location: G#118

Born in Peebles, Scotland in 1856 to Ralph and Isabella (Kerr) Murray and educated in England, she moved to Ontario, Canada in 1866 at age 10, with her family. Her father was a mining engineer (also listed as a minister) when in Peebles. After nursing her father back to health after an accident, nursing her mother who was a invalid, and dressing wounds of neighbors before the doctor arrived, her family began telling her she should become a doctor.

In 1891 she graduated from the Medical College of Queen's University, being one of the first females to attend there, and began working for doctors in Canada. After a quick stop in Schenectady on her way to Boston for an interview, she returned to Schenectady in 1893 when the job didn't materialize and opened her practice above a Jay Street tailor shop (although listed 242-230-1/2 State Street) and then to 14 Mynderse Street, where she practiced for the next forty years. There was no hospital in Schenectady when she began. If someone needed an operation, they had to be taken by wagon to the railroad station, be put in a baggage car, and ride to Albany. She always made time to take care of the poor.

She quickly integrated into the medical societies and clubs in the area. Her entrance to the county medical society was met with skepticism. By 1905 she was Vice President of the society. In 1935 she was elected to become Vice President of the Queens University Alumni Association and also a member of the Board of Councilors of the Women's Medical Society of New York.

Dr. Janet Murray.

She made the news on August 19, 1921, when she was involved in a car accident, ironically in front of a doctors office. Her and a woman companion were bruised and cut when she crashed her Kissel Coupe car into a telephone pole in front of Dr. William H. Seward's on West Main Street. They were coming home from a trip in Utica. It was raining hard and the lights of an approaching car blinded her. They were taken care of by Dr. Seward and the Kissel car was taken to the L.R. Mack garage.

She retired to the Old Ladies Home (Heritage Home for Women) in March 1937 and died there on February 20, 1940, at age 83 after a ten day illness. While there she volunteered her services. She had practiced medicine for 64 years in Schenectady.

Mordecai Myers

May 1, 1776 - January 20, 1871
Location: B#36

Myers was born in Newport, Rhode Island but spent his early years (1776-1783) in New York City with his poor Jewish immigrant parents. Unfortunately for him, he was the child of Loyalists during the American Revolution and spent 1783-87 in the woods of Nova Scotia. He tried becoming a merchant in Richmond, Virginia and served in the military under Col. John Marshall (later Chief Justice). When he returned to NYC in 1787, he never looked back and had several successful careers in military and politics. He tried business in NYC and served in a military company under Capt. John Swartwout. He had the distinction of being at Washington's inauguration as President.

During the War of 1812, as Captain of the 13th Pennsylvania Infantry, he was wounded severely in the left shoulder in the American defeat at the Battle of Chrysler's

Portrait of Myers by John Wesley Jarvis.

Field in Ontario, but recovered. His life was saved by Dr. Albon Man of Constable, New York, a highly respected physician at the time, who instead of amputating, removed 30 fragments of his humorous. The 38-year-old Myers was brought to Man's home and Myers was tended to in Man's office. He also noticed 17-year-old Charlotte Bailey, who was told to put a curtain in the window to prevent the sun from shining too brightly on Myers. She was the daughter of Man's bother-in-law. He married Charlotte (1796-1848), and they had ten children; he outlived six of them. He was the great-great-grandfather of Robert Lowell, the Pulitzer Prize winning poet.

Myers is credited with saving nearly 200 lives when two schooners capsized near Sackets Harbor in 1813. While he rescued most, some 40 or 50 were dead. The survivors were drunk from raiding the hospital stores while their boats were capsized.

In 1815 he retired from the service due to his disability and received a pension for half pay as Captain. He was the first Jew elected to the New York Legislature, from 1828-1834 (six terms), representing New York City, where he became friends with Martin Van Buren. He moved to Kinderhook to retire and was elected their Mayor in 1838.

The financial crisis of the 1830s and 1840s severely hurt him and he sold his home and moved to Schenectady at age 72. Schenectady Democrats, knowing his reputation as a war hero and politician, urged him to run for Mayor, which he won in 1851 and 1854 (as a Whig). He was the first and only Jewish Mayor to date in Schenectady politics. While Mayor he helped poor people get access to vaccinations, and talked Albany's Erastus Corning, then President of the New York Central Railroad, to slow speeding trains entering the city.

He was accepted as a member of the Freemasons, achieving the 32nd Degree, and was the State's Grand Master of the Grand Lodge, from 1853 to 1856. He decided to run for Congress at the age of 84 in 1860, but lost.

In 2013 Neil Yetwin, a history teacher at Schenectady High School, authored a book on Myers titled, <u>To My Son: The Life and War Remembrances of Captain Mordecai Myers, 13th United States Infantry, 1812-1815</u>.

Detail of Myers monument in Vale.

William Ten Broeck Mynderse

August 1, 1871 - April 23, 1931
Location: L#50

William was the son of medical doctor Barent Aaron Mynderse (1829-1887) and Albertina Sanders Tenbroeck (1835-1900), they married on May 29, 1860. Albertina was the daughter of Leonard William Tenbroeck and Helen Livingston. William had a brother Herman and a sister Helen.

He married Sarah Hulme Wilson, daughter of Harold Wilson and Mary Elizabeth Livingston Sanders, on September 7, 1905 at Clermont, New York. They had a daughter, Helen Livingston Mynderse, born on February 2, 1914. Mary E. Sanders was a daughter of Judge John Sanders, a writer of note and editor of *New York History*. He married Jane Livingston, a direct descendant of Robert Livingston, first "Lord of the Manor," Columbia County, New York.

William went to Union College, class of 1893, and was a member of Delta Phi Fraternity. He was a noted and prolific architect of Schenectady from 1910 to 1926. The following paragraphs list some of his works.

In 1910, he designed a two-story home on Wendell Avenue and Union Street for Edward F. Cohen; a two story Parish House for St. George's Episcopal Church at 78 North Ferry; alterations to a store building at 245-47 State Street for Patton & Hall; remodeled interior and new front at 218 State Street from J. Levi and Sons; alterations of a home and wing to provide a garage at 48 Washington Street for W.L.R. Emmett of General Electric; designed a two-story home at Morris Avenue for L.E. Jeffers; alterations for a home owned by Prof. E.E. Hale at Union College; designed a garage at 3 Gillespie Street for F. Mackintosh; a garage for JR Lovejoy, unknown address.

In 1913 alone he designed a garage on upper State Street; Apartment Building at 7 Lafayette Street; a two-story home on Wendell Avenue for E.G. Waters; similar size on Lowell Road for Charles Van Brunt at 19 Washington Avenue; a garage for W. Howard Wright at 15 Stanford Road; a four-story store and apartment building (3 stores and 21 apartments) at 791-95 Albany Street from Mrs. Josephine. A. Rickard; a two-story home at 44 Lowell Road for Mrs. H.H. Benham; a two-story home at 15 Ardsley Road for W.D. Sargent. The same year he designed a two-story home for F. M. Case at 5 Washington Road in Scotia, New York.

In 1914, he designed a one-story club house for the Mohawk Golf Club on Troy Road; a store and office building at 420-22 State Street for E.H. Cohn; and a two-story home for Mrs. C.D. Hoskins at Avon & Lowell Roads. He designed his own house, called the Holland House, on Sunnyside Avenue in Scotia. It was made to look like Washington Irving's "Sunnyside."

In 1915 he designed a store and loft building at 115 S. Centre Street (Broadway) for D.L.W. Watkins; a one story church in Scotia for St. Andrew's Church; a new store front at 218-22 State Street for Albert Levi; a two-story residence for H.J. Haigh on Lowell Road; a store and flat building (2 each and addition) at 117-19 S. Centre Street; a two-story home on Washington Road (Scotia) for Frank H Field; four stores on Center and Franklin Streets for Samuel Graubart; the three- and four-story addition to the Old Ladies Home (Heritage Home for Women) at 1519 Union Street.

In 1916 he designed a three-story house for J.W. Kellogg at 10 Front Street in Schenectady; a home at 3 Avon Rd for F.J. Cole; two-story home for W.C. Frame at Sunnyside Road; a two and one-half story for Chas Fair on Lowell Road; a single family home for D. L. Whitestone at 7 Douglass Road; a two and one-half story home in Scotia; and a two-story home on Lowell Road for Charles Farr.

In 1917 he designed the Mary McClellan Hospital, paid for by his brother-in-law Edwin McClellan; he designed a two-story home on Troy Road for C.W. Stone; a two and one-half story home for Abel Clements on Sunnyside Avenue; two-story store and cafe at 115 S. Center Street owned by D.L.W. Watkins; an addition to a home at 3 Avon Road for F.J. Cole; alteration and addition to 7 Douglas Road for S. L. Whiteston; a store and flat at State and Princetown streets for Emanuel Ebrarowitz; an addition to the Club House for Schenectady Golf Club.

In 1918, he built two story building for Union College.

In 1919, he designed a home on Washington Road in Scotia for C.B. Davis.

In 1920, the home for G.E. inventor Charles W. Stone, called Stone Ridge, that later became part of Bellevue Maternity Hospital in 1942; a two story home at 2 Parkwood Boulevard for G.R. Fonda.

In 1922, he designed three nurses' homes for the Mary McClellan Hospital in Cambridge, New York, one of them for Miss Southerland, Superintendent on premises.

In 1926, he designed the 1st National Bank of Scotia building at 201 Mohawk Avenue in Scotia.

His wife Sara was President of the Board of Management of the Old Ladies' Home and served on the board for 45 years, starting in 1922 and was the longest ever of any member. She retired in 1950.

Eliphalet Nott

June 25, 1773 - January 29, 1866
Location: Plot 15:15 (Union Plot)

The Rev. Eliphalet Nott.

The Rev. Eliphalet Nott was born in Ashford, Connecticut, the son of Stephen Nott, a merchant, farmer and tanner. His mother was Deborah Selden, daughter of Samuel Selden, a highly respected gentleman from Lyme, Connecticut. Eliphalet was the second son and youngest of nine children, and was left an orphan at an early age, being brought up in hard farm life by a relative. His older brother worked to become a clergyman, and young Eliphalet was destined to follow, although his first love was the natural sciences. He lived with his brother for four years, learning Latin and Greek.

He married Sarah Marie Benedict, daughter of Rev. Joel Benedict of Plainfield, Connecticut, who died while they were in Albany on March 9, 1804, at age 39. He then married Gertrude Peebles in 1807. She died in January 1841. His third wife was Urania E. Sheldon (born September 25, 1806) was only 35 when he, age 69, married her in 1842. She was formerly a principal of the Schenectady Academy that was supposed to have been merged into Union College in 1795. It was reconstituted in 1818. He had two sons, Joel B. and B.C. Nott.

He graduated in 1794 from Brown College (then Rhode Island College) with a Masters Degree at age 19, and studied theology for six months. He settled in Cherry Valley, Otsego County, New York, as a preacher and teacher and established the Cherry Valley Academy. He received a call to preach at Albany in the First Presbyterian Church and stayed for nearly seven years.

When he was at Albany, he became noted for an eloquent sermon given on the death of Alexander Hamilton and which is considered a classic in English oratory. Both Aaron Burr and Hamilton were members of his church. Nott spoke out against the dueling that took place in Hoboken, New Jersey, the site of many a duel. His sermon is available online at: *https://archive.org/details/discourseoccasio00nott*.

In 1804 he was selected as President of Union College in Schenectady, where he stayed for 61 years until he died, the longest term ever to this day. He had been on the Board of Trustees for a number of years prior. He decided to move out of the downtown campus he built, called North College, and purchased 250 acres for what is now the Union Campus on upper Union Street. Designed by famous French architect Joseph Ramée, it became the first planned college campus in America. He was able to secure funding for $200,000 for the fledgling college in 1814 from the New York State Legislature, and the new college grew. Nott also served as President of the Rensselaer Institute (present day Rensselaer Polytechnic Institute) in Troy from 1829-1845.

Nott was also an inventor. He was an early promoter of Robert Fulton and his steam river navigation, and the steamer *S.S. Novelty* was built under Nott's guidance and proved to be more efficient that Fulton's boilers. The speed at which it ran from New York to Albany impressed everyone. He invented the Nott cast iron stove, first to use Anthracite coal; a three-wheeled coach, which he donated to his friend Mary Delevan in later years; and thirty patents for other inventions between 1832 and 1839. He amassed a personal fortune, and in 1854 donated much to the college he loved as a permanent endowment ($610,000). It provided for the support of nine professors and six assistant professors, and for the purchase of books and other materials for students.

He published a number of works including "Counsels to Young Men" in 1810, and "Lectures on Temperance" in 1847.

Nott introduced practical education into the education system, as classical education was on the way out and students were able to get degrees in engineering, chemistry and other professions that Nott thought would be more adequate for the rise of American ingenuity.

Nott is recognized as an early abolitionist. He hired Moses Viney, a runaway slave from Maryland who found his way to Schenectady, as his coachman and, after the passage of the Fugitive Slave Act in 1850, Nott paid for his freedom. Viney was left a sum of money when Nott died, but he still served Nott's widow Urania, who had taken control of much of the school after her husband started having strokes in 1860. In an 1860 diary entry by Jonathan Pearson, who worked at the school, he wrote that Nott was "completely under Urania's thumb now, and has to do just as she says." Not everyone was happy about her having such control, but there is little written about her. She was the principle architect in forming the Home for the Friendless (now Heritage Home for Women) and was the first directress from 1868 to 1885. She was also principal of the Utica Female Seminary in 1842 when she married Eliphalet. She is also buried at Vale.

Union College has the Eliphalet Nott Scholar award given to a undergrad student who earns an academic average of 3.67 or better in the previous academic year.

In 1933, a boulder with his name on a plaque was given to the Connecticut Governor, who designed in a small state park the new Eliphalet Nott Memorial Highway. The boulder was part of the foundation of the house in which he was born in Connecticut. Nott Highway joined several other state highways named for famous people, such as Jonathan Trumbull, Ethan Allen and George Washington.

Nott Road (Rexford), Nott Street and Nott Terrace are named for him.

Nott Memorial is the centerpiece at the college grounds. Built in 1858, it is considered an architectural wonder and one of the few sixteen-sided buildings in the world, and is a National Historic Landmark. It was designed by Edward Tuckerman Potter, grandson of Nott. It was planned to be demolished, but was restored under Union College President Roger Hull in 1993.

Nott was buried next to Col. William A. Jackson in Vale.

The Nott Memorial on the campus of Union College. (Courtesy of Richard Vang.)

Abraham Oothout

May 27, 1744 - June 19, 1822
Location: P#36

Abraham was the son of Jonas Oothout and Elisabeth Lansing. He married Magarita Lansing (1747-1786), daughter of Gerrit Janse Lansing and Elsje Abrahamse Lansing on November 27, 1767, and they had eight children. After the death of Margarita he then married 37-year-old widow Lena Lansing on November 14, 1787, the daughter of John J. Lansing and Cathlina Schuyler. Lena had two children from a previous marriage (a third, a son, died at age 28).

Oothout moved to Schenectady from the Albany area in 1759.

According to A History of Schenectady During the Revolution by Willis T. Hanson, the chief Revolutionary figures of Schenectady were Colonels Cornelius Van Dyck, Abraham Wemple, Abraham Oothout and Lieutenant-Colonel Christopher Yates.

On May 6, 1775, Oothout was elected a member of the first Committee of Safety. He served also on the second Committee and the Committees taking office January 15, 1777, June 2, 1777, and January 5, 1778. He was a deputy from Albany County to the first Provincial Congress. He served throughout the war as a Captain in the Second Regiment, Albany County Militia, being appointed soon after January 26, 1776.

On June 27, 1775, he was appointed to attend the council with the Indians at German Flats, and on February 24, 1776, he was appointed with Christopher Yates to collect donations from the inhabitants to pay for sleds to transport the troops from Albany to Lake George. In the fall he was in command of a detail to Fort Ann, Fort Edward and Skenesborough.

On April 24, 1777, he was detailed as a wagoner for duty from Albany to Lake George. On May 21, 1777, he was a member of a court-martial at Albany. He served with the troops against General Burgoyne at Saratoga, Stillwater and Bemis Heights.

On June 20, 1778, he was regularly commissioned Captain, and in the summer commanded a detachment to Stone Arabia. On June 24, 1779, he was again appointed a member of the Committee of Safety, and on June 2 was appointed Chairman of the Board, which office he resigned on July 8, because of the pressure of public business. On July 1, 1780, he was appointed one of the Commissioners of Conspiracies. In August, 1780, he marched with the troops to Fort Plain (after the raid on that section), and in the fall of 1781 was stationed at Fort Hunter. After the battle of Johnstown he marched in pursuit of the enemy. Towards the end of the war he was promoted to the rank of Colonel in the 2nd Albany County Militia to succeed Col. Wemple, who resigned.

In 1794, Oothout petitioned the court and was appointed guardian of Lena's two children. Oothout went on and became the third Mayor of Schenectady in 1810-11, and was one of the original 126 founders of Union College.

John Nicholas Parker

September 20, 1854 - February 23, 1907
Location: Unknown

John was born in Providence, Saratoga County, New York, on September 20, 1853, the son of Robert Parker and Margaret Timeson. His parents were very poor and could not afford to send him to school. He worked at small tasks, on farms and on the Erie Canal for one dollar per day. He was a clerk in the Parker Hotel in Rexford, New York, that his uncle owned. He then established a small business which became John N. Parker & Company, one of the largest wholesale hay dealing concerns in the state.

John purchased a hotel in Rexford Flats in 1876, operating until 1887, and which later became the McClane Hotel. Then he purchased the old Aqueduct Hotel, formerly owned by his uncle Hiram until 1894, then sold it.

He then formed the Schenectady Paving and Contracting Company, which he kept until his death. He also had an interest in the Niskayuna Ice Company and was a director of the Schenectady Trust Company.

John was first the Highway Commissioner in the Town of Niskayuna and served two terms on the Board of Supervisors. Governor Levi P. Morton appointed him Division Superintendent of the Canals for the Eastern Division in 1895, which office he held for 12 years. He resigned shortly before he died. When he died he was Assistant Superintendent of Public Works for the State of New York.

He was a member of St. George's Lodge, No. 6, F. & A.M.; St George's Chapter No. 157, R.A.M.; St. George's Commandery No. 37, K.T.; and Oriental Temple, Nobles of the Mystic Shrine. He was also a charter member of the Shaughnaugh-ta-da Tribe No. 122, International Order of Red Men, and the local lodge of the Benevolent and Protective Order of Elks.

He married on October 14, 1881 to Katherine Blair of Craig, the daughter of John Blair, a prominent contractor. She died on December 19, 1903. With her he had sons John R., born in 1882 (married Fanny S. Sanford on July 3, 1907), and James C. (born 1887), a real estate dealer in Schenectady, and a daughter Ethel B. (born 1884) who married George G Schieffelin.

John remarried on November 15, 1905 to Mary B Lorad in New York City.

His son James R. Parker was nominated for the New York Assembly by the Republicans in 1909. He was a lawyer and partner of ex-Senator William W. Wemple.

John was a Republican Boss of Schenectady County for a decade, and many politicians attended his funeral, led by St. George's Commandery and other organizations in line such as the Shaughnaugh-ta-da Tribe of Red Men, the Schenectady Elks and Schenectady County Republican Committee. It was the longest funeral procession in years according to local papers. He was 53 when he died of Bright's Disease (today known as acute nephritis, a kidney disease) and heart trouble. He was sick for two years. In 1906 it was reported in the paper that he was near death after staying at a sanitarium in Saratoga for months. He had a full Masonic Burial.

When he was nominated to be on the railroad commission in 1905, the governor refused, citing that Schenectady County "has grown to be of great importance in State politics and is of such proportions now as to demand recognition. It is one of the banner Republican counties of the State, and the Republican boss of such an important county deserves something better than a measly $2,400 a year canal job. As a railroad commissioner Boss Parker would receive $8,000 a year, besides which he would have considerable patronage."

In 1903 the Erie Canal had a derrick boat called the *John N Parker*. It raised sunken boats in the Erie Canal. In 1900 there was a John N Parker Club of Schenectady, named for the county Republican campaign club. At an outing at the Aqueduct, the steamer *Kitty West* was ready to leave, but a sword of First Sergeant Williams dropped overboard. He disrobed and dove in twice to receive it at the Liberty Street bridge.

Hinsdill Parsons

February 10, 1864 - April 28, 1912
Location: M3#4

Hinsdill Parsons was born in Hoosick Falls, New York, where his father J. Russell Parsons practiced law. His father was manager of the Walter A. Wood Company and a powerful Democrat in Rensselaer County politics. There were five sons in the family. Both Hinsdill and his brother James grew up in Hoosick Falls and both studied law at Trinity College in Hartford. Hinsdill graduated in 1884. While in college, Parsons joined Phi Beta Kappa and Delta Psi fraternities. He attended Albany Law School and graduated in 1885; he was admitted to the New York State Bar in the same year. In September 1889, he married Jessie Mary Burchard in Hoosick Falls.

Hinsdill was a patent attorney for his father's company. When he moved to Schenectady he worked for the Schenectady Railway Company, becoming Superintendent of the company for eighteen years.

In 1894 he went to the legal department at General Electric. In May, 1901, he was given control of G.E.'s legal affairs and was elected Vice President of the company. At

Hinsdill Parsons.

this time, Parsons was also elected President of the Schenectady Railroad Company, retiring from that position when it was sold to the New York Central and Delaware & Hudson railroads on July 25, 1905. During his tenure with G.E., Parsons was involved with various company anti-trust legal issues.

He was one of the most influential people of Schenectady. As the head of the law department, he handled all of the company's legal affairs in both the Schenectady and New York offices. He was also president of the Schenectady Illuminating Company and the Mohawk Gas Company.

Hinsdill Parsons was killed instantly on April 28, 1912 in a car accident. He was driving a high-powered automotive (90 horse power Simplex) along the Albany-Boston Turnpike near Clinton Heights, back of Rensselaer (East Greenbush). A rear tire blew out and overturned, killing him by crushing his head. His chauffeur, James Nicholson, had one foot amputated, and ironically his son was hit by a car later in the year, and his private secretary Benjamin H. Weisbrod escaped without injury. Hinsdill was known to like speed and many had predicted he would die this way. It was projected that he was driving faster than 60 miles per hour from eye witnesses, including an ex-Sheriff.

The monument for Hinsdill Parsons and his wife Jessie Burchard at Vale.

On April 30, 1912, out of respect, all power in the G.E. plants in Schenectady, Pittsfield (Massachusetts), Erie (Pennsylvania), Lynn (Massachusetts), Harrison (New Jersey), and Fort Wayne (Indiana), were turned off at 3:30 p.m. for two minutes while workers paid tribute. All flags at these plants were at half mast. The Schenectady Illuminating Company and the Mohawk Gas Company closed their offices from 2 p.m. to 4 p.m. The Schenectady Railway Cars were stopped for five minutes.

He was a member of St. George's Episcopal Church, and active in charities and contributed to institutions. He was a member of the Mohawk Club and the Mohawk Golf Club, University, Metropolitan, St. Andrew's and St. Nicholas' clubs, and the Down Town Association in New York City. Parsons served on the board of directors for the Electric Bond and Share, the Washington Water Power, and the Knickerbocker Trust Companies (he reorganized and saved the company during the 1907 panic), was a trustee for the General Electric Investment Club, was co-President of the Bully Hill Copper Mining & Smelting Company, and was a member of the American Academy of Political and Social Science. He was only 48 when he died.

He lived in NYC in the winter and in summer lived at 21 Front Street in Schenectady, and each weekend usually all year.

His brother James Russell Parsons, Jr., was Deputy Superintendent of Public Instruction in New York State and Secretary of the University at Albany. He was appointed to a federal position, Consul General in Mexico, by President Teddy Roosevelt. Ironically, James was killed in Mexico City on December 5, 1905, while riding in an open carriage with his wife and son. The vehicle was hit by a fast moving trolley car and James was thrown out of the vehicle, and his head hit a trolley pole, killing him instantly.

Hinsdill was reputed to be a millionaire. He did not have a will and one-third of his estate went to his widow and the rest to three brothers and a nephew. He married Jessie Mary Burchard in 1889, she was the sister of Anson W. Burchard who was assistant to the president of G.E. When she died on July 28, 1951 at age 83, she left an estate valued at $865,768, and she left $105,192.35 to St. George's Episcopal Church. She owned homes on 19, 21, and 23 Front Street, which she donated to the church. Most of her wealth was in securities and bonds, so it appears Hinsdill did leave her in good financial shape even without a will.

A fire department division, the Hinsdill Parsons Hose No. 8, was formed in Bellevue.

When he was buried at Vale, the choir of St. George's Church sang "Oh Paradise" at the grave. Many notables attended the funeral, including Charles Steinmetz, C.A. Coffin, President of G.E., and managers of all the G.E. plants.

His archives were found in the attic of 21 Front Street in 2000, and are now at the University of Albany Archives of Public Affairs.

Jonathan Pearson

February 23, 1813 - 1887
Location: X1:1.3 (Union Plot)

Jonathan was born in Chichester, New Hampshire, the son of Caleb Pearson, a Revolutionary War filer and mill builder. Jonathan found his way to Schenectady by way of his father, and entered Union College in January 1832, graduating with honors in 1835. He lived at 187 Union Street.

In 1836, he was a tutor at the college; Assistant Professor of Chemistry and Natural Philosophy in 1839; Professor of Natural History in 1849; Treasurer of the college in 1854; and in 1873 was transferred to the Deptartment of Agriculture and Botany.

Jonathan Pearson was a noted authority of local and colonial history, and his writings are still one of the more important references today, particularly for Schenectady colonial history. When he first attended Union College he wrote in 1832, "Dorp is a strange place on the whole, a dirty, sandy, and mean city. It reminds me often when the wind blows of a blustering winter's day, from the sand riding in clouds above the city and fills one's eyes."

As the librarian and treasurer of Union College he was known as "one of the most ardent of woman haters" in his younger days, and this dislike included not only women, but marriage and children as well. He wrote in November 1835, "Of all hells, deliver me from one where there is the squalling of children. I can listen to the jargon of a multitude, but …"

However, two months later he expressed his idea that "Perhaps it might not be wicked to wish for a wife who, in addition to all her other accomplishments, had that very charming grace, a snug little fortune. In fact, wealth in the world is the highest adornment, and the most powerful attraction that a young woman can have."

He also wrote: "Old maids are a commodity which ought to be shipped to Bottony Bay with the other refuse of society." Within one year however he reversed his feelings based on his experience with a Ms. Lord from Utica. Whatever happened, he wrote "woman softens the savageness of man's nature and tames him down into a sociable being—a man who lives a bachelor until 30 years of age and has not mingled in female society cannot ordinarily profit by marriage."

By 1840 he wrote of his narrow escape from love: "Came as near getting in love some months ago as I could and still miss it. Came of only by the skin of my teeth. My heart got some miserable twinges. The good for nothing, black-eyed, rosy-cheeked thing tried her prettiest but my Captain Reason wouldn't budge an inch—plaguey long story, hangs thereon, but I won't tell it."

Jonathan Pearson.

Eight months later he writes: "At Utica. And what for? To see Lord—the prettiest, the best in the world." He married Mary Lord Hosford in April 1841 and had three sons.

He still however had opinions of female attire. In 1845 he wrote, "What the backs of the young misses of today will arrive at is indeed a serious question. They protrude already more than a camel's rump and increase daily. A full dressed woman nowadays juts out behind more than a foot—her waist may be as large as a quart mug—her hips and appurtenances may be from the size of a barrel to that of a good fat hogs-head, but thanks to the fashion, all this rotundity is no solid matter, else they could never enter a door or sit upon a chair; its nothing but down, hair, feather, cotton, wool, or, in some cases, wind—the latter a most admirable contrivance for life preservers only it might hold the wrong end up in the water."

Beginning with a study of his own family history, he spent a great amount of time researching and deciphering the Dutch records in Albany and Schenectady, translating most of the vast mass of records in "Mohawk Dutch"—a compound of Netherlandish, Indian, French, and English speech—in the archives of the churches and public offices in the Mohawk Valley. He published Early Records of the County of Albany (Albany, 1869); Genealogy of the First Settlers of Albany (1872); Genealogies of the First Settlers of Schenectady (1873); History of the Reformed Protestant Dutch Church of Schenectady (Schenectady, 1880); and A History of the Schenectady Patent, edited by J. W. MacMurray (Albany, 1883).

Pearson kept personal journals for 43 years, detailing his life when he arrived in Schenectady and all those years after. His genealogy and history publications are still today considered some of the best insights into early Schenectady history and many can be freely downloaded from the Internet.

Albert Johnson Pitkin

March 22, 1854 - November 16, 1905
Location: M64

Born in Northampton, Ohio, his father Caleb was a Presbyterian minister and his mother Elizabeth Bancroft died when he was 9 years old in 1863.

At 17, he learned machinery in a stationary engine works in Webster, Camp and Lane Machine Company in Akron, Ohio, and a year in the locomotive shops of the Akron & Columbus Railway.

He worked at Baldwin Locomotive for five years, and then became chief draughtsman for the Rhode Island Locomotive Works. Later he moved to Schenectady in 1882 to work for the Schenectady Locomotive Works as a mechanical engineer. Albert became Superintendent of the engineering department at 30. When Edwin Ellis died he was made Vice President and General Manager. His refinements of locomotive engines gave the company an edge. He advocated larger boilers and increased gate areas. Pitkin introduced the cross-compound engine and was the chief designer of the 4-4-0 type. The cross-compound used one high-pressure and one low-pressure cylinder, thus using the steam twice and resulting in great economies in the use of both coal and water. He was known as the "Father of the cross-compound locomotive."

He became the second President of American Locomotive Company when Samuel Callaway died in 1904, but Albert died a year later at his home at 194 Riverside Drive in New York City.

He was married on September 1, 1878 to Carrie M. Lane and had three children: Agnes B., born Dec 16, 1879; Arthur F, born Nov 4, 1881; and Elizabeth B., born Nov 26, 1883.

He had several patents on engines and valves. He describes his compound engine in the 1897 patent:

My invention relates to compound locomotive-engines in which the high and low pressure cylinders are connected by a receiver pipe located in the smoke-box of the locomotive. In all such locomotive-engines as heretofore constructed condensation steam occurs in the high-pressure cylinder, which is carried over into the low-pressure cylinder, thereby occasioning a loss of power. This condensed steam is not revaporated in any receiver-pipe heretofore used with which I am familiar, although it is a fact that the temperature of the gases in the smoke-box of a locomotive is very much higher than that of the steam passing through the receiver.

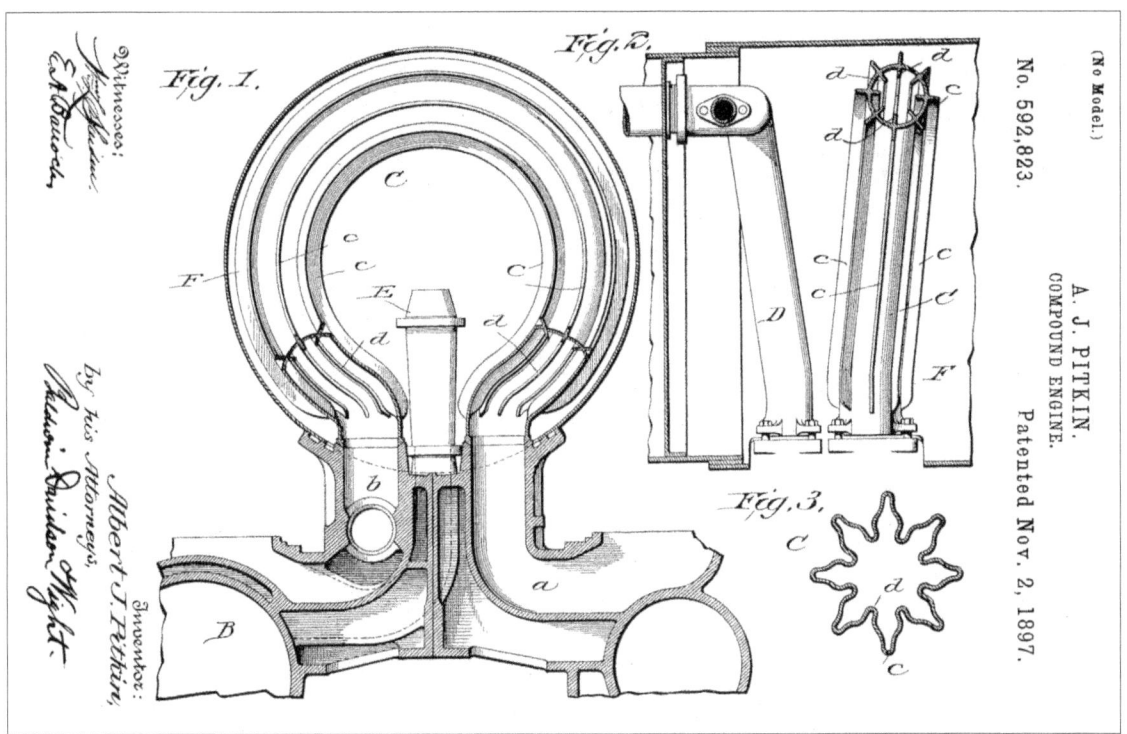
Patent drawing for Pitkin's compound engine. (Courtesy of U.S. Patent Office.)

David S. Proper

? - 1863
Location: D 39

Proper was a volunteer firefighter of the Neptune Engine No. 4 Company, who enlisted in the 134th New York Company F during the Civil War. He and his fellow fireman Robert D. Corl were killed at Gettysburg on July 1, 1863. His body was brought home and buried by donations from other volunteer firefighters in Schenectady. Orderly Sergeant William H. Howe, of Co. F, writes from Gettysburg, July 6th:

When we got to Gettysburg we went right in the fight and through kind Providence I was spared to come out safe, without a scratch. Our regiment and the 154th fought Stonewall Jackson's brigade and the Louisiana Tigers, only our two regiments against these two brigades, the best troops the rebels have. They fired grape and shell at us and we let them get about sixty yards from us, and then we gave them a volley, but they drove us and when we fell back they killed a great many of our boys. We fought not over one hundred yards from the town. The first volley they fired they shot Jake Trask through the breast and he laid right over and died in five minutes after. Poor Jake!

They took me prisoner and then made me dress the wounds of our boys there. Our first day's fight I was taken prisoner, and there I had to stay right by the battlefield and our men firing shell down there. John Kennedy was taken prisoner and taken to Richmond, and our First Lieutenant, Otis Guffin, was wounded and will probably die. Our regiment numbers now 75 men. The last accounts our company numbers about 20 men; they are with Co. A.

I am now at the 11th Corps Hospital waiting on our boys, but will join my regiment in a day or so and take command of company F. When we went in the fight our Lieutenant Colonel Allen Jackson had command of our regiment. When our men retook the town, I left with the wounded and got away from the rebels; I could not bear the idea of going on to Richmond. Our boys were killed all around me, and I escaped without a scratch. Oh what a great battle this has been, and how many of our poor boys killed. All our men killed were buried where they fell, and in a nice place too, by the fence in a pasture. Our poor Sergeant Jacob Trask was buried in a nice place by himself. He died a brave soldier and a good man, and will be remembered by his comrades. Send word to Bill Ostrom and tell him where he can get Dave Proper's body. He was buried by a brick yard near the gas house. Any of the citizens can tell him where they will find him. Our boys are all buried by one another. I pray God I may never see another such a battlefield. There was at one time about 150 pieces of artillery firing all the afternoon. Our regiment was at one time supporting a battery when they were firing at Stuart's cavalry. Our regiment was on the march for twenty days, and we marched over 220 miles. I think this fight will use up the rebel army. They lost three to our one in this battle. Our cannons piled them in heaps. I heard this morning that our regiment had gone to Baltimore to do Provost duty. I am going to join the regiment when I can hear where they are. These names I give you of the killed and wounded are those I have seen. There are more but I do not know who they are until I get to the regiment. These are only of Co. F: KILLED—Adjt. Parmer, Jake Trask, Alonzo Van Aernam, David Proper, John Hyert. WOUNDED, F.—Sergt. Cramer, leg; Sergt. McMillan, arm; T. Miller, leg; Sam Swales, breast; Ben. Carroll, leg; Wm. White head and leg; John Halpin, arm; Charles Heldebrant, hip; Cris Kohn, hip; Henry Battinger, foot; James Van Epps, James Myers, Michael Hogan, both legs. All these privates are wounded.

The *Schenectady Evening Star & Times* reported the funeral.

The remains of Robert D. Corl and David S. Proper, of the One Hundred and Thirty-fourth, who died of wounds received at Gettysburg, were consigned to their last resting place Friday afternoon. The funeral was large and the exercises unusually interesting. A number of our returned volunteers of the 18th and 30th regiments turned out in uniform, as did also Numbers One and Four of the Fire department. There were a large number of private carriages in the procession, which was led by the Drum Corp. The remains were interred in Vale Cemetery. Brave soldiers! They have yielded up their lives on the altar of their country. They could not have a nobler epitaph than the mere statement of the fact.

> THE BODIES of Robert Robert D. Corl and David S. Proper reached here this morning and are temporarily deposited in the dead house, from which they will be taken to-morrow afternoon at 2 o'clock to the Methodist Church under escort of the firemen of this city and returned Volunteers, where funeral services will be performed, and from there to the Cemetery for final interment. Late members of the One Hundred and Thirty fourth Regiment N. Y. Vol. who died of wounds received at Gettysburg.

Notice in the *Evening Star & Times*, July 23, 1863.

Cornelia "Clara" Clarissa Putman

January 19, 1751 - July 1, 1833
Location: G 122 (M 45?)

Clara Putnam, as she was known, was born in Tribes Hill in Albany County at the time and was the daughter of Arent Victoorse Putman and Elizabeth Peck, of Dutch Descent.

Clara is famous for being the unwed wife of Sir John Johnson, son of William Johnson, from 1765-1773. She was John Johnson's house keeper at the start and she is mentioned in most Johnson biographies in a paragraph or two. It has been written that she bore two children from Johnson, a son William (1770-1836) and daughter Margaret (c. 1772-?), who married James Van Horne in 1790 in Schenectady. When Sir John returned from a visit from New York with a wife from a family of stature, to please his father, she moved out to the town of Florida in Albany County, now Montgomery County.

There are fictional books written about her, including Clarissa Putman of Tribes Hill by John J. Vrooman (*http://catalog.hathitrust.org/Record/009135909*).

Johnson gave her money and land and is reported to have paid for a house to be built for her. She and John reportedly kept in touch until his death in 1830.

Her house is still standing and has been recently renovated at Tribes Hill (see *http://mohawkvalley.blogspot.com/2006/10/clarissa-putmans-house-part-1.html*). She late removed to Schenectady and lived on State Street on the site of the old Van Horne Hall, near the northwest corner of the present Erie Boulevard and State Street intersection.

Simon Quinlin (Quinlan)

1831 - August 26, 1895
Location: F2 68A

Simon was born in Liverpool, England and was educated there before he came to American in 1851, working in New York City and Syracuse for a decade, then moving to Chicago in 1861. He became wealthy in the real estate business and the theatrical business as a member of the firm of (Richard) Hooley & Quinlin. His daughter Mary Ellen ("Ella") married actor James O'Neill in 1877 and was part of the public feud between O'Neill and a former girlfriend, Nettie Walsh, who tried to say they had been married.

He was always eager to help people and would lend his name to ventures, such as Quinlin & Pollard, wholesale Grocers in Chicago.

Simon married Esther M. Carpenter of Schenectady (and East Palmyra, New York), and later purchased a farm of eight acres and built a summer home there named Elk Heights. They had no children but educated many orphan children, including giving $1,000 to the De La Salle Institute in Chicago for a life scholarship for one boy who was being educated there.

The Benevolent and Protective Order of Elks (BPOE), an American fraternal and social club, was founded in 1868. It began as the Jolly Corks, a private club in New York State, to bypass the closing hours of the public taverns. Simon joined the Chicago Lodge No. 4 shortly after it was created on October 4, 1877, and was number 27 on the membership roll. He served as Esteemed Leading Knight, Treasurer, Trustee and Exalted Leader of No 4.

In 1881 he served as Esteemed Leading Grand Knight, and in 1882 was one of the Grant Trustees. In 1886-87 he was District Deputy Exalted Grand Ruler for the State of Illinois, and as District Deputy Exalted Grand Ruler at Large in 1888-89. He was elected the Exalted Grand Ruler in 1889 and 1890, serving two full terms. His tenure was controversial, as the Order was going through turmoil on the opposition of the migration of the Grand Lodge. He was appointed Grand Chaplain by Astley Apperly in 1894, and reappointed by Meade D. Detweiler in 1895.

He died in East Palmyra of stomach cancer, after leaving his house against the advice of his doctor to attend a special session at Jamestown on June 18, 1894. He was 64 years old. He was buried with full Masonic honors in East Palmyra by Newark Lodge No. 83 F. & A.M. A large delegation of Elks from Syracuse Lodge attended the funeral.

Local Elks Lodge members maintain the burial site of Exalted Grand Ruler Simon Quinlin.

Henry Ramsay

May 18, 1808 - July 12, 1886
Location: K#109

Henry Ramsay was born in Guilderland in Albany County, New York. He was an American civil engineer, and for a short time New York State Engineer and Surveyor in 1853. He moved to Albany with his parents at age 6. He was educated in the first Lancaster School established in the U.S. at Albany, opened by William Anderson Tweed Dale under the personal supervision of Joseph Lancaster. In 1823 he went to Albany Academy for free because of his grades, but left in 1826. He taught for a year at the Lancaster School, then became principal of a school in Glenville, and returned to Albany as bookkeeper in French Webster's hardware store. He moved to New York City in 1829 without any money, but found a job as a clerk for $10 per month, and started to make maps and practice civil engineering.

In 1831 he married Isabelle Westervelt, daughter of Jacob Westervelt, Sheriff of New York County. He became bookkeeper in the Merchants' Exchange Bank and then became Deputy Sheriff under his father-in-law. In 1836 he moved to Schenectady, bought 14 acres on top of State Street (where the former Armory was), and amassed a great fortune, creating the Henry Ramsay Scholarship at Albany Academy. He was also Assistant Engineer of the Seneca River Survey. He went back to New York and returned four years later in 1839.

In 1842, he was appointed Chief Engineer of the Mohawk & Hudson Railroad between Albany and Schenectady, New York. He laid out the course of the New York Central Railroad at Schenectady, to avoid the inclined plane at that terminus. He then became Assistant Engineer on the Erie Canal enlargement, the section extending from Little Falls to the tower aqueduct. He defined the subdivision of the Great Hardenbugh Patents in 1844-46 by Eugene and Montgomery Livingston during the anti-rent wars in Ulster and Delaware Counties. In 1849, he moved to Schenectady, and was for several terms City Surveyor. He was later nominated to become Mayor by the Democrats, but he declined.

In 1853 he was chosen by the Board of State Offices to locate the wharf or water line of Newtown Creek and East River. On December 10, 1853, he was appointed New York State Engineer and Surveyor, to fill the vacancy caused by the resignation of William J. McAlpine. He served from January 1, 1856 to December 31, 1857. When he retired from the State he was appointed Chief Engineer of the U.S. Petroleum Company at Pithole, Venango County, Pennsylvania, and at Duck Creek, Ohio, driving the first take in the oil field of Thomas Holmden. He retired in 1867.

When he died at age 79 he was considered one of the oldest and wealthiest citizens of Schenectady. He was considered an eccentric, spoke several languages and traveled a great deal, especially to the Holy Land. He was called Robinson Crusoe by sailors who were familiar with him.

He found a huge boulder two miles from Schenectady, probably a glacial erratic, and had it moved to his family lot in the cemetery and inscribed, it weighed 12 tons.

He and Isabelle had ten children, though one died, but had five sons and four daughters: Julia R; Wayne R., Wilfred, Anna, Henry, DeWitt, Isabella, Mary and Paul.

A PLEASURE RIDE ON AN EARLY AMERICAN TRAIN

Appendix 1: 101 Notables in Vale Cemetery 137

Henry Ramsay's inclined plane depot, the first at Schenectady.

Replica of *Mohawk & Hudson*, New York's first train, on a NY Central flatbed during the 1908 Hudson-Fulton Celebration.

The boulder monument of Henry Ramsay at Vale.

Stephen J.H. Reed, M.D.

November 4, 1880 - October 3, 1918
Location: I*2 14

Stephen Reed was the son of Caroline Reed of 38 Moyston Street. Had a sister, Mrs. J.T. Thorbyon, and a brother Fred L.F. Reed. He was born in Schenectady and attended public schools, graduating from the Union Classical Institute (High School) with the class of 1903. He graduated from Albany Medical College with the class of 1907 and was Class Marshal. He had a senior appointment at Ellis Hospital and was a medical intern at Manhattan State Hospital on Ward Island in New York from February 4, 1908 to October 21, 1908. He was the house physician to Physicians Hospital in Schenectady from October 22, 1908 to May 10, 1909, and junior assistant physician to Hudson River State Hospital in Poughkeepsie from May 10, 1909 to May 15, 1911. He was also the President of the Montgomery County Medical Society, and served as Coroner of Montgomery County, beginning November 14, 1911.

During his second term as Coroner he was commissioned a Lieutenant on August 27, 1917 and went to officer training camp at Fort Benjamin Harrison. He went to Romania and was two days out of San Francisco on a transport going by way of Siberia when the ship was ordered back to port because of the Russian Revolution. He was then stationed for a short time at the Presidio, and during the winter of 1917-18 served in Camp Bowie.

In the spring of 1918 Capt. Reed was assigned to the 130th infantry of the 33rd division and sailed for France in May 1918. He was on duty at a dressing station at Hill 281 in France, and was killed in the first line trenches and buried in the French Military cemetery Gloieus near Verdun. He was reburied in Vale on August 1, 1921 with full military honors, after his body was flown back from France.

Stretchers 108th Sanitary Train, carrying wounded to Field Hospital. (Courtesy, U.S. National Library of Medicine.)

Dirk Romeyn

January 12, 1714 - April 16, 1804
Location: I*1, Plot C, Grave 2

Dirk was born in Hackensack, New Jersey, the youngest child of Nicholas Romeyn and Rachel Vreeland. He was educated at Princeton, graduating in 1765, and licensed by the American classis in 1766. He became the seventh pastor for the Dutch Reformed Church in Schenectady at the age of 40 in 1784. He was paid $350, with free house rent, garden, pasture for two cows and a horse, and seventy loads of firewood delivered at the door. He did get periodic raises.

He originally was pastor of churches in Hackensack and Schraalenburgh, New Jersey for about ten years beginning in 1775.

Under his leadership the Schenectady Academy was established in 1785 at the northwest corner of Ferry and Union streets, later to become Union College, the first chartered college in New York State. He also served as Professor of Theology in the Seminary of New Brunswick.

He married Elizabeth Brodhead on June 11, 1767 and had two children, John Brodhead Romeyn and Catherine Theresa Romeyn. While at the church he married 945 couples, baptized 3,541 children and received to the church 248 members. He was the last to conduct services in Dutch.

Charles Shumway Ruffner

June 22, 1880 - January 20, 1939
Location: M3#113

Charles Ruffner was born in Chicago, the only child to Vivion Whaley Ruffner, who worked in the Tobacco business (1858-1889), and Nellie Shumway (1860-?). He was the great-grandson of Ensign Wait Beach, Capt. Bezaleel Beebee's Company, Col. Philip Burr, Bradley's Connecticut Battalion. He attended Centenary College at Palmyra, Missouri, and after that, the University of Missouri, graduating with a B.S. in electronic engineering in 1900. He married Hazel R. Wesson of Denver, Colorado in 1911.

He was affiliated with power companies in the Midwest until 1919. He worked for Telluride Power Company in Telluride, Colorado and helped build transmission lines across the continental divide. He became the Director of Operations for the Central Colorado Power Company in 1909, and two years later went to St. Louis as President and General Manager of the Mississippi River Power Distributing Company. He became the Vice President of two successor companies, the Electric Company of Missouri and the Union Electric Light and Power Company. He went to New York City in 1919 to become Vice President of the North American Company.

In 1921 Ruffner became Vice President and General Manager of the Adirondack Power and Light Corporation in Schenectady. In 1926 he resigned as President. He was also President of the Mohawk Hudson Power Company from 1925 to 1930, and of the New York Power and Light Corporation from 1927 to 1929. In 1929 he was named President of the Empire State Gas & Electric Association, and in 1931 Vice President of the Niagara Hudson Power Corporation.

He joined Schenectady Trust Company in 1932 as Vice President, and in 1933 became President. In 1937 he became Chairman of the Board of Directors. He was also a director of the New York State Economic Council, the Boy Scout Council, the YMCA, and the Bureau of Municipal Research, of which he was Treasurer. He was also President of the Schenectady County Clearing House Association, and in 1935 and 1936 was Chairman of Group V of the New York State Bankers' Association. Ruffner was active in the Schenectady Chamber of Commerce, and was a member of the Mohawk Golf Club, Mohawk Club, the Electro-chemical Society, Phi Delta Theta, Theta Nu Epsilon, Tau Beta Pi, the Engineers' Club, the Freemasons, and the Sons of the American

Revolution. He was also a Fellow of the American Institute of Electrical Engineers, of which he had been Vice President and Manager.

Ruffner lived on Rosendale Road in Schenectady, but died in his sleep in Fort Myers, Florida at age 58, after two years of poor health.

The gravestones of Charles and Hazel Ruffner in Vale.

James Teller Schoolcraft

May 3, 1855 - February 11, 1937
Location: M3#21

James was born in Schenectady and was educated in the public schools. He began law in the offices of Alexander Thomson before he was admitted to the bar at 21 years old.

He was elected District Attorney in Schenectady County just past his 21st birthday, and held it for two terms. During his tenure he prosecuted charges against County Clerk J. Fonda Viele for irregularities in his office. Later he formed a partnership with Charles Hastings.

President Grover Cleveland appointed him Postmaster in 1894, which he held for one four-year term. During that year he also became a Director in the company that purchased the *Weekly Gazette* and organized the Daily Gazette Company, publishers of the *Schenectady Gazette*, now called the *Daily Gazette*. He held offices in the paper for several years.

The climax of his career was in 1914 when he was nominated as Mayor on the fusion ticket from Democrats, Republicans and Progressives, and defeated Mayor George R. Lunn's bid for reelection. He served one term, 1914-15.

He and partner Hastings went into real estate in 1906, and until 1922 was a partner in the firm of Schermerhorn and Company. He developed the tract known as the Vedder Plot in Bellevue, and erected the three-story office building on Broadway which housed the Boston Store.

The two partners practiced law in the Ellis Building at 277 State Street and Erie Boulevard for 33 years. After Hasting's death, Schoolcraft gradually decreased his workload. He was also first Secretary of the Board of

Trade, the forerunner of the Chamber of Commerce. He was a member of St. George's Lodge No. 6, F. & A.M, and of the First Reformed Church.

He married Elizabeth Dickinson of Schenectady on May 7, 1879, who died in 1920. They had three sons: Prof. James Teller Schoolcraft, Jr., who worked at the University of New Hampshire; Leland; and J. Leslie Schoolcraft (died in 1963) former GOP committee chairman. They had two daughters: Mrs. Samuel B. Stewart of Schenectady and Mrs. Robert B Shepard of Glenridge, New Jersey. James lived at 1370 Union Street, where he died after a week's illness of the flu on February 11, 1937. He was 82.

Amalia Schoppe

October 9, 1791 - September 29, 1858
Location: ST4

"The Schenectady Life of German-American Author Amalia Schoppe, née Weise (1791–1858)," by Dr. Hargen Thomsen, Hebbel-Gesellschaft eV Wesselburen, Germany. (Published in *Heritage*, February 2011, pp. 9-12. Edited by Don Rittner.)

Photograph of Amalia Schoppe. (Courtesy of *Heritage* magazine.)

When Amalia Schoppe died on September 29, 1858 in Schenectady, New York, she was nearly forgotten in her homeland Germany, although during the 1820s and 1830s she was one of the country's most popular authors of light novels and children books. In her new hometown, where she lived since 1852, few people knew about her writings (none of them were translated in English), but regarded her highly for her warm-hearted, helpful personality. Her gravestone, located in Vale Cemetery, shows it up until now, as it was "erected by her affectionate pupils," as the engraving on the back states.

Amalia Weise was born on October 9, 1791 on Fehmarn, an island in the Baltic Sea, now a part of Germany, but then belonging to Denmark. Her beloved father, a physician, died at a very young age and left his family without money or any other support. As a result her mother had to give her away to an uncle in Hamburg, who turned out to be a violent drunkard, who beat her, locked her in his half-rotten house, and gave her barely enough to eat. For four years she had to stay under these conditions, until her mother married a rich merchant in Hamburg and took her back. Amalia turned "from rags to riches," literally from poverty to luxury in one moment, but not for long.

It was the age of the Napoleonic wars. Hamburg was occupied by the French to enforce the continental blockade against England, which caused many perils for an international dealing merchant like Amalia's stepfather. He went bankrupt in 1806 and 15-year-old Amalia, grown headstrong and independent through the many twists of fate, decided to look after herself. She acquired work as a private tutor for girls in distinguished families.

At this time Amalia met Rosa Maria Varnhagen, eight years older than she, and who also worked as a tutor. They developed a lifelong friendship, and that included Rosa Maria's future husband, the Jewish born physician David Assing. Through her friendship, Amalia also got to know her brother Karl August Varnhagen von Ense, officer, diplomat, writer, collector of manuscripts and married to the famous "femme de lettres" of the Berlin salon, Rahel Varnhagen. When Varnhagen visited his sister in Hamburg, he brought with him his friend Adalbert von Chamisso, author of the famous "Peter Schlemihl," and the young Swabian doctor and poet Justinus Kerner. And so, in the summer of 1809, Hamburg had its own circle of romantic poetry in which the 17-year-old Amalia was the "baby of the family." The romantic spirit, which she encountered there influenced her deeply, and she, on the other hand, impressed through her independent, unbound and inspired personality, which, in this period, was not common for young girls. Justinus Kerner wrote in1811 a poetic description of his journey ("Reiseschatten"), in which Amalia appeared as a mysterious "girl from the sea," half mermaid, half ancient priestess. In the same year she published her first poems in an anthology of the circle, but at the time she never thought of writing as a profession.

In the years of turmoil that followed she escaped from war, when German, Russian and French troops fought over Hamburg in 1813/14. She also left because she had given birth to an illegitimate son in 1813. The father, Friedrich Heinrich Schoppe, forced himself upon her since she was fourteen and finally raped her. She married him in 1814, only to take care of her son, making clear to her husband that she did not love him.

The ill-matched couple tried to live together several times and separated several times. Two more sons were born in 1818 and 1821, and they finally separated permanently without getting divorced. Schoppe drowned in the Elbe in 1829; it is unknown if it was an accident or suicide.

Around 1820 Amalia decided to make a living from writing, because it was the only way to take care of her family (three sons and her mother). She began to publish in journals, calendar books and anthologies, at first journalistic articles, poems and stories. In 1823, she published her first children's book, and in 1824 her first novel. They were a success and for the next twenty years she wrote one book after another in a speed that she seldom read over what she had written. To her credit, there are approximately sixty novels and story collections and about the same number of children books, most of them in two or three volumes; also a smaller amount of nonfictional books and two periodicals that she edited, the "Neue Pariser Modeblätter" (1827–1845), a fashion magazine (an early predecessor of "Vogue"), and the "Iduna" (1831–37), a journal for children.

In these journals Friedrich Hebbel (1813–1863), the poet and dramatist, published some of his first poems. The son of a poor craftsman he lived in a small village in the wider surroundings of Hamburg. He hadn't a chance to improve his talents until Amalia managed to get him to Hamburg in 1835, from where he could start his career and which made him the most famous dramatist of his generation—today much more famous because of his diaries. Amalia's helpfulness extended over many people, young authors, as well as common folks, but this particular case provided her a small place in German history of literature and made her name remembered even when her books were long forgotten.

When in 1848 a revolution crushed the authoritarian political system of the Metternich era, Amalia was on the side of the revolutionary movement. She stopped writing novels, but rather documented the events in journalistic articles. Even uproar, war, and the reactionary "rollback" in 1849 couldn't affect her democratic convictions. "Even if my body is like a dying leaf on the tree of life," she wrote to a friend, "my mind has kept all his fire, all his youthfulness and I'm longing towards the changing world, as if I had to live through many new phases."

But in the end the revolution was suppressed. Following her last son Alphons (the other two were already dead at that time) she immigrated to America in 1851. "I can stand it no longer in this weathered and decayed Europe," she wrote to her old friend Justinus Kerner, "and with my last breath I will soak up the freedom, for whom I lived, strived and suffered." Deceived of her savings by swindlers, she and Alphons moved from New York to Schenectady in 1852. Alphons found work as an engineer on the Albany-Susquehanna Railroad. Amalia, blessed with a gift to make friends wherever she became acquainted, included Eliphalet Nott and the scholars at Union College. She gave lessons in German to the prosperous ladies of the city, and organized help for poor families. Her last letters to her German friends show great affection to the new country and the people in it. When she died in 1858, she was buried in a section of the cemetery that was reserved for students of Union College, showing that she hadn't lost her inner youth until her last days. Her headstone stands with three others just outside the gates of the Union College burial section.

Henry R. Schwerin

May 28, 1842 - May 10, 1863
Location: C#15

Henry was in the 119th New York Infantry. He was listed as severely wounded in his right leg on May 2, 1863 at Chancellorsville, Virginia, but died of those wounds on May 10th in the field.

DEATH OF CAPTAIN SCHWERIN OF SCHENECTADY N.Y.—At a special meeting of the members of the Senior Class of Union College, on May 19th 1863, the following preamble and resolutions were unanimously adopted. Whereas, It has pleased Almighty God in his all wise, but inscrutable Providence to remove by the hand of death, our friend and class-mate, Henry R. Schwerin, Capt. in the 119th Regiment, N. Y. S. V. therefore, Resolved, That we deeply mourn the loss of one, who by his faithful and energetic endeavors, for the prosperity and advancement of class interests, by his greatness of heart and purity of life, and by the noble, patriotic and Christian-like motives, which prompted him *to enter the service of his country, to aid in the suppression of this unholy rebellion, has forever endeared himself to each and every member of the class of 1863. Resolved, That we extend to the afflicted family, and bereaved friends of the deceased, our sincere and tender sympathy, and desires for them in the bitterness of this great grief, the consolation which a chastening, but loving Father can alone impart. Resolved, That as a public taken of our respect and sorrow, we wear the usual badge of mourning for fifteen days. Resolved, That a copy of these resolutions be transmitted to the family of the deceased, and that they be published in the Schenectady and Albany papers. Signed AMASA J. PARKER, Jr., CHARLES G. CLARK, FRANK THOMPSON. Committee on Resolutions.*

Capt. Henry Schwerin. (Courtesy of New York State Military Museum.)

Christian Steenstrup

December 8, 1873 - November 28, 1955
Location: E-94

Christian was born in Aalborg, Denmark. He left college preparatory school and entered a machine shop at 14, and then spent five years as an apprentice and studied at a technical night school. He came to America in 1894 at age 21. He once dug ditches for a living in Bridgeport, Connecticut.

He married Agnes Hjerrild and had two daughters, Agnes and Laura, and a son, Carl H. Christian and his wife became naturalized citizens in 1904. In 1939 Agnes married the General Electric patent attorney who filed all of Christian's patents. Laura worked in the Lansingburgh School district and Russell Sage College. Carl married Alice Olga Reese of Brandywine Avenue, and worked at G.E., following his father's footsteps in the refrigerator department.

Christian joined G.E. in 1901 as a toolmaker and made his first contribution by inventing an automatic indexing device to eliminate the slow hand-method with punch presses.

Before World War I he went to Sweden to study steam turbines. When he returned he was in charge of building several giant power units.

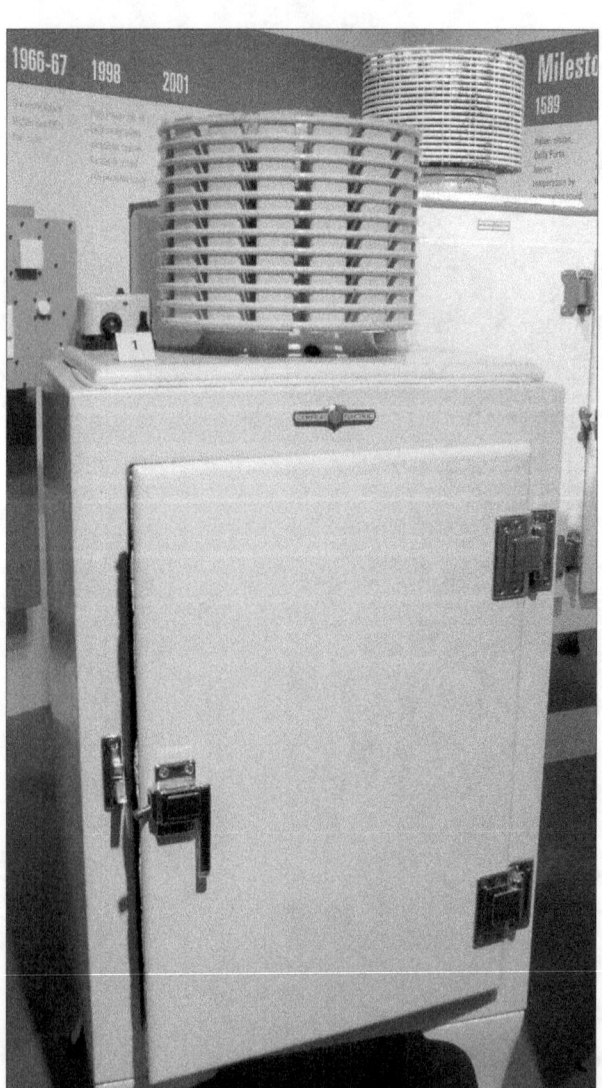

The G.E. "Monitor Top" refrigerator. (Courtesy of Museum of Innovation and Science, Schenectady.)

His invention of the hermetically-sealed home refrigerator that he proposed in 1925 was profitable for G.E. In 1927, G.E. introduced his "Monitor Top" refrigerator, so-named by the public because of the resemblance of the exposed compressor on top of its cabinet to the cylindrical turret of the Civil War gunship, the *Monitor*. The product was priced at $525. Before that they cost over $1,000.

He became the Chief Engineer of the Electric Refrigeration Department, which was organized in 1927. So successful was the sealed unit that from 1928 to 1938 the number of electric refrigerators in the U.S. rose to 11,250,000. In 1925 only 150,000 electric refrigerators were in use in the country. During the same period the number of registered autos rose only 4,500. He also invented the ice cube tray in 1935 and 1940, and an ice cream maker in 1934.

During WWII he spent most of the time working on war projects.

In 1940 when he turned 67, the city of Bridgeport, where he worked earlier, gave him a birthday party with a huge birthday cake shaped as a monitor top refrigerator.

He was the founder of the suggestion award system in American industry. It paid out more than $8 million to G.E. employees. He was twice the recipient of G.E.'s coveted Coffin Award, once for his refrigeration work, and another time for developing a method of hydrogen copper brazing which made the process practical for commercial work. He had 128 patents, and retired on September 1, 1945 after 44 years with G.E.

He won the Modern Pioneer Award of the National Association of Manufacturers for his sealed refrigeration unit that made refrigerators affordable.

He died at his home at 2250 Grand Boulevard and was cremated.

Appendix 1: 101 Notables in Vale Cemetery

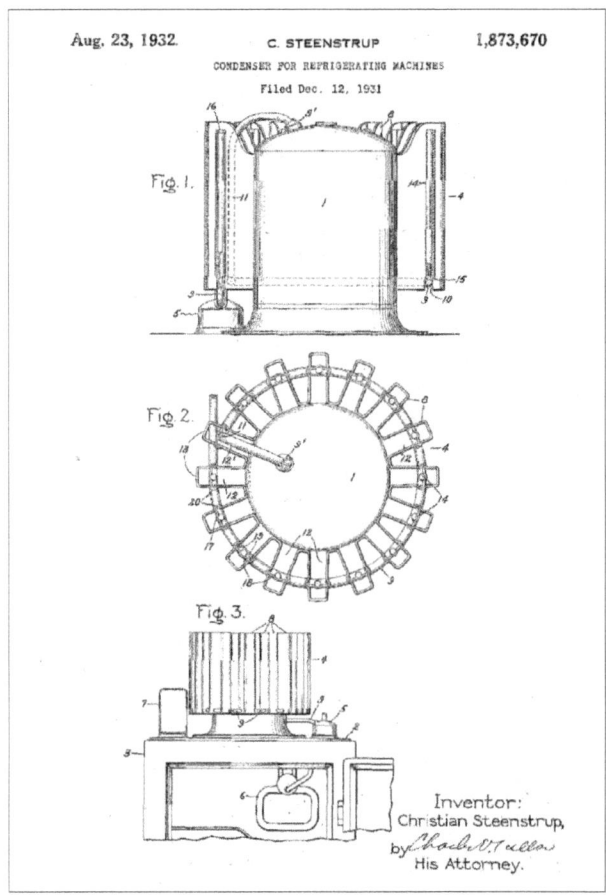

Patent drawings for the "Monitor Top" condenser and the ice cube tray. (Courtesy of U.S. Patent Office.)

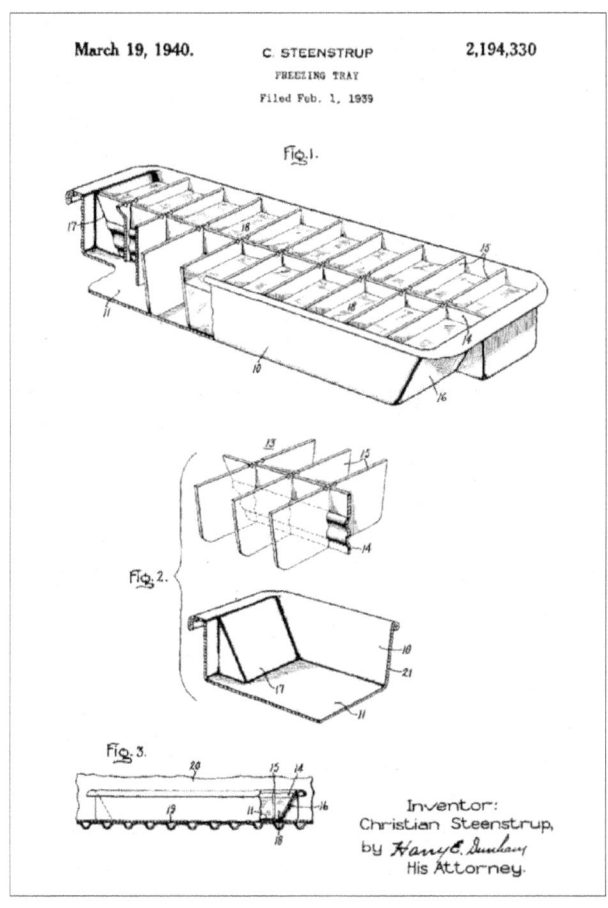

Charles Steinmetz

April 9, 1865 - October 26, 1923
Location: M3 45

Charles Proteus Steinmetz. (See also the back cover image.)

Born in Breslau, Germany of poor parents, Carl Heinrich Steinmetz, a lithographer, and Caroline Neuwbert. His original name was Carl August Rudolf, but was christened by the University Club where he was a member as Charles Proteus, a name he kept. Charles Steinmetz grew up to become one of the leading scientists of the world.

He attended school in Germany and at five was introduced to mathematics. When he graduated, his name was the only one on the list of honor pupils. He entered the University of Breslau in 1882. When he joined the student Mathematics Society he was given the name Proteus, a custom then to give nicknames to all new members. It was during the latter years at school Steinmetz became a socialist.

When his friend Henry Lux was rounded up by Bismarck's agents in Berlin and sent to prison, Steinmetz and Lux continued corresponding in secret code using invisible ink that Lux created. Steinmetz became editor of the student newspaper *The People's Voice*, and articles offensive to the government were published and they confiscated the issues. When Lux was released, more and more evidence was gained on Steinmetz, and after the government told the university they had a case, the school quietly tipped off Steinmetz. In May 1888 Steinmetz secretly was smuggled across the border to Prague, and then Vienna, where he stayed a year or two, then went to Zurich, Switzerland for a year.

Attending school there he made friends with a young American who had wealthy parents and they became roommates. It was the American who convinced Steinmetz to go back to America with him, his friend paying the way. Both he and his friend sailed on a French liner in the steerage section, and arrived on June 1, 1889. Immigration officials were not going to let Steinmetz in, but the American convinced them, and they ended up in Brooklyn, and then moved to the Bronx.

Two weeks later, Steinmetz was working for Rudolph Eickemeyer at Yonkers as a draftsman for $12 per week. In 1892 General Electric bought Eickemeyer's company, and Steinmetz became a G.E. employee at the Lynn Works. In 1893 he was transferred to Schenectady. He became the company's chief consulting engineer. He became a U.S. citizen in 1894. In 1912 he was appointed President of the Board of Education in Schenectady, and in 1915 was elected President of the Common Council on the Socialist ticket.

When Charles Proteus Steinmetz arrived in New York on June 1, 1889 aboard the French boat *La Champagne*, he spoke no English. He tired to learn it during the 8-day voyage, but to no avail. During the end of the year he joined the American Institute of Electrical Engineers and the New York Mathematical Society (American Mathematical Society). In the latter he took an active part, reading many of his original papers. But eventually he became more involved in engineering, and his first public appearance was the meeting of the American Institute of Eclectic Engineers, at age 26, where he read a paper called "Armature Reaction of Alternators," and criticized the theory as incomplete because third harmonics was not considered, which he then worked out and presented later. It was the beginning of the scientific career of one of the most brilliant scientists in America. He was invited to read that paper by David E. Lain, an employee of Eickemeyer, where Steinmetz held his first job as a draftsman.

Steinmetz never received his degree in Germany since he had to leave, but Harvard gave him a Master of Arts in 1902. The President of Harvard remarked, "I confer this degree upon you as the foremost electrical engineer in the United States, and therefore in the world." In 1903 Union College gave him a Doctor of Philosophy degree and he became Professor of Electrical Engineering at the college. He became an honorary member of the Union College chapters of Phi Gamma Delta, Sigma Xi, Tau Beta Pi and Eta Kappa Nu. In 1902, he became President of the American Institute of Electrical Engineers and of the Illuminating Engineering Society from 1915-16, the National Association of Coras, Vice President of the International Proration Schools in 1915, and many more institutions and organizations. In 1922, he ran as a Socialist for the State Engineer and Surveyor but was defeated. He offered Soviet leader Lenin technical help for his country in 1922.

Steinmetz wrote ten books in math and engineering and many scientific papers over his lifetime.

He never married, due to a genetic disease that made him a humpback, but he did adopt a family, the Hayden's, and they lived at 117 Wendell Avenue in a house built for him by G.E. It was torn down in the 1930s when the State of New York and the City of Schenectady couldn't agree who was going to make it a museum in his honor. It was the adopted Hayden's father who befriended Steinmetz in New York and Steinmetz adopted his son J. Leroy Hayden and family.

Ernst J. Berg, who lived with Steinmetz in the early years, wrote this about Steinmentz:

Early work in close contact with Dr. Steinmetz, and a common home in bachelor days, afforded me opportunity to appreciate his remarkable mind and to admire the lovable qualities of human nature which he revealed in daily life. Kind and gentle in character, his main motive was always to be helpful. He had a strong idea that life could be made much easier and pleasanter than it was and particularly desired the reduction of manual labor by the introduction of machinery. His sympathy with the working class led him into difficulties in Germany during his early life, and resulted eventually in his coming to this country.

He was unusually fond of children. He would often suggest plans for a dance and would enjoy the sight of the gaiety and a chance to admire pretty girls and their beauty and wit. During childhood, prevented by over-anxious parents from playing with children, he seemed to retain the desire throughout his maturity, and would play with them any time, no matter how pressed with more serious matters.

In his early years here, while still in his youth and surrounded by other young men, he was often the leader in boyish pranks and sports. He would take active part in sailing and boating and water contests, thought it is doubtful if he learned to swim well, or even at all. He was an enthusiastic bicyclist and many a time rode as far as Lake George in a day, then 65 miles by the road. He was a reliable guard against detection when friends decided some nights to change a few signs about the streets of the city. In all kinds of ways he was boyish, even at the age of 30.

Steinmetz and friends in front of his house on Washington Avenue.

The Steinmetz monument at Vale.

On religion, he wrote in November 1922, "Science and religion, regarded as increasingly antagonistic, are not necessarily incompatible but are different and unrelated activities of the human mind." He went on to say that there "could be no scientific foundation of religion, but the belief must always remain the foundation of religion."

Steinmetz listed what he considered his three most important works:

- The Investigations on Magnetism (The Law of Hysteresis)
- The Development of the Symbolic Method of Alternating Current Calculations (Complex Quantities)
- The General Theory of Electrical Transients.

Steinmetz was a proponent of electric cars; he himself owned a Detroit Electric and created the Steinmetz Electric Car Company in 1917 that flourished but collapsed after his death. Steinmetz also created artificial lightning after a lightning bolt almost destroyed his summer retreat cottage on the Mohawk River in Glenville, where he often stayed for 25 years.

Steinmetz was known to keep odd and ugly pets, from alligators to cacti. He was also an accomplished photographer and often did trick photography.

As President of the City Council he was responsible for improving the schools of Schenectady, making sure every student had a desk, and he was responsible for the creation of the city's Central Park.

Steinmetz died in October 1923, a couple of weeks after he returned from an exhaustive trip to San Francisco and other cities giving addresses to large crowds. Many people attended his funeral at Vale.

His reputed $100,000 salary apparently was never realized, as he only drew enough money to pay his bills. In his will, very little was bequeathed to his half-sisters and the Hayden family, although they did get the house. A true socialist to the end.

A pair of his eyeglasses is at the Efner Research Center in City Hall. A chemistry set and desk is at the Unitarian Church in Schenectady, and a table is in the home of the Chestnut's on Wendell Avenue.

Virginia Sweet

February 12, 1921 - July 12, 2009
Location: M1 177 grv 3

Virginia "Ginger" Sweet was born on February 12, 1921, the daughter of Harry P. Sweet and Jessica S. Sweet, and became interested in flying when she was 12 after reading about the adventures of Amelia Earhart. She had two sisters, Betty and Helen. After an elementary education in a one-room school house in Quaker Springs, New York, she received

Lt. Col. Sweet.

diplomas from Duke University and the Sorbonne in France with degrees in languages. She taught French, Spanish, and Latin for a number of years.

While living at 1083 Parkwood Boulevard with her parents, she joined a civil pilot training program at Schenectady Airport in 1940. She was the first female in Schenectady County to gather pilot ratings. She ranked 9th of the 60 students in the flying school. The only other female in the program was Beth Eaton of Rosendale Road. Virginia was also a department store model. She then went back to college for her senior year at Duke University, where she was majoring in French. After 200 hours of flying she joined the Women Air force Service Pilots (WASP) in class 43-W-4 in Houston, Texas. After that she went to basic and advanced training at Avenger Field in Sweetwater, Texas, where she graduated and was assigned to Romulus, Michigan, in the Third Ferry group in Air Transport Command (ATC).

She attended instrument school, officer training school, and pursuit operational training, as well as qualified as a pilot for the P-39, P-40, P-51 Mustang (her favorite, see below), and P-63. However, by the time she left the service she flew 52 different military aircraft as a pilot in command. She was also qualified as co-pilot for the B-17 Flying Fortress, B-24, B-25, B-29 Superfortress, and the PBY-5 Catalina flying boat. She was a pilot with the WASPs, carrying materials from factories to air bases so that men could fight overseas. As a pilot she would often fly aircraft that needed repairs badly and was referred to as flying "shot up." 38 women flyers were killed performing this service.

The "99" annual Amelia Earhart Scholarship of $200 was presented to Virginia in NYC in 1949 by Maj. Gen. Robert M. Webster, Commanding General of the Eastern Defense Command of the Continental Air Command, United States Air Force. In April 1945, Virginia, along with female pilots Ruth Groves, B. Davis, Elizabeth Haas and Louise Bowden, who once bailed out of a dead engine P-51 over the Tennessee Mountains, were ferrying surplus army planes into the Albany Airport to be sold by the Albany Aircraft Company.

After World War II she served a reserve commission in 1949 and spent five years on active duty during and after the Korean War.

After 30 years of service, she retired from the USAF Reserve in September 1979 as a Lieutenant Colonel.

Her military service as a WASP was not recognized until 1977, when the Department of Defense acknowledged the WASPs as members of the military.

On July 1, 2009, the President of the United States signed B "S.614" to award the WASPs the Congressional Gold Medal, the highest honor Congress can bestow upon a civilian.

After WASP deactivation, she continued with her aviation career, adding some 55 different civilian types of aircraft to her flight log, along with 14 sailplanes and gliders. She also held a commercial pilot certificate, with ratings for single and multi-engine land and seaplanes, gliders, and an instrument and instructor certificate.

Virginia was an advanced ground school instructor and was a flight examiner for many years. She taught flying at Lake Champlain, at Rensselaer Polytechnic Institute to ROTC cadets, and at most of the airports in the Capital District.

On the morning of July 12, 2009, less than two weeks after receiving the Congressional Gold Medal, she died at the Baptist Health Nursing and Rehabilitation Center in Scotia, after a short illness. She was buried with military honors.

Abraham Swits

October 1, 1730 - August 17, 1814
Location: G#50

Abraham was the son of Jacob Swits and Helena DeWitt. He married Neeltie Van Antwerpen, daughter of Pieter Van Antwerpen, on February 24, 1748. They had a daughter, Helena, on July 15, 1750.

He married his second wife Elisabeth, the daughter of Wouter Vrooman, on December 26, 1753. They had three children: Walterous (Walter), on November 10, 1754; Maria, on September 18, 1756; and Susanna, on May 13, 1759.

He married his third wife, Margaret, daughter of Jan and Eva Delamont, on November 22, 1760. They had seven children: Eva, on July 24, 1761; Jacob, on November 3, 1762; Catrina, on May 1, 1764; Johannes, on March 21, 1768 (another source says December 1, 1775); Jannetje, on August 23, 1770; Elisabeth, on March 12, 1772; and Andries, on November 8, 1773.

Abraham owned a brick house and lot on the north corner of Maiden Lane and State Street, extending to Liberty Street. He also had a blacksmith shop across Maiden Lane.

Swits was First Major of the Second Regiment of the Schenectady Militia. The militia was established to keep British and those loyal to the crown from establishing a foothold in the Schenectady area (although Schenectady was part of Albany County then, it was technically the Albany Militia). Colonel Abraham Wemple was commander. The Second Regiment saw action between the Battle of Normanskill in 1777 and the Battle of Johnstown in 1781.

Swits is famous for the Battle of the Normanskill, in which he and a group of about 100 Continental troops from Schenectady descended on the barn in the Town of Guilderland belonging to Nicholas Van Patten, and where a large group of loyalists were congregating. During darkness on August 11th/12th, Swits and his militia, including 40 Rhode Island troops, routed the Tories, killing David Springer and taking 13 prisoners, while about 100 others escaped.

The regiment also took part in the first and second battles of Saratoga in September and October of 1771 as part of General Glover's brigade.

Swits served at Fort Plain in August of 1780 after the settlements of Canajoharie were destroyed. Later, he was in command of 200 men in the defense of Ballston, after the British under Monroe burned and sacked the town on October 12, 1780. He stayed stayed for about six weeks, according to John Wemple's pension claims. After that he performed garrison duty at Fort Paris in August, 1781, and at the Upper Fort in Schoharie.

His sons Walter (Lieutenant) and Jacob (General) also both fought in the Revolution. Swits died August 17, 1814, aged 83 years.

Walter (Walterous) Swits

November 10, 1754 - October 31, 1823
Location: 1 F front grave 5

Walter Swits was the son of Major Abraham Swits and served with the Green Mountain Boys in the Northern Campaign under Colonel Seth Warner in 1776.

On May 1, 1776, Swits applied to the Committee of Safety to be dismissed from Captain Gerrit S. Veeder's Company on a plea that he not been fairly enlisted. The company was supposed to be led by Capt. John A. Bradt. On the testimony of Lt. Bates that the enlistment was regular, the committee, however, refused to interfere. Others were not happy about Veeder's appointment as well. Solomon Pendleton, commissioned as Second Lieutenant in a company formed under Capt. Bradt, also wanted to resign because Veeder was given charge rather than wait for Bradt to return. On May 6, Swits complained to the Committee that the officers of the company had refused to "take a sufficient man in his place." In June 1776, he finally served as a Lieutenant in Capt. Bradt's Company of State Rangers.

Around February 15, 1777, he enlisted as a Lieutenant in Captain Giles Wolcott's Company, Colonel Seth Warner's Regiment. Seth Warner was one of Ethan Allen's Green Mountain Boys, second in command at the capture of Fort Ticonderoga, took part in the siege of St. John's, commanded the rear guard at Hubbardtown and repelled British reinforcements at Bennington. The Green Mountain Boys defended settlers in the New Hampshire Grants against New York authority. Warner was an outlaw and was wanted in New York State for striking Justice of the Peace John Monroe when he and a posse tried to arrest Warner's cousin. Swits remained in this company until September 1780, when he resigned and returned to Schenectady.

In March 1782, he commanded a company of 46 men raised to keep guard at Forts Volunteer and Squash in Schenectady. The locations of these two "forts" is unknown. There was a Fort Volunteer during the War of 1812 in Sackets Harbor, Jefferson County. The references, however, indicate both Volunteer and Squash were in Schenectady. Harmon Peters stated that in March, 1782, he entered service as a volunteer in a company of 46 men commanded by Walter Swits, raised to keep guard at Fort Volunteer and Fort Squash at Schenectady. The company was divided 23 men to each fort.

Swits was placed on pension roll, 1818, for service as a Lieutenant in the New York Line. His widow received a pension.

James Cuff Swits

c. 1820 - 1893
Location: Potter's Field

James was a 6-foot 7-inch Mohawk Indian and herb peddler during the 19th century. He was born on the farm of Hendrick Swits, on the south side of State Street, opposite Jay Street. He took the name James Hartley Swits, but was called James Cuff by most everyone.

Not much is known about him. Some report that his father was African-American and his mother a full-blooded Mohawk, some report vice versa. He lived alone in a one-room shack outside the city near Albany Street and Brandywine Avenue. He scoured the area for herbs during the spring and summer, and had many customers for his home remedies. He was a regular fixture in downtown Schenectady.

He stopped once a week at Dr. Harman Swits at 218 State Street (replaced by the Carl Building) to deliver his standing order, and later his Jim Cuff's Syrup of Tar and Wide Cherry was bottled by the Orisena Company at 209 State Street (see the advertisement on the next page). He had no financial interest in the medicine with his name on it. He also collected milkweed that people liked to eat boiled like spinach. He was arrested once on March 19, 1859 for being drunk and threatening to shoot people in a bar, but his weapon was a corncob pipe.

On February 26, 1893, he was removed from his hut and placed in the county almshouse on Steuben Street. He died in March of pneumonia. He was buried in Potter's Field at Vale. A stonecutter friend, Thomas Wallace, made a small stone for him with his likeness in profile (see page 45) and a simple epitaph, "Admitted to that equal sky." The headstone was switched when an attempt to rob his grave by students went wrong. They forgot the name of the switched headstone and so his actual burial location is unknown.

His famous cough medicine was sold for many years after he died. One advertisement says the formula was "turned over to The Orisena Co." Since he is buried in Potter's Field, one can only assumed he didn't make much for giving it up.

James Cuff Swits.

Advertisement for Jim Cuff's Syrup of Tar & Wild Cherry.

William A. Thornton

1802 - 1866
Location: G 13

William Thornton was born in Albany, New York. Thornton was married to Helen Smith (1810-1885) and they had three children: Adelia Thornton Casey (1839-1875), who was married to James Seaman Casey); William Adrian Thornton (1841-1872); and George DeWitt Thornton (1844- 1883). William attended Union College and Albany Law School and became a lawyer in Newburgh, Orange County, New York.

Thornton's military career was published in Graduates of the U.S. Military Academy, page 236. He was student 403 and graduated 12th in his class.

Military History. — Cadet at the Military Academy, July 1, 1820, to July 1, 1825, when he was graduated and promoted in the Army to Bvt. Second Lieut., 1st Artillery, July 1, 1825.

Second Lieut., 4th Artillery, July 1, 1825. Served: in garrison at Ft. Monroe, Va. (Artillery School for Practice), 1825-26; on survey of Dismal Swamp Canal, 1826; at the Military Academy, as Asst. Instructor of Infantry Tactics, Sep. 21, 1826, to July 16, 1829; on Ordnance duty at Watertown Arsenal, Mas., July 16, 1829, to Sep. 26, 1831; in garrison at Ft. Monroe, Va. (Artillery School for Practice), 1831-32; in on the "Black Hawk Expedition," 1832, but not at the seat of war; a in garrison at Charleston harbor, S. C., 1832-33, during South Carolina's threatened nullification; on Ordnance duty at Watervliet Arsenal, N. Y., Mar. 27, 1833, to October 15, 1836; (First Lieut., 4th Artillery, January 31, 1835) in the Florida War, on Quartermaster duty, 1836-37; on Ordnance duty at Watervliet Arsenal, N. Y., May 15, 1837, to July 7, 1838; as Asst. Ordnance Officer on Niagara Frontier, July 7 to October 27, 1838; in command of Mt. Vernon (Captain, Ordnance, July 7, 1838) Arsenal, Ala., and putting in order the armament of the Gulf Defenses, 1838-40, — and of New York Ordnance Depot, 1840-48; as Inspector of Contract Arms, 1840-54; in command of Watertown Arsenal, Mas., 1842 (during the Dorr Outbreak (Bvt. Major, May 30, 1848, for Meritorious Conduct) in Rhode Island), and 1848-51, — and of New York Ordnance Depot, 1851-54; as Member of Ordnance Board for the trial of Small Arms, January 13 to February 19, 1855; in command of St. Louis Arsenal, Mo., 1855; as Chief of Ordnance of the Department of New Mexico, Aug. 31, 1855, to October 1, 1857; as Member of Ordnance Board for testing the strength of heavy guns and gun carriages, January 6-19, 1858; in preparing building materials, at Watervliet, N. Y., for an Arsenal in California, 1858; in command of New York Ordnance Depot, (Major, Ordnance, May 28, 1861) and as Inspector of Contract Arms, 1858-61; and as Member of Board to test the merits of James and Schencle's Rifled Cannon, 1859.

Served during the Rebellion of the Seceding States, 1861-66; in command of Watervliet Arsenal, N. Y., May 14, 1861, to Dec. 17, 1863; as Inspector of (Lieut.-Colonel, Ordnance, Mar. 3, 1863) (Colonel, Ordnance, Sep. 15, 1863) Contract Arms and Ordnance, Dec. 17, 1863, to Apr. 6, 1866; and in command (Bvt. Brig.-General, U. S. Army, Mar. 13, 1865, for Faithful and Meritorious Services in the Ordnance Department) of New York Arsenal, June 19, 1865, to Apr. 6, 1866.

Died, Apr. 6, 1866, at Governor's Island, N. Y.: Aged 63.

In a *Troy Times Record* article on January 26, 2012, Robert Pfeil, then Watervliet Arsenal museum curator, stated that

Major William A. Thornton took charge of the arsenal in 1861. He increased production of cartridge boxes, belts, combustible cartridges, paper-wrapped cartridges, artillery carriages and ammunition.

When the Hudson River flooded the arsenal in April 1862, it stopped the machines at Watervliet for the first time since the beginning of the Civil War, but by the end of April the arsenal had completed an order for Ft. Monroe Virginia that included 10 18-pounder siege carriages modified for 30-pound Parrotts, 600 10-pounder shot, 360 rounds of case shot for 12-pounders and 608 12-pounder shells ...

Production at the arsenal was held up only once more during the Civil War in July 1863 during the Draft Riots. While 2,000 men burned and looted Troy, Thornton swore in 400 of his most reliable workers and, together with 65 regular army soldiers on duty, made a show of force that discouraged any mob from considering Watervliet an easy or desirable target.

Thornton kept a diary on his military expedition to New Mexico in 1855-56. The diary is available online at *http://www.kancoll.org/articles/thornton.htm*. He contracted a lung disease during this expedition, from which he never fully recovered.

The Thornton monument at Vale.

George W. Tompkins

1842 - 1934
Location: Section M-1, Lot 59

George Tompkins (also spelled Thompkins) was born in Otisville, New York, the son of Emer and Elizabeth (Eaton) Thompkins, and came to Schenectady after the Civil War, opening a bakery on the northwest corner of Jay and Union streets. Tompkins was awarded the Medal or Honor for bravery during the Civil War.

He enlisted at age 21 as a Private on August 11, 1862 in Port Jervis, New York. He mustered into F Company of the 124th New York Volunteers, known as the "Orange Blossoms," on September 5, 1862. He was promoted to Corporal on March 1, 1865.

At the Battle of Petersburg, Virginia, on March 25, 1865, Cpl. George Tompkins was with his regiment attacking the position held by the 59th Alabama Infantry near Hatcher's Run, Virginia. In front of the Confederate lines, Lt. Col. Daniel Shipman Troy of the 60th Alabama Infantry held the flag of the 59th Alabama Infantry and was urging the men under this command forward, when he was shot by Tompkins. Tompkins picked up the Confederate flag. He was given the Medal of Honor on April 6, 1865, at the urging of Maj. Gen. George G. Meade in a letter dated March 28, 1865 to the Adjutant-General of the Army in Washington, D.C.

His Medal of Honor citation reads:

The President of the United States of America, in the name of Congress, takes pleasure in presenting the Medal of Honor to Corporal George W. Tompkins, United States Army, for extraordinary heroism on 25 March 1865, while serving with Company F, 124th New York Infantry, in action at Petersburg, Virginia, for capture of flag of 59th Alabama Infantry (Confederate States of America) from an officer who, with colors in hand, was rallying his men.

Tompkins is one of only five 124th New York Soldiers to receive such an award (the others were Sgt. Thomas W. Bradley, Pvt. Archibald Freeman, Pvt. Nathan M. Hallock and 1st Lt. Lewis S. Wisner). The medal was pinned on him by General Grant at Petersburg, Virginia. The flag Tompkins captured was returned to the State of Alabama in 1905.

Tompkins saw three years of battle, participating the Battles of Bull Run, Antietam and Gettysburg. He was discharged on June 3, 1865 as a Corporal.

He spent his last years living with his daughter, Mrs. Alfred J. Boss, at 459 Duane Avenue, and was almost 93 when he died. His death reduced the membership of the Horsfall G.A.R. Post to seven members. Tompkins was Commander of the post at one time.

Hancock 2nd Army Corps Silver Identification Badge named to Congressional Medal of Honor Winner Private G. W. Tompkins, Company "F", 124th Regiment, New York Volunteers. The coin silver badge is in the shape of a cloverleaf, the motif of the 2nd Corps. It has a decorative engraved border with "Hancock" engraved at the top and "2. A. C." in the center. The reverse is hand-engraved script "G. W. Tompkins" and "Co F. 124th Regt. N.Y. Vol's."

Cornelius Van Dyck

October 3, 1740 - June 9, 1792
Location: L1 H2

Cornelius was the son of physician Dr. Cornelius Van Dyck and his second wife Margaret Bradt, who had three children. Dr. Van Dyck married his first wife, Marytje Mabie, daughter of Johannes Mabie and Anna Borsboom, on November 12, 1721. They had six children. She was 1/4 Mohawk; his second wife was 1/16 Mohawk.

The younger Cornelius married Thanna (Tansake) Yates, the daughter of Joseph Yates, on February 20, 1762. They had no children. Much of this history on Cornelius comes from the thorough writings of James Nohl Churchyard at *http://www.nyhistory.net/*.

On May 27, 1775, Cornelius was appointed Captain of the militia by the Committee of Safety of Albany County. Two days later he was recruiting a company to defend Fort Ticonderoga.

On May 29 the Schenectady Committee of Safety, at a request from the Albany Committee, voted to raise a company for service at Fort Ticonderoga to assist in retaining possession of the cannon and military stores that were found by Ethan Allen and the Green Mountain Boys when they captured it on May 10. Cornelius was given command of the company he raised, but instead of giving them a uniform, each soldier was given a ribbon that designated them a soldier in the Continental service.

He and his men stayed in Schenectady, and at the end of June he was commissioned Captain by the provincial Congress and assigned to the Second New York Line.

On July 13, 1775, General Schuyler sent him orders to bring his company to Lake George, but Van Dyck was on a recruiting mission. When the company was told to go without him they refused, so Van Dyck was asked to return immediately to lead them, which he did.

They marched to Ticonderoga, then to Crown Point, performing guard duty there, and then proceeded to the fort at Isle Aux Noix (a narrow island in the Sorel (Richelieu) River), forming part of the detachment that reduced the fort at Chamblee in Canada.

The regiment was in garrison at Chamblee covering the lines of communication when Montgomery was directing the siege and assault of Quebec on New Year's Eve, 1776. Capt. Van Dyck served during the remainder of the campaign as a military aide-de-camp. When he returned to Schenectady on May 7, 1776, he was again elected a member of the Committee of Safety. He was commissioned a Colonel of the New York Militia on July 1, 1776.

However, on November 21, he was commissioned a Lieutenant Colonel in the Continental Army, being assigned to the First New York Line. He was acting as commandant at Fort George for some of the time. On August 21, 1777 he was a member of a council of war held at German Flats under Gen. Benedict Arnold. The regiment helped raise the siege of Fort Stanwix under the command of Arnold and remained in garrison at Fort Stanwix, along with other smaller forts up and down the Mohawk Valley, until November. They went into winter quarters in Schenectady and missed the battle of Saratoga.

In late March 1778, Gen. George Washington ordered the regiment to join him at Valley Forge. They left Albany in early April and arrived at Valley Forge on May 5, 1778. The regiment mounted a picquet guard post at Cuckold's Town, three miles to the southwest of the main camp. During the Battle of Monmouth (June 28, 1778), the First New York was on the left flank and took part in the action. Lt. Col. Van Dyck was placed in charge of the burial detail the next day, after the British slipped away. His report is the basis of the casualty figures cited for that battle.

During the summer the regiment provided garrisons on both sides of the Hudson. In October it was decided that the regiment should return to the upper Mohawk Valley, and arrived at Fort Schuyler (Stanwix) in early December 1778. Col. Van Schaick returned to Albany, leaving the command of the regiment to Lt. Col. Van Dyck until the next April. In February 1779 an outlying fort was built at the Oneida Castle. This was called Fort Van Dyck and garrisoned through April.

None of the officers or men of the First New York Regiment appear on the roster of the Sullivan Expedition of May to November 1779. However, Col. Goose Van Schaick, commander of that regiment, led a raid against the Onondagas in April of 1779, which preceded Sullivan's expedition. He left Fort Stanwix and, in a march of 180 miles in five-and-a-half days, destroyed the Onondaga Castle of about 50 houses, took 37 prisoners, killed between 20 and 30 warriors, picked up 100 muskets and returned without losing a man. For this achievement Col. Van Schaick, his officers and the soldiers were voted the "Thanks of Congress" on May 10, 1779. Van Dyck was in command at Albany during the period of Sullivan's expedition.

The First New York Regiment was at the siege of Yorktown. Lt. Col. Van Dyck and the Marquis de Lafayette were officers-of-the-day there for September 29, 1781. On the storming of the redoubts late in the afternoon of October 14, 1781, the regiment was divided. One half was committed to the French under Baron de Viomesnil, and the other half to the Americans under the Marquis Lafayette. These troops assaulted the works with such rapidity and daring that the redoubts were carried with inconsiderable loss.

Cornelius continued in the Continental Army after the surrender at Yorktown. By the Resolution of Congress of September 30, 1783, he was brevetted to the rank of Colonel, but only enjoyed it for a couple of months, since Washington ordered the army disbanded on November 3, 1783. He was probably with the army on June 8, 1783, but he does not appear to have been with those at Fraunces Tavern on December 4, 1783 for Washington's farewell to his officers. Instead, he was at a meeting of St. George's Lodge of Freemasons in Schenectady on December 6, 1783.

Van Dyck's services during the Revolution as a militia officer, civil official, and Continental Army officer span the period from before the Battle of Bunker Hill to the disbanding of the army. He saw action from Canada in the north, to Virginia in the south. He was an original member of the Society of the Cincinnati and endorsed his name on the parchment roll of the society. Today, it is the oldest patriotic society, founded in 1783 by officers of the Continental Army and French counterparts, promoting the knowledge and appreciation of the achievement of American independence.

He returned to Schenectady and the citizens demonstrated their esteem by electing him to represent Albany County to the New York State Legislature in 1788-89, in the Anti-Federalist Party. His name appears on the half-pay roll of the Army.

He was a Charter Member of St. George's Lodge of Freemasons in Schenectady. He is named as the Junior Warden in the original charter, dated September 14, 1774. He is noted as being present on December 14, 1779, and at several meetings between the 6th and 20th of December, 1783. He was the Master of the lodge in 1787 and 1788.

Congress initially promised 450 acres to each Lieutenant Colonel at the end of the war. New York added generously to this amount, and Van Dyck was allocated a total of 2,700 acres of former Indian land. On July 24, 1790 he received a bounty land warrant for this land in partial payment for his services during the Revolution. On this record he is termed "Lt.-Colonel." He apparently did not use his brevet rank of full Colonel. He sold this land to Levi Jerome on October 20, 1791.

Col. Cornelis Van Dyck died on June 9, 1792, at age 51. His wife died June 16, 1813, aged 73 years. In 1920 the Col. Cornelius Van Dyck Chapter of the Sons of the American Revolution and St. George's Lodge No. 6, F. & A.M., mounted a bronze plaque on the old tombstone, briefly noting the principle achievements of his military and civil careers.

Dirk Van Ingen

September 19, 1738 - February 27, 1814
Location: IL G#6

Dirk, originally from Rotterdam, Netherlands, lived on Church Street in the second house north of the Dutch church.

He was married on September 29, 1759 to Margaret Van Seysen (Sice) (1738-1815), the daughter of Joseph Van Seysen (Sice) and Elisabeth Peek. They had eight children: Francina (October 7, 1770 - ?); Joseph (October 3,1762 - ?); John (November 11, 1764 - 1839); Abraham (November 20, 1773 - March 18, 1853); Willem (November 23, 1760 - January 10, 1800); Jacob (December 28, 1766 - 1843); Elizabeth (October 11, 1772 - ?); and Judith (June 1, 1777 - February 25, 1844).

He married a second time on June 30, 1790 to widow Geertruyd Mynderse Wemple (1745-?), daughter of Jacobus Mynderse and Sara Yates. Her first husband was Myndert M. Wemple, with whom she had two children: Alida (1781-1775) and Maria (1781-?). In her will she leaves everything to daughter Alida, suggesting that Maria had already died when the will was written.

On November 7, 1775, Dirk was elected as member of the Second Committee of Safety, and appointed Chairman on December 29. He was a clerk of the committee, taking office on June 2, 1777, and served on several subsequent committees. From May 9, 1777 to January 18, 1780 (reduced to supernumerary), he served in the general hospitals of the Northern Department for eight months as a junior surgeon, and the remainder of the time as senior surgeon. From May to June 1778, he was at the Schoharie forts, where he took charge of the wounded after the Battle of Cobleskill. On June 24, 1779, he was again elected a member of the Committee of Safety, and on July 2 was appointed Clerk of the Board. During the fall of 1780, he was in charge of the hospital at Schenectady (the site was at the southwest corner of Union and Lafayette streets), where he dressed the wounds of Col. Brown's soldiers, who were brought down after the Battle of Klock's Field.

Van Ingen was also part of the group that formed the old Academy, and later Union College. He was treasurer of both institutions in the 1790s. He was a collector for the Dutch Reformed Church in 1801.

Originally buried at the old cemetery at the First Reformed Church at the intersection of Green and Front streets, he was later moved to Vale in 1879.

His son John became Sheriff of Schenectady County and was in the Second Albany County Militia. His son Abraham became an attorney in Schenectady.

His son Joseph acted as a surgeon's mate under his father, from November 1778 to May 1, 1779, and had the rank of First Lieutenant. He also served as clerk and surgeon's mate under Dr. Stephen McCrea, doctor and surgeon general of the Flying Hospital, Continental Army, from November 1779 to May 1780. He was back with his father from May to June 1780. He was later a clerk in the Quartermaster Department of General Clinton's Brigade, from June to August 1, 1780; a clerk to the Commissary General from August 1, 1780 to May 1 1781; a conductor of ordnance and military stores under apportionment by General Clinton, from May 1 to September 1, 1781; and a First Lieutenant in Captain Hale's company, Colonel Willett's Levies. He served in Sullivan's Campaign against the Native Americans and was in the Battle of Newtown. He often performed as a surgeon at the Schenectady hospital, and while he was conductor of ordnance, was in charge of the U.S. Gunsmiths' or armories shop on Ferry Street. Gunsmiths were repairing guns there for about a year. It was written that he was remembered wearing a "kind of mixed coat and a cocked hat with a cockade thereon."

Benjamin Van Vranken

1825 - Janujary 19, 1901
Location: L12

Benjamin Van Vranken was a businessman in the construction trades. Benjamin laid out the first foot of sewer in the city of Schenectady in August 1884, and when finished, constructed the first 10 miles of sewer line in the city.

He also owned a grocery business at the corner of State and Jay streets, known as the Van Vranken Building, later selling it to John J. Hart, former City Recorder.

In 1867 he invented an improved "Empire" brick-making machine.

In 1886 he was awarded a patent for a new design for a toilet, sewer flush tank and siphon, which he advertised nationally.

He was married to Angelica Speir (1827-1893) from Saratoga, the daughter of Joseph and Eleanor McDearmid Speir. They had three children: Isabella Van Vranken Duell (1853-1922); Anna Van Vranken Olmstead (1855-1911); and Grace, who married Arthur Knight, golfer and inventor of the Schenectady Putter.

Van Vranken was Superintendent of the second section of the Erie Canal in the Schenectady area, which included 32 miles from the head of the Lower Mohawk Aqueduct to the head of Lock 27.

He dropped dead in a store on Wall Street in Schenectady. He had held several city and minor state political offices, was active in the Democratic Party, was a leader in the old Fourth Ward, and was interested in many large contracting ventures throughout the state.

Garrit S. Veeder

1751 - 1836
Location: M1 38

The following is from the Pension Application of Garrit S. Veeder.

On this eighteenth day of October in the year of our Lord one thousand eight hundred and thirty-two, personally appeared in open court, before the Judges of the Court of Common Pleas, in and for said County now sitting Garrit S. Veeder, a resident of the town of Rotterdam in said County aged eighty-one years who being first duly sworn according to law, doth on his oath make the following declaration in order to obtain the benefit of the act of Congress passed June 7th 1832.

Garrit was born in the then township, now City of Schenectady, in the now County of Schenectady, then County of Albany, on July 4, 1751. The record of his age is contained in his Bible & in the Register of Baptisms, kept by the Reformed Protestant Dutch Church in Schenectady.

From the time of his birth, until the commencement of the revolutionary war, he lived in said township—since said war he has lived in said township, & he now lives in the town of Rotterdam aforesaid.

He entered the service of the United States and served as herein stated. In the month of July 1775, he received the appointment of First Lieutenant in the company of Minute men commanded by Captain John Mynderse in the Regiment whereof Abraham Wemple was colonel. He served as such lieutenant until the spring of the year 1776 when he received the appointment of captain has herein after stated—while in the service as such Lieutenant he marched to Johnstown in the beginning of the year 1776, with a detachment of militia from Schenectady, on this occasion Sir John Johnson surrendered himself a prisoner of war & disarmed his tenants & dependents. He also while such lieutenant marched to Albany & other places in the vicinity of Schenectady aforesaid and performed his quota of duty at the Schenectady garrison. In confirmation of said appointment he received a commission as such lieutenant which is signed by Nathaniel Woodhull President of Congress & is hereinto annexed, & bears date the 20 October 1775.

He received the appointment of Captain in the Continental Line by commission dated 1st March 1776 in the regiment of forces of the United Colonies raised in and for the defence of the Colony of New York, commanded by Colonel Cornelius D. Wynkoop. The lieutenants of said company were Solomon Pendleton & David Bates & Ephraim Snow Ensign. This appointment he accepted & served under in the winter of the year 1777, he received the appointment of Captain in the Continental Line "during the war"—which appointment he declined to accept, but still continued to serve as captain as aforesaid until the end of the revolutionary war.

He was in the engagement at the taking of Burgoyne and his army, and had then the command of a detachment of men at Bemis's Heights.

He was marched to the Norman's Kill to Caughnawaga, Fort Plain, Fort Plank, Stone Arabia, Schoharie, & had then the command of the Middlefort—also to Beaverdam, Ballston, and at many other posts & passes to intercept the enemy, and repel their incursions upon our frontiers.

His commission as Captain as aforesaid has several times been used by others to substantiate the claims for pension of George Shannon and other soldiers who served under him and who were found entitled to the benefits of the acts under which they applied. In consequence his said commission became mutilated, and he has now only fragments thereof which are hereto annexed. This commission was signed by John Hancock, President of the Provincial Congress & Countersigned by Charles Thompson Secretary.
He declares that he is the identical person mentioned in the first named commission as "Garrit N. Veeder" and in the last named commission as "Garrit, S. Veeder".

The following are the names of some of the regular officers whom he knew, or who were with the troops where he served, and such continental and militia regiments or companies with which he served, or as he can recollect, viz: Col. Wemple, Gen. Schuyler, Major Swits, Generals Gates, Arnold, Poor, & Patterson & Larned of the Connecticut line also

Colonels Daton, VanSchaick, Willett & he never received any written discharge from the service. Besides his commissions he had a muster roll of his company which is hereunto annexed—He had several other but they are now lost.

He has no documentary evidence, and knows of no person whose testimony he can procure who can testify to his service except those whose affidavits are annexed or who can testify to [?] services.

The following are the names of persons to whom he is known in his present neighborhood, and who can testify as to his character for veracity, and their belief of his services as a soldier of the revolution, to wit: Joseph G. Yates, James V.S. Reyler, Jacob Swits, John Lander, Rev. Jacob VanVechten.

He hereby relinquishes every claim whatever to a pension or annuity except the present, and declares that his name is not on the pension roll of the agency of any state.

[Signed] Garrit S. Veeder
Subscribed and sworn to the day and year first aforesaid, John S. Vrooman.

Letter of inquiry answered September 3, 1936.

The data furnished herein pertaining to Garrit S. Veeder were obtained from papers on file in pension claim, S.7792, based upon his service in the War of the Revolution.
Garrit S. Veeder was born July 4, 1751 [old style] in Schenectady, New York. The names of his parents were not stated.
While a resident of said Schenectady, Garrit S.Veeder was appointed sometime in July, 1775, first lieutenant in Captain John Mynderse's company, Colonel Abraham Wemple's New York Regiment, and was commissioned, March 1, 1776, captain of the fourth company in Colonel Cornelius D. Wynkoop's New York Regiment; he was at the taking of Burgoyne, and continued in the service until the close of the war.

He was allowed pension on his application, executed October 18, 1832, at which time he was a resident of Rotterdam, Schenectady County, New York. He died February 18, 1836.

On February 26, 1855, C.N. Northrup, writing from Chattanooga, Tennessee, referred to Captain Garrit S. Veeder of Schenectady, New York, War of the Revolution as "my grandfather by marriage."

Moses Viney

March 10, 1817 – January 10, 1909
Location: Colored Plot (African-American Burial Plot)

Moses Viney was a former slave who moved to Schenectady to live his life as a free man. Born in a slave cabin in Easton, Maryland, Viney and his family were purchased on a Baltimore auction block by William Murphy, a plantation owner. He was separated from his family at 14 and spent several years working the fields before he became a butler for the Murphy's.

After he heard rumors that the Murphy slaves were being sold to the Deep South, he decided he was going to win his freedom and head north. After saving $20 from stacking wheat, he and two others left on Easter morning, 1840, working their way north to Troy, New York. After failing to find his contact there, he continued west to Schenectady and worked on a farm in Glenville until 1843, when he was hired by Union College President Eliphalet Nott as a coachman and messenger for the next 25 years.

When Congress passed the Fugitive Slave Act in 1850, slave catchers began moving north in search of former runaway slaves. When Viney spotted his former master Richard Murphy in Schenectady, Viney rushed to Nott, who then hired Judge Douglass Campbell and lawyer James Brown to look into the issue. Deemed legal by the men, Nott sent his grandson Clarkson N. Potter to Maryland to negotiate a payment for his freedom. Instead of paying the $1,600 ransom, Nott sent Viney to Canada to escape the slave catchers.

Moses Viney. (Courtesy of The Efner History Research Library, Schenectady.)

Nott wrote an affidavit on December 5, 1850 for Viney to carry to Canada.

This certifies that Moses Viney, a colored man, has been in my employment for eight years. He leaves the United States on account of the late fugitive slave law. He is a man of great integrity, and great industry and capability. He is a moral and religious man in whom entire confidence can be placed. Should the funds he has taken not be sufficient for his support till he gets employment, he is hereby authorized to draw on me at sight at the Mohawk Bank at Schenectady, State of New York, for any sum not exceeding one hundred dollars, and I will honor the draft.

While in Canada he worked for a family named Palement until 1852, and eventually Murphy accepted an offer of $250 for Viney's freedom. Viney returned to Schenectady to live out the remainder of his life.

Besides driving Nott as a coachman, Viney delivered messages for the president around the city and campus and was the designated driver for all important persons visiting Union. He also had great relations with the students of the college, and had a reputation for helping students get up in the morning after nights of the usual college escapades. Two of these students were Frederick William Seward, son of Secretary of State William Seward, and future president Chester A. Arthur.

Moses was taken ill by a series of strokes between 1859 and 1864, and so switched his role from driver to preparing Nott's meals and masseuse to Nott, becoming so good at massage therapy that he became an assistant to a local doctor.

When Nott died, Moses was the last to leave the cemetery. But his grief gave him also complete independence. Nott had left Viney $1,000 from his estate, and in 1847 Viney and his wife Anna purchased a home on Lafayette Street. Viney was hired again as a coachman by Urania Nott, the president's widow.

Viney's wife died in 1885, and Urania Nott died two years later. Mrs. Nott left Moses $1,000, the president's chair and other mementos. He used the money to buy her horse and carriage and started his own livery service.

Viney continued to stay connected to Union and appeared each year at the annual alumni dinner, much to the delight of the alumni.

He retired in February 1901 at age 84, his health frail. He died on January 10, 1909.

John Weber

June 15, 1875 - July, 1966
Location: L3#102

John was born in Elizabeth, New Jersey, the son of August Weber of Zurich, Switzerland, and was educated in common schools. He was an apprentice at the trade of machinist, and took a course at the Albany Business College after his parents moved to Schenectady in 1896.

His father worked for Edison, perfecting porcelain attachment and other features of Edison's electrical inventions. He created his own factory in Schenectady in 1896, at the end of Campbell Avenue, for the manufacture of the electrical instruments and appliances of his own invention.

John married Laura Fabry of Schenectady.

In 1905, with a capital stock of $25,000, he, his father and his brother, August, Jr., incorporated Weber Electric Company of Rotterdam. August, Jr. was president and John was Vice President, Secretary and Treasurer. Most of the 300 employees were women.

In 1919 he invented and patented a porcelain incandescent electric lamp socket casing. He and his brother, along with their father, invented electric sockets, casings and switches. They held several patents.

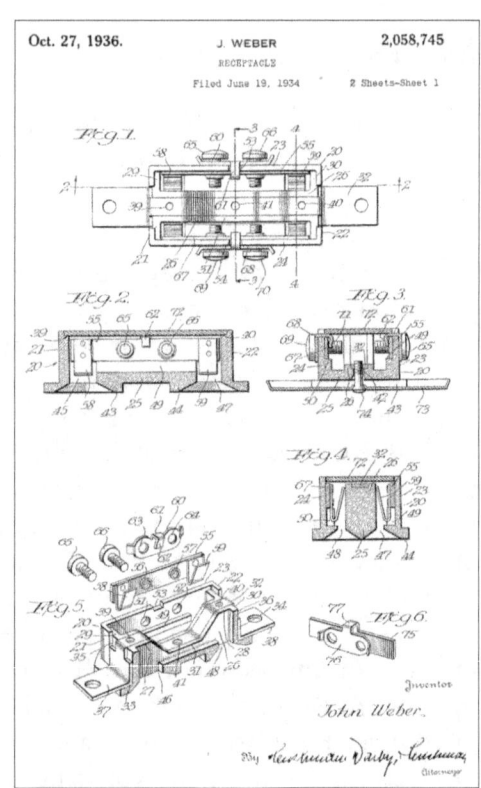

Patent drawing for a Weber receptacle. (Courtesy of U.S. Patent Office.)

In 1936 Weber Electric Company, a manufacturing institution employing 300 persons for more than 40 years, closed. Closing the plant was a personal decision; they were operating the plant without any returns for three years, but out of consideration for their employees delayed the closing. With added manufacturing costs they could no longer compete, as they made only wiring devices and had no diversity of products.

John was 91 when he died. He was a member of St. Georges Lodge No. 6, Free and Accepted Masons.

Myron F. Westover

July 10, 1860 - October 21, 1933
Location: M3#57

Myron Westover was born on a farm in Vinton, Iowa, the son of William and Sarah (Covert). After three years in the university classical course, he taught school for several years to save money. He then went into law at the University of Iowa, and in 1882 earned an L.L.B. He was admitted to the Iowa bar in 1882 and practiced in Britt, Iowa until 1883, and then Dakota City until 1884.

In 1888 he became Secretary to the President of the Thomson-Houston Electric Company in Boston until 1894, when he started at General Electric as Secretary, serving for 34 years. He sponsored the first company group insurance plan in 1919, was in charge of all insurance matters, and was a member of the pension board when it started. His reputation was so great that most of the large companies he placed insurance claims with never questioned the claim and approved it. He retired in 1928.

He was a Republican and was a member of the Schenectady Board of Trade. He also belonged to the Phi Gamma Delta fraternity, and belonged to several clubs, such as the Mohawk Club, the Mohawk Golf Club and the Camp Fire Club of America. He was

Myron Westover.

a lover of the outdoors, and in particular had a vast knowledge of geology. As a result, he discovered many mines for minerals needed by G.E. for products being developed.

Myron was also an educator and a student of local history. He published Schenectady, Past and Present in 1931, Pathways of Time, Schenectady, 1798-1948 in 1948, and eleven papers on the history of Schenectady. He was President of the Schenectady Historical Society and active in the society.

He married Lou E. Ham of Iowa City, Iowa. She was an organizer and first President of the Schenectady Women's Club in 1900, and died in 1939. They had one son, Wendell. They lived at 10 North Ferry Street (1912) and 10 Stratford Rd (1914). When he died at age 73, he was at 1156 Wendell Avenue.

Albert Westinghouse

1842 - December 10, 1864
Location: L2 41

Albert was the brother of the famed George Westinghouse, Jr., inventor of the air brake and creator of the Westinghouse Corporation. Albert was George's best friend, and when Albert was killed in the Civil War, his death was a huge blow to the Westinghouse family.

Albert served as Second Lieutenant in the Second New York Veteran Cavalry Regiment (Empire Light Calvary), Company B, during the Civil War (September 22 - December 19, 1863). Mustered in as Second Lieutenant on September 22 1863, he was promoted to First Lieutenant on December 19, 1863. His regiment was in the battles of Fort Blakely (April 2, 1865), Mansfield (April 8, 1864), Pleasant Hill (April 9, 1864), Spanish Fort (March 27, 1865; Albert was already deceased) and Monett's Ferry (April 23, 1864). He was killed at McLeod's Mills on December 10, 1864.

Westinghouse monument at Vale.

Sergeant Luman L. Cadwell (1836-1925) was an American soldier who fought alongside Westinghouse. Cadwell received the country's highest award for bravery during combat, the Medal of Honor, for his action at the Alabama Bayou, Louisiana on September 20, 1864. He was honored with the award on August 17, 1894.

On September 20, 1864, Cadwell, along with Westinghouse, swam across the 150-foot Alabama Bayou near New Orleans in order to retrieve a small boat, which his company used to gain access to a Confederate camp stationed on an island in the middle of the Bayou, and to destroy buildings, supplies, artillery and capture Confederate forces. They were able to cross 30 men with the boat and rout the rebels. A.L. Gurney, Lt. Col., was in command. Why Westinghouse wasn't honored as well is a mystery. He was killed two months later. The following is Gurney's complete report.

HDQRS. SECOND VETERAN CAVALRY NEW YORK VOLS.,Morganza, La., September 22, 1864.
 CAPT.: Pursuant to orders I left camp with a detachment of my regiment at 7 a. m. the 19th instant, with five days' rations, camp equipage, &c., and halted at 10 p. m. at Poydras' College, on Fausse River, where I established a camp and sent orders to the detachment of cavalry at Grossetete Bayou to report to me by direction of Gen. Lawler. At 9 p. m. the 20th instant left my camp with 225 men (leaving fifty men to guard camp) and moved out to Bayou Maringouin, where I searched every house. At the house of Wiley Barrow I left the bayou and went straight back into the swamp, and after passing over a very muddy road through an almost impenetrable swamp, arrived at Bayou Alabama at 7.30 a. m., having been five hours going over eight miles of road. Halted my command one-third of a mile from the bayou and dismounted my men to fight on foot. Went forward myself to ascertain the position of the enemy; found an island in my front from which some of the enemy were bathing. Width of the bayou to the island about fifty yards. On the opposite bank a camp fire, one piece of artillery in position, a hut surrounded by camp kettles, &c., and three or four men in the water. A flat-boat lay at the opposite bank directly under the piece of artillery. Posted sharpshooters behind trees, stumps, &c., to keep the artillery silent and cover a crossing. Brought up my men, while Lieut. Albert Westinghouse, Company B, and Sergeant Cadwell, Company B, both of my regiment, swam the bayou and brought across the flat-boat, by which I was able to cross thirty men at a time. The enemy disappeared in the woods upon seeing us. Sixty men across and I commenced moving at a double-quick into the woods; came upon the camp of Capt. Ratliff after one mile and a half march and captured it with but a slight skirmish. The camp consisted of wooden buildings, houses, barns, negroes quarters, and a saw-mill, all of which I burned, except a few quarters occupied by old negroes. Captured at this camp 1 piece of artillery, a few carbines, sabers, and pistols, a large amount of ammunition, including artillery, carbine, and pistol powder, percussion caps, &c., five dozen pairs pants, eight dozen shirts, large supply of commissary stores, camp equipage, &c., also 15 horses, 3 prisoners of war, and a large mail. I was unable to bring away but a very small quantity of the captured stores on account of the bad roads. Many places my men had to dismount and lead their horses, having many bayous to ford and never finding a bridge. I spiked the piece of artillery and sunk it in the middle of the bayou, first dismounting it; water about fifty feet deep and very soft bottom. Destroyed everything of value not brought away. Found at the camp Mrs. Ratliff, the captain's wife. Returned by another road, striking the State road at Robert I. Barrow's, five miles above Livonia; halted at sundown at John Lombard's, where we fed and rested for the first time since the day before. My men were very much fatigued, the work performed by them being of the

most laborious character. Resumed the march at 7 a. m. the next day and arrived at my camp on Fausse River at 1 p. m. Broke camp on Fausse River at 7 a. m. 22d instant, and arrived at this camp at 12 m. I was informed by Mrs. Frank Harding that her husband was arrested by Confederate authority and confined for during the war for taking the oath of allegiance to the United States and for friendliness to our soldiers.

The order was issued for his arrest upon an application signed by Mr. Pullman, of Grossetete Bayou, Mr. Mathews, at junction of Fordoche and Grossetete Bayous; Mr. Ciberth, of Fausse River; Rev. Mr. Smiley, Grossetete; Robert I. Barrow, State road above Grossetete. Mr. Howard, whom I arrested, conducted Capt. Pryne and men to arrest Frank Harding and assisted in the arrest. I would respectfully recommend that the parties causing the arrest of Mr. Harding be arrested and confined until Mr. Harding is released and return to his family, which is very large and poor.

The following were the troops under my command on this expedition: Second Veteran Cavalry, New York Volunteers, 234 men; First Texas Cavalry Volunteers, 75 men; total, 309.

Very respectfully, your obedient servant,

A.L. GURNEY, Lieut.-Col., Cmdg.
Capt. B. WILSON, Assistant Adjutant-Gen., U. S. Forces.

Albert Westinghouse died leading a raid on a railroad near the Leaf River in Louisiana. Fortunately, fellow officers who remained stationed in Louisiana arranged to have "his remains taken up and stored" in a metallic coffin until they could escort him home for proper military burial.

The following is a description of his death written by a Corporal of Company B, in a letter to home dated December 28, 1864, from Morganzia, Louisiana, detailing a month-long mission and the battle at McCloud's Mill (sometimes listed as McCleod's Mill, Missouri).

Dec. 10th. We kept them going back about 2 miles the major told our Lieut [Westinghouse] he was in command of the first squadron to draw sabre and charge on them & Capt Dolan to support us. At the word draw sabre we pulled the bright steel blade for the first time in a fight. At the word charge we put spurrs to our horses and our 1st Lieut says boys follow me swinging his sabre at arms length above his head. The smartest horses got into there rear and the last blow our Lieut made struck a reb in the back which fetched him to the ground. Another reb was in the front of our Lieut drawed his revolver shot the Lieut through about half way from the pit of his stomache to the hollow of his neck he dismounted his horse took his hat in his hand started back when I met him he said go on boys I'm shot. He soon died. We drove them until we seen there line of infantry. We was ordered by Capt Dolan to return when we came back Charley & myself with two others took up the Lieut carried him back with us a 1/4 of a mile laid him down. He was to heavy. The most of our men that was there at the end of the charge was Co A & B and a few from other Co's. Dont think we numbered over 40 men in all the rest. Was back over a mile in the rear we captured 4 rebs one ambulance and two mules took the ambulance and got the Lieut. Took him with us and we marched back. Took another road down the river road some 25 or 30 miles and very still I can tell you and encamped for the remainder of the night.

Dec 11th. We burried the Lieut and heard by the women that lived there said our men was near there yesterday driving cattle so the Col sent out a guard of men. Soon found that we was on one direct road to the army. About noon we started got to Paschaglia (Pascagoula) river crossed on a flat boat a Louisiana regt was waiting for us.

In December of 1864, Mrs. P. Clute asked the City Council to "aid in the removal of the remains of her husband and two other soldiers from New Orleans to this city." Albert was one of them.

George Westinghouse

October 6, 1809 - March 12, 1884
Location: L2 41 9

George Westinghouse.

George Westinghouse, Sr. was the son of John Ferdinand Westinghouse of Pownal, Vermont, and was the fifth of twelve children. George married Emeline Vedder in 1831. They took a wagon to the Ohio frontier to strike it rich, but returned five years later, and he began working with tools and machinery. They had ten children.

George Westinghouse, Sr. is the father of the famous inventor George Westinghouse, Jr., but had his own successful career as an inventor and businessman, beginning in 1836 in the rural town of Central Bridge in Schoharie County, New York.

In 1856, farmer and agricultural toolmaker George moved east from Central Bridge to Schenectady to take advantage of the new Erie Canal. He established a new firm, the Schenectady Agricultural Works, G. Westinghouse & Co., that made agricultural machinery, mill machinery and small steam engines. They worked out of an old cement mill on the south bank of the Erie Canal, now part of the General Electric parking lot and I-90 Interchange. In 1883 it was incorporated into the Westinghouse Company.

In 1860 he received a patent for a horse power machine, a grain separator, a crank box, and six more after. In 1864 he patented a threshing machine design that became a staple of his product line. In 1865 he was granted a sawmill patent. In 1872 he earned a patent for the improvement of threshing machines. An 1872 advertisement mentions drag saws as one of their products. They also made architectural cast iron.

After his death in 1884, ownership went to his three sons, including George Westinghouse, Jr. The buildings were eventually sold to General Electric and torn down. This is ironic, since George Jr. and Thomas Edison fought each in the famous "Battle of the Currents" (the establishment of Direct Current vs. Alternating Current) during the late 19th century. Westinghouse won the war.

George Sr., Emeline and the children lived at 16 State Street. Their son John and his family lived at 20 State Street.

A Westinghouse threshing machine.

Westinghouse warehouse on the Erie Canal in Schenectady.

Home of George Westinghouse on State Street.

Joseph Whistler

October 19, 1822 - April 20, 1899
Location: P37

Joseph Nelson Garland Whistler, son of William and Julia (Fearson) Whistler, was born on October 19, 1822 at Green Bay, Wisconsin. After his education at College Hill, Poughkeepsie, New York, he entered the U.S. Military Academy at West Point, graduating with the class of 1846. After graduating he was appointed to the Eighth Infantry as Brevet Second Lieutenant on July 1, 1846.

Joseph N.G. Whistler married Eliza Cobham Hall of Albany, New York. She was the daughter of Maj. Nathaniel Nye Hall and granddaughter of the Hon. Francis Bloodgood. They had five children: Garland Nelson (1847-1914), who served in the Mexican War and the Civil War and attained the rank of General and was an expert in the field of high explosives; Willie (1850- 1857), who died at age seven when he fell from a cherry tree while visiting his grandparents; Margaret (1861-?); Julia (1863-?); and Kenner Garrard (c.1863-?).

During the Mexican War in 1846, Joseph Whistler served in the Third Infantry and fought in the Battles of Vera Cruz, Cerro Gordo, Contreras, Cherubusco, Chapultepec and the capture of Mexico City. He was brevetted First Lieutenant on August 20, 1847 for "gallant and meritorious conduct."

After the Mexican War, he was stationed in New Mexico, where the Army was involved with numerous skirmishes with the Apache and Navajo Indians for a decade.

When the Civil War broke out, he was captured by the Confederates while he was headed to a new post at Indianolo, Texas. He was paroled as a prisoner of war (August 27, 1862, exchanged for 1st Lt. J.W. Hill, 2nd N.C. Infantry Bn.), and during the War served as Assistant Instructor of Infantry Tactics at West Point from September 1861 to March 1863.

He was promoted to Captain of the Third Infantry on May 14, 1861 and, in 1863, joined the Volunteer army as Colonel of the Second New York Heavy Artillery. From August 11 to September 16, 1863, and from July 9, 1864 to August 20, 1865, he commanded First Brigade, Defenses South of the Potomac, XXII Corps, Department of Washington, D.C.

He served in the Washington, D.C. and Richmond campaigns and was wounded at the Siege of Petersburg on June 19, 1864. He was mustered out of the volunteer army with the rank of Brigadier General on March 13, 1865.

After the war he received numerous brevets, serving in the 31st, 22nd, 15th, and 5th Infantries. He was commander of Ft. Buford in the Dakota territory.

In the fall of 1871 the first expedition to the Yellowstone River, as escort to Gen. T.J. Rosser's surveying party of the projected Northern Pacific Railway, was organized at and started from Fort Rice. The column was composed of Companies D and H, 17th; B, 20th; and A, C, H and I, 22nd Infantry; two Gatling guns and twenty-six Indian scouts, all under command of Whistler. The transportation consisted of 104 wagons. The expedition marched from Rice, September 9; reached the Yellowstone, at the mouth of Glendive Creek near where the town of Glendive is now situated, October 2; from there returned to Rice, arriving on the 16th, having marched over 600 miles.

He retired on October 19, 1886 with the rank of Colonel.

He died at Fort Wadsworth, New York on April 20, 1898. He was remembered by his comrades as "a man of sterling worth, a thorough soldier, an enthusiastic sportsman, a gentleman of the old school; … To those who served under him he was like a father. To those of his own age 'Beau' Whistler was a beloved comrade."

Whistler was an Original Companion of the Military Order of the Loyal Legion of the United States (MOLLUS), a military society for Union officers who served in the American Civil War and was formed on April 20, 1865, shortly after the assassination of President Abraham Lincoln. The organization still exists today (*http://suvcw.org/mollus/mollus.htm*)

Joseph was the grandson of John Whistler, an Irish-born soldier who served under General Burgoyne during the Revolutionary War and was captured at the Battle of Saratoga. His first cousin was the famous artist James Abbott McNeill Whistler of America's Guilded Age (1870-1900).

During WW I, a battery was named for him, Battery Whistler (1919-1942) It was a reinforced concrete, Taft-Period 12-inch coastal mortar battery on Fort Rosecrans, San Diego County, California. The battery was named in 1916. Construction started on March 15,1916, was completed and transferred to the Coastal Artillery for use August 19, 1919, at a cost of $ 118,000. It was deactivated in 1942.

Frank E. Wickware

March 18, 1888 - November 2, 1967
Location: I1 8-15

Frank Wickware was born in Coffeyville, Kansas. The *Schenectady Union-Star* called Wickware "the best colored pitcher in the world." Racism prevented him from playing in the majors and an alcohol problem prevented him from getting into the Baseball Hall of Fame

A right-hander with a blazing fastball, he was a formidable pitcher during the second decade of the 20th century. He began in the Chicago baseball arena in 1910, after playing with the Dallas Giants. He posted an 18-1 record for the Leland Giants. He had several nicknames: Smokey, Rawhide, The Red Ant, Big Red, Smiley and Wigware. At the age of 22, he was known for his velocity, coolness on the mound under pressure and with a smooth delivery. He was a big winner with the Chicago American Giants, and pitched two winter seasons in Cuba.

Frank was a star and in demand by all the leading teams of the time, and continued to be a formidable pitcher throughout the decade. According to James A. Riley, in his <u>The Biographical Encyclopedia of the Negro Baseball Leagues</u> (Carroll & Graf Publishers, Inc., 1994), in a game in July 1913, after jumping to the Mohawk Giants of Schenectady, New York, he excited the crowd when he called in his outfield with two outs in the ninth inning and struck out the last batter to end the game. Thirty days later the Chicago Cubs came to town for a scheduled exhibition game with the Rutland, Vermont team, but Rutland had already hired Wickware as a ringer to pitch against the Cubs. Once the Cubs figured it out they refused to play if he pitched.

Another recorded incident with the Mohawks shows how popular he was. The western champion Chicago American Giants and the eastern champion New York Lincoln Giants were in a playoff for the colored championship. Both teams signed Wickware as a ringer to pitch for them in the championship series. When each of the opposing managers learned of his counterpart's plans, they argued over who had the legal claim to Wickware, and the game was protested.

Wickware as seen in the *Schenectady Gazette*, 1913. (See also the image on the back cover.)

During the 1914 season he pitched for four different teams and was credited with no-hitters against both the Indianapolis ABCs and the Cuban Stars.

However, his real claim to fame was when he out-dueled Walter Johnson 2 out of 3 games in 1913 and 1914, when both hurlers were at the top of their game. One of those victories, a 1-0 game called on account of darkness after five innings, came on October 5, 1913, with Johnson just having completed a sensational season, with a 34-7 record and a 1.09 E.R.A. with the Washington Senators, and was American League M.V.P. that year. There were 6,000-8,000 spectators watching the game, according to the local newspaper, played at Island Park, on Van Slyck Island (later Iroquois Island) in the Mohawk River. It was the last game of the Giant's first season. Johnson and a team of all-stars came to Schenectady and would lose to the Mohawk Giants 1-0 in a game that was called due to darkness after 5½ innings. The game was touted as "a test of the best white pitcher versus the best colored twirler." The game looked like at one point it would not play at all, since the Giants had not been paid for several games and refused to play unless they were paid. Alfred Nicholaus, a local restaurant owner at the corner of the Erie Canal and State, and silent partner in the Mohawk Giants team, rushed part of the funds to the striking players and the game went on.

Ironically, Johnson and Wickware came from the same place—Coffeyville, Kansas—and Wickware was often called "the black Walter Johnson."

Because of his habit of jumping teams, his statistics from his prime seasons are fragmented, but it seems he was 15-14 against quality teams. His personal habits didn't win fans with managers, and his drinking problem took a toll. By 1917 it looked like he was through, when he was with the declining Chicago Giants his pitching became erratic, with loss of control. It appeared he was done, but by late summer he had joined the Chicago American Giants and was back in form. The next season he was thrown out because he quit running on a ground ball, when he would have beaten the throw.

Wickware's career was further affected by his time serving in the Army during World War I. He was a Private in Company B of the Second Development Battalion. During the 1920s he was declining both as a pitcher and in popularity. He made a pitching appearance with the Calgary Black Sox in 1921, and in 1925, at age 37, he was with the New York Lincoln Giants for his last year in black baseball. In April he and Oliver Marcelle were with teammate Dave Brown on the night Brown killed a man in a barroom fight. Although not involved in the incident, the next day at the ball field, he was interrogated but released.

In his latter years he was known as "Rawhide" Wickware. He briefly managed the New Bedford, Massachusetts team in 1930. He left baseball and lived in Schenectady during the 1940s, but faded into obscurity and died in 1967. His career, which spanned 1910-1925 as a pitcher, was with several teams: Dallas Giants (1909), Leland Giants (1909-1910), Chicago American Giants (1911-1912, 1914-1918, 1920-1921), Brooklyn Royal Giants (1912-1914), Mohawk Giants (1913-1914), Louisville White Sox (1914), New York Lincoln Stars, Indianapolis ABCs (1916), Jewell's ABCs (1917), Chicago Giants (1917), military service (1918-1919), Detroit Stars (1919), Norfolk Stars (1920), New York Lincoln Giants (1920, 1925), Canadian League (1921), St. Louis Giants, and Philadelphia Giants.

Because of racism, Wickware was never able to play the white major leagues. An article by Frank G. Menke discussed the loss of three great pitchers because of it. He wrote of him on June 8, 1915 in the *Springs Gazette Telegraph* of Colorado Springs, Colorado.

> *Frank Wickware is another negro pitcher who would rate with the Walter Johnsons, Joe Woods, and Grover Alexanders if he were a white man. Wickware performed some marvelous pitching feats in and around Schenectady, NY and has since moved on to Chicago where he has become a sensation among the semipros.*
>
> Has Marvelous Speed and Curve.
> *Wickware has marvelous speed, a weird set of curves and wonderful control. And he has a trick that has made him feared among batters. He throws what seems to be a "Beanball" but his control is so perfect that he never yet has hit a batter in the head. But when the batters see the ball propelled with mighty force, come for their heads, they jump away—and the ball, taking its proper and well timed curve, arches over the plate for a strike.*
>
> *Wickware has compiled a wonderful strike-out average. He figured in about 30 games, over a stretch of three years from 1912 and struck out something like 250 batmen—an average of about 8 1/3 to a game. In one game he fanned 15 men. He has allowed on an average of only five hits to a game for the last 20 games pitched and over a stretch of 15 games he allowed only 26 runs, less than two runs a game.*

Of the two famous duelers, Walter Johnson would go on to be honored as one of the "Five Immortals"—first five players elected to the Baseball Hall of Fame. Wickware went into obscurity and died in Schenectady.

While living in Schenectady he worked for the Army Depot. He was indicted with others in thefts from the depot in 1948 when he was 60 years old. The others were Harry R. Bryant, age 28, and Frank Bulley, age 56. Wickware was living at 31 Weaver Street. It appears they all stole combat boots. Wickware received the heaviest sentence, with 4 months in prison, while Bryant received two and Bulley received one.

He was married to Elizabeth McCan, and they were divorced in 1964 *in abstentia*. In a notice that he published in the *Schenectady Gazette* newspaper on February 12, 1964 he states,

> *Please take notice, that a petition has been presented to this court by Frank E. Wickware, your husband, for dissolution of your marriage on the ground that you have absented yourself for five successive years last past without being known to him to be living and that he believes you to be dead.*

It appears that she left him.

In 1957 the *Gazette* reported the death of Sara Frances Williams Wickware, 66, of 412 Grand Street, his second wife. She was buried in Fisher Cemetery.

When he died in 1967 at age 79, he was still living at 412 Grand Street with his third wife Verdie, and it was said he died after a long illness. His obituary was short. He had been living in Schenectady for 40 years and was employed all those years at the Army Depot until he retired.

In 1971 the *Schenectady Gazette* published a picture of Mrs. Verdie Wickware planting flowers on his grave.

John Martin Wiederhold

1843 - December 14, 1917
Location: Unknown

John and his brother George (September 17, 1848 - December 27, 1921) came to America in 1862, and to Schenectady in 1869 from Amesbury, Massachusetts. John was the older of the two.

In 1870 John and George formed the Wiederhold Brothers company and made hoop skirts. Their retail store was at State and North Ferry streets in 1874. A large, three-story brick factory called the Victory was built on Broadway opposite Hamilton and, now gone, was built when John took in Charles Washburn in 1882. The building made muslin underwear for 35 years and closed in 1916 before it became a Saveway market.

George went to New York City around 1880 to open his own garment factory there. He came back after retirement and lived at 12 North Street. He is also buried at Vale.

In 1886, the firm of John Wiederhold & Co., manufacturers of ladies' underwear, children's garments, dress wrappers, aprons, hoop skirts, etc., was located at 180 Centre Street, now Broadway. They employed one hundred women and girls, and were fully equipped with sewing machines and other necessary machines and implements.

John was a member of the Schenectady Lodge of Elks and New Hope Lodge of Masons. He had two children, Edward J. and Marguerite. John lived at 612 Union Street, and died from pneumonia at age 73.

Ironically his son, Edward J. Wiederhold, a graduate of Cornell in 1906, also died of pneumonia, on November 16, 1918, only a year later. The son had studied at Albany Law School and New York Law School, but became manager of his father's firm after he died. The company was then doing only government orders.

Shop of the Wiederhold Brothers at State and North Ferry Streets (bottom right).

Clark Witbeck

January 26, 1852 - August 22, 1937
Location: M3 43-44

Witbeck ad from the 1950s.

Clark Witbeck was born on a farm near Cohoes, New York and moved to Schenectady with his parents at an early age. He attended Union Classical Institute. His father opened a hardware store who later sold it to Clark.

He was the founder of the Union National Bank in 1898, and was Chairman of the board until he died. When he was young, he was a founder of the Mohawk Golf Club, and at one time maintained a racing stable. He had a standard stallion named General Electric, registered with the U.S. Trotting Association, that he bred. He also had a standard mare named Faustelle. His other hobbies included horticulture. He was a member of the Mohawk Club, the Rotary Club and St. George's Masonic Lodge. He was active in the Community Chest and a member of the board of the Ingersoll Memorial Home.

Clark founded the Clark Witbeck Hardware Company in 1899 at 413 State Street, and moved into the Beaux Arts-inspired building at 215-217 State Street in 1905. In 1954, they were at 132-140 North Broadway, with a branch in Rochester. By 1964 they were at 1482 Erie Blvd.

Witbeck was in business for more than half a century. He was active in the New York Sate Hardware Jobbers Association and National Wholesale Warehouse Association, being President of the state association at one time.

He died at his home on Troy Road. He married Sophie L. Rosa, who died a few months before him.

Henry Deforest Wright

1908 - September 6, 1995
Location: M3 18 5 (Landon Plot)

Henry DeForest Wright, was a prominent Schenectady business leader. He served for 34 years as Chairman and Chief Executive Officer of Schenectady International Inc., a family-founded business that grew into a global chemical manufacturer with affiliated companies in 10 countries. He became President of the SI Group, formerly Schenectady International, after the passing of his father, W. Howard Wright.

In addition to his business activities, Wright was active in the Schenectady community, establishing scholarships and donating property to Union College.

He and his wife lived on Stratford Road and then moved to 1248 Lenox Road in 1944. Their daughters were Adeline Wright of Schenectady and Aleda Campbell Wright of Saratoga Springs, New York; his stepdaughters were Jean Steele of Baltimore, Maryland and Patricia Hoopes of Bolton Landing, New York; his stepson was Edward Gilmour of Santa Fe, New Mexico.

He was a resident of Gulf Stream, Florida when he died on of natural causes at his home. He was 87.

Richard P.G. Wright

March 5, 1776 - May 29, 1847
Location: F 23 7 (Colored Plot)

Richard Wright was an African-American and a native of Madagascar. One source says he was born in Bristol, Massachusetts. Until 1810 he was known as Prince G. Wright, which may indicate he was a slave at one time. Richard managed a hairdressing business in Providence, Rhode Island, and settled in Schenectady, where he lived for over 40 years. It is known that he was in Schenectady as early as 1811, when he published in the newspaper a notice that he was disowning his wife Lydia for improper conduct.

He was a hairdresser and barber serving a white community, and he was so esteemed that in 1825 he was testifying for J. Stillman's Finest Edge Razor (he sharpened them), which he used at his barbershop. His barbershop was at 2 Canal Street (now South College Avenue) near the canal, and he lived only a block away at 84 Ferry Street. Both sites are gone.

He was a prosperous, well-respected member of the Schenectady community, but he was a well-known abolitionist as well. His abolitionist tendencies are clear in the name of his son Theodore Sedgwick Wright, named after a prominent Massachusetts jurist and legislator, who in 1783 successfully defended an enslaved woman against her master, from whom she had fled. He sent his son to a school headed by three white Methodists who had opened their school to black children. The school did not succeed but introduced the young man to integration. Richard's house in Schenectady served as a station on the Underground Railroad.

> **NOTICE.**
> FROM the very improper conduct of my wife LYDIA, I am reluctantly compelled to notice her in a public manner —This is therefore to caution all persons from trusting or harboring her on my account, as I am determined to pay no debts of her contracting after this date.
> RICHARD P. G. WRIGHT.
> Schenectady, August 16, 1811.   3

Newspaper notice by Wright disowning his wife.

Both he and his son were abolitionists that participated in groups that were racially integrated (American Anti-Slavery Society) and dedicated to affecting social change through action (Committee of Vigilance). He is listed as being in attendance at the Third Anti-Slavery Society meeting in New York City in May, 1836. He was a founding member of the Anti-Slavery Society of the City of Schenectady in 1838, and his name appears in several anti-slavery conventions and meetings.

In 1845 it was reported that Richard had helped slave Charles Nelson from Mississippi. Nelson was in Saratoga with his master on their way to Niagara Falls. The master left Charles in a hotel alone where he met Wright, who asked Nelson if he wanted to be free. He arranged an escape with Mason Anthony, who took him to Rokeby, Vermont, via a known Underground Railroad route from Schenectady to Greenfield where Anthony lived.

This may have been part of the reason why Richard also participated in Schenectady's white Masonic lodges in the 1820s and 1840s. In 1794, Richard was raised in African Lodge No. 459, the first Masonic Lodge comprised of black American men. Members of this lodge signed a petition in 1777 against slavery, and in 1788 against slave trade and kidnapping, to the Massachusetts legislature in 1788. Richard again appears in the Masonic books in 1818, when he is listed as a visitor in Tyrian Mark Masters Lodge No. 66 of Schenectady. This lodge was founded in 1814 and disbanded in 1823. His involvement in other lodges is also noted, such as Cyrus Royal Arch Chapter No. 57, Delta Lodge of Perfection, and St. George's Lodge No. 6. He is recorded as the earliest "black member" in 1844, along with his son, in St. George's. He received the degree of "Perfection" from the old Lodge of Perfection, originally established in Albany by Henry A. Francken, Deputy Sovereign Grand Inspector General, and revived in 1821 in the city of Schenectady. Richard was one of the treasurers of the revived lodge in 1822. The lodge lasted until 1825, when it moved back to Albany and the Schenectady members became honorary members. He held offices in both Royal Arch and Scottish Rite Masonic bodies.

According to historian Jeffrey Croteau, the Wright's had a long history of Masonic participation.

R.P.G. Wright's and T.S. Wright's Participation in Freemasonry, 1794-1847

- June 23, 1794 – R.P.G. Wright raised a Master Mason at African Lodge No. 459
- December 14, 1818 – R.P.G. Wright visits Tyrian Mark Masters Lodge No. 66
- October 23, 1820 – R.P.G. Wright listed as visitor at Morton Lodge No. 87 when G.F. Yates is initiated as E.A.
- October 27, 1820 – R.P.G. Wright listed as visitor at Morton when G.F. Yates is passed as F.C.
- November 6, 1820 – R.P.G. Wright listed as Tyler Pro-Tem at Tyrian
- November 7, 1820 – R.P.G. Wright listed as Junior Overseer Pro-Tem at Tyrian
- January 2, 1821 – R.P.G. Wright listed as Master Overseer Pro-Tem at Tyrian
- March 6, 1821 – R.P.G. Wright listed as visitor at Tyrian when GF Yates raised to M.M.
- January 25, 1822 – T.S. Wright petitions Morton Lodge No. 87
- February 1, 1822 – T.S. Wright initiated as E.A.
- February 22, 1822 – T.S. Wright passed as F.C.
- February 23, 1822 – T.S. Wright raised as M.M.
- April 14, 1822 – committee appointed to investigate character of T.S. Wright at Tyrian
- May 7, 1822 – T.S. Wright elected to Tyrian
- May 10, 1822 – T.S. Wright advanced at Tyrian
- June 20, 1822 – R.P.G. Wright visits Cyrus Royal Arch Chapter No. 57
- September 7, 1822 – R.P.G. Wright installed as Grand Treasurer of Delta Lodge of Perfection
- November 11, 1823 – R.P.G. Wright elected Grand Tyler of Delta
- September 22, 1841 – R.P.G. Wright listed as member of Delta, with degrees of G.E.P. & S.M. and P. of J. listed next to his name
- September 23, 1841 – R.P.G. Wright elected and installed as Grand Tyler of Delta Lodge of Perfection
- March 18, 1844 – R.P.G. Wright petitions to join St. George's Lodge No. 6
- March 28, 1844 – R.P.G. Wright affiliates with St. George's
- August 28, 1844 – T.S. Wright affiliates with St. George's
- April 7, 1847 – St. George's minutes record death of T.S. Wright
- June 16, 1847 – St. George's minutes record death of R.P.G. Wright.

R.P.G. Wright's gravestone at Vale.

Twenty years after he died, a Prince Hall Masonic lodge was chartered in Schenectady on January 27, 1869, and named the R.P.G. Wright Lodge No 29. By 1929 the lodge disappeared. Naming a lodge after him was indicative of how highly esteemed Wright was in Schenectady.

When President Martin Van Buren died in 1847, a procession was led in his honor in Schenectady. Wright arranged for a group of men and it was noted in the newspaper:

An urn carried by four colored persons, properly robed, which, being followed by a horse led by two colored men, also in proper costume, presented an imposing and solemn appearance. This part of the procession we understand was under the direction or Mr. R.P.G. Wright, a colored gentleman, who displayed much taste in its arrangement.

When Richard he died in 1847, this small obituary was published in a local Albany newspaper:

R.P.G. WRIGHT died at New-York on the 29 of May. The funeral took place at Schenectady, and was numerously attended by all classes of citizens. Mr. Wright was noble in his personal carriage, gentlemanly and kind in his entire deportment, though a very black man. His simple, sincere Christian character was such as to win for him the cordial respect and confidence of the community in which he lived for forty years. He came from Massachusetts to Schenectady when a young man. He has left behind him no truer friend of the interests of his injured people. His death took place two months only after that of his son, the late lamented Theodore S. Wright of New-York. They were most tenderly attached to each other in life, and were not long sundered by death!

Both he and his son Theodore may have died of cholera, just two months apart in 1847. He was 75 when he died and living in New York, probably with his son. He was brought to Schenectady for burial.

While not buried in Vale, Theodore Sedgwick Wright is worth mentioning as part of his father's abolitionist legacy. Theodore was an African-American minister and abolitionist in New York City. Educator Walter Merrill wrote, in his entry to the <u>Encyclopedia Britannica's Dictionary of American Negro Biographies</u>, "except for Frederick Douglass, few American Negroes of his generation labored more effectively for the freedom and equality of his race than Theodore S. Wright."

He was the first African-American to attend Princeton Theological Seminary, from which he graduated in 1829, the first African-American to graduate from any theological seminary in the country. He then became the second pastor of the First Colored Presbyterian Church in New York City, a lifelong career for him. It is now St. James Presbyterian Church in Harlem.

Throughout his life Theodore traveled and gave lectures condemning racial prejudice. He wrote several entries and speeches for William Lloyd Garrison's *Liberator*, the leading anti-slavery newspaper in the United States during the antebellum period.

He also became a founder or officer of several important and influential anti-slavery organizations, such as the New England Anti-Slavery Society, the American Anti-Slavery Society, the Phoenix Society, New York City's Committee of Vigilance, the Union Missionary Society and the predominately white American Missionary Association. He was active in politics in the Liberty Party and circulated petitions to the New York Legislature, and attended important conventions, such as the New York State Anti-Slavery Society convention held in Utica, on September 20, 1837.

Engraving of abolitionist Rev. Theodore Sedgwick Wright, son of R.P.G. Wright.

Locally, he spoke at the dedication of the First Free Church of Schenectady, the first black church in the city, on October 26, 1837. He was also instrumental in the erection of the Liberty Street Presbyterian Church in Troy in 1834. A day school for "colored children" and an evening school for adults were opened in the basement.

Like his father, for many years Theodore Wright used his house at 235 W. Broadway in New York City as a station for the Underground Railroad. Theodore Sedgwick Wright died on March 25, 1847. His house is still standing.

The grandson of Richard P.G. Wright, Richard T.P. Wright, died on the November 25, 1842, and was buried in Schenectady after a sermon at the "Free Church."

Thomas Wallace Wright

August 3, 1842 - September 13, 1908
Location: College Plot X

Thomas Wright was one of nine children of Alexander and Mary (Wallace) Wright. He was born in Galloway, Scotland. His early life began in Canada, and he went to college at the Collegiate Institute at Galt, Ontario. He then went on to the University of Toronto, getting his B.A. in 1863. He entered the Yale Sheffield Scientific School in January of his senior year, 1872, and in 1883 was awarded a Civil Engineer degree at Yale.

After Yale, he was a civil engineer in the Lake Survey at Detroit, Michigan, and later taught engineering at Lehigh University, in Bethlehem, Pennsylvania. In 1885 he was appointed Professor of Applied Mathematics and Physics at Union College in Schenectady, and stayed at that postition until 1905 when he retired, becoming Professor Emeritus.

He received an M.A. from the University of Toronto in 1891, also the same year his degree of Doctor of Philosophy was received at Union.

He authored three textbooks:

- Elements of Mechanics including Kinematics, Kinetics and Statics With Applications, 1896.

- The Adjustment of Observations, 1906

- Textbook of Mechanics for Colleges and Technical Schools, 1890

He married in Detroit to Frances E. Boughton, daughter of George Winfield Boughton, a farmer of Novesta, Michigan. She died on February 20, 1877, and he married again at Galt, Canada on June 20, 1879 to Margaret Taylor, daughter of Adam Hood.

He had five children, three daughters and two sons. The sons also went to Union.

He died of paralysis at his home on September 13, 1908 at 66 years of age.

W. Howard Wright

1875 - February 25, 1959
Location: M3#29

A native of Detroit, Michigan, he came to Schenectady in 1885 when his father Thomas W. Wright accepted a professorship in physics at Union College. In 1895 Howard graduated with a degree in chemistry and began working for General Electric. In a short time, from 1900 to 1906, Wright quickly progressed to Chief Chemist as he and his G.E. peers—including Thomas Edison and Charles Steinmetz—pioneered the age of electric motors, generators and transformers. Among Wright's responsibilities was the analysis of certain raw materials and rating the performance of varnishes made from the recipes he developed.

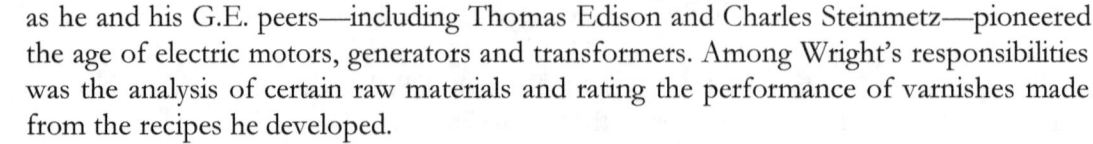

In 1903, based on his recommendations, G.E. funded the construction of a facility to manufacture insulating varnishes and compounds. As orders for G.E.'s electrical devices flooded in, their in-house varnish production could not sustain the demands placed upon it. George E. Emmons (Manager of the Lynn, Massachusetts G.E. works) and Howard Wright studied the problem. Emmons proposed that Wright set up a business to supply insulating varnish to the G.E. plants. In 1906 he left and started the Schenectady Varnish Company to manufacture versatile and economical electrical insulation materials, at Congress and Ninth Avenue. The company quickly became a success.

As the company grew and expanded to manufacture clear coat and agricultural varnishes, Howard began searching for the site of a new facility. He located a six-acre site in Schenectady on the main line of the New York Central Railroad. The first edifice on the present Schenectady plant site was built in 1907. By 1925, the original staff of three had grown to 50, and there were several prime accounts sustaining the business.

During this period, a method was discovered for applying a coating of the company's Schenectady Spar Varnish to the wire forming the coils of motors and transformers. The product worked exceptionally well, which eliminated the need for the bulky tape-wrapped wire formerly used, and permitted a large reduction in the size and weight of the electrical devices. Schenectady Spar Varnish became the industry standard for wire enamel.

In 1968 the W. Howard Wright Research Center opened on Balltown Road in Niskayuna.

He died at Ellis Hospital at age 84 and was considered the city's "Elder Citizen," a title bestowed on him by the Chamber of Commerce in 1950, due to his leadership in civil, charitable and business activities for nearly 50 years. When he died, his estate was worth $1,631,084.

Since 1968 Union College has had a W. Howard Wright Chemistry Scholarship for students from Saratoga, Schenectady and Warren counties that study chemistry. He was a Trustee of the college and Chairman of the executive committee, the building and grounds committee and Chairman of fund campaigns. He was one of the organizers of the Schenectady Chamber of Commerce in 1922, and served as the third President in 1925-26, and he had previously been a director of the Board of Trade. He was a Director of the Schenectady Trust Co., served on a local management committee of the Works Progress Administration, was a member of the Bureau of Municipal Research and a director of Ellis Hospital. He also was Chairman of the City Planning Commission from 1952-55, and a member since 1946. Was a member of the First Reformed Church. In 1950 the Mayor of Schenectady proclaimed "W. Howard Wright Day," for giving "unstintingly of his time and talents to make Schenectady a more prosperous industrial center and a finer place in which to live." He was a Trustee of the Children's Home Society. The Wright Foundation continues to provide charitable donations to many local non-profit agencies.

The company name was changed from Schenectady Varnish Works to Schenectady Chemical, then to Schenectady International, and since 2006 is simply called the SI Group.

He was married to Beula Deforest, the daughter of Mayor Henry Schmermerhorn DeForest. They lived at 1273 Stratford Road and had a summer home at 938 Charlton Road in Charlton, Saratoga County, since 1931. They had a son, Henry Deforest Wright, who lived at 1248 Lenox Road, and a daughter, Elva W. Miller. of 1164 Stratford Road. Another daughter, Lucie, died at age 5, and they had another daughter, Vivian. His son Henry, who succeeded him as President of SI Group, is also buried at Vale.

John B. Yates

October 18, 1833 - October 18, 1899
Location: S#9

John B. Yates was a distinguished officer and engineer during the Civil War. He was the son of Rev. John Austin Yates and was an 1852 graduate of Union College. He was married to Ellen Bell Yates (1842-1888), and they had three children: May (1862-1875); Sandy (1867-1875); and Annie (1869-1875).

He began his career as an axe man on the Utica & Schenectady Railroad, and then later was a rodman on the Detroit & Milwaukee. He enrolled in Company A of the First Michigan Engineers when the Civil War started, and was commissioned as Captain on September 12, 1861. He was promoted to Major on May 28, 1863, and Colonel on November 3, 1864.

His regiment was the main reliance for bridge building for Gen. Sherman during the march from Atlanta to the sea. Sherman later wrote to the War Department:

> *I well remember the First Michigan Engineers and its colonel Yates. That regiment had not only to make its marches with the army, but very often had to work breaking up railroads and building bridges all day and catch up at night. Its journal of operation during the campaign in Georgia and the Carolinas would illustrate the absolute limit of man for physical labor. I have sometimes reproached myself for cruelty in imposing, or allowing to be imposed on it, such hard and con-*

stant labor, and now desire to endorse this paper with an emphasis that will show that I was conscious of the fact. I will be much pleased if Col. Yates can be suitably rewarded for his past most valuable services.

William T. Sherman, commanding.

After the war, President Johnson appointed Col. Yates as Military Superintendent of Railroads for the State of Tennessee, a position he kept thorough the Reconstruction period. When he returned home to Schenectady, he was made Division Engineer for the Erie Canal. While there he came under investigation by Gov. Samuel Tilden for the "Erie Canal Ring," and retired from politics after that. He later worked on the engineering staff of the New York Central Railroad.

He died on October 19, 1899, in Amesburgh, Ontario, and was buried in Vale on October 23, 1899. He was working under contract in Canada with the U.S. Government on improvements along the St. Clair River.

Yates saw a lot of battle. Eyewitness accounts are included in <u>History of the Services of the First Regiment Michigan Engineers and Mechanics, During the Civil War, 1861-1865</u> (White Printing, 1921) by Charles Robert Sligh).

The ten companies under command of Yates was attached directly to Sherman headquarters on the march to Savannah, Georgia, often building bridges and laying pontoons. The regiment destroyed a vast amount of RR tack leading out of the city and assisted in constructing defense and fortification, and while under fire a dam in front of Savannah. On this memorable march, the regiment was required to keep pace with the movements of the army traveling over 20 miles a day and during the time was employed in tearing up RR track, twisting rails, burning bridges, repairing and making roads through marshes and building bridges. They left Atlanta on Nov 16 and arrive before Savannah Dec 11.

Nov 20th. [1864] Marched to near Eatonton factory. Went into camp for the first time since leaving Atlanta before dark. Major Yates called upon company commanders to enforce the orders against entering houses, pilfering and shooting without orders.

December 11th. Major Hannings, with Companies C, E, I, and B moved over to the Charleston & Savannah railroad.

After finishing the dam across the canal the balance of the regiment moved out from under fire and went into camp near General Sherman's headquarters. Since that time. until we reached Savannah. the regiment was employed in building 'corduroy' roads and destroying the railroads for several miles in the rear of our lines. On December 23d Major Yates and Captain Rhodes moved into the city with the right wing, followed by Major Hannings with the left wing on December 24, companies in the following order: A, E, D, I, B, G, H, K, F, C, Company A in front. We have very comfortable quarters in the suburbs of the city and the men are enjoying a good rest. The ever-active Major Yates has been everywhere present and an efficient commander.

Feb 12th. [1865] Four companies of left wing returned to Wooliston to report to General Davis for work on the railroad. Right wing moved to the north branch of Edisto River. The enemy threw shot and shell while we were at work on the bridge. Colonel Yates had a narrow escape, a piece of shot tearing a hole in the waist of his coat while examining the crossing. Worked during the night on the bridge.

March 19th. [Mingo Creek] Moved forward, repairing the road. About noon halted for rest and dinner, after which moved forward about two miles to where the 14th corps were engaged with the enemy. The action had been going on an hour or two, and was quite heavy. Soon after our arrival the enemy pressed the center of our line. Colonel Yates had been assigned a position on the left. While moving to the position assigned small crowds of pack animals, coming out of the woods, and from the front, seemed to indicate to an observe the likelihood of our repulse. The Colonel, with the companies of his command then with him, advanced towards the woods in line of battle to bear a part with the infantry in holding the ground. While doing this the movement of infantry in front and on the right with the accompanying noise of battle seemed to show that the enemy would soon be upon them. The Colonel following the movements of infantry on his right took a better position. Then facing the enemy he ordered the men, who had been provided with shovels from our tool wagons, to throw up hastily a temporary earthwork in their front. They worked lively. At the same time it was reported that the enemy were massing on our left. Colonel Yates exhorted his men to stand form, but saying "We will whip the rebels." The men stood form and kept in line. After the enemy had been checked and the troops deployed in front, we moved to our position on the left, where a very strong line o works were soon thrown up. The action from this time (5:30 P.M.) until dark was very heavy indeed, The rebels, massed in front, made several charges to take our battery, holding on desperately for half an hour, during which time the guns poured in grape canister, shot and shell. The noise occasioned by the incessant rattle of musketry, mingled with the loud, sharped crackling of artillery and the dense smoke made it for a time on the sharpest battles of the war.

Colonel Yates, in over four years of service, was never sick or absent from his command a single day until after the surrender of Johnson to Sherman, when he was granted a thirty day furlough.

Christopher Yates

July 8, 1737 - September 1, 1785
Location: S#8

The following information is from A History of Schenectady During the Revolution (E. L. Hildreth & Co., 1916) by Willis T. Hanson, Jr.

Christopher Yates.

Christopher Yates was born at the old homestead in Alplaus, New York, the son of Joseph Yates and Eva Fonda. During the American Revolution he lived in the house he built, now at 26 Front Street in Schenectady (see the photograph on the next page). In this house was born his son, Joseph C., first Mayor of Schenectady (1798) and Governor of New York State (1823-1824).

Christopher Yates was a surveyor by profession and "one of the best informed and most efficient patriots in the Mohawk Valley." On May 6, 1775, he was elected a member of the first Committee of Safety, and at the first meeting on the 9th was chosen Chairman. On May 24 he was appointed one of a committee to go to Guy Park to deliver an answer to a speech made by the Mohawk Indians. On June 30 he was appointed by the Provincial Congress one of a committee to determine the ranks of the various officers serving in the New York regiments. On July 26 a letter was addressed to him by the Committee asking whether or not he had resigned, and on August 9 he tendered his resignation. On November 7 he was elected a member of the second Committee of Safety, and on December 29, was appointed Deputy Clerk.

On January 13, 1776, he was appointed Lieutenant Colonel of the Second Albany County Militia, and on March 5, Henry Glen was instructed to apply to Congress for his commission. On May 7, 1776, he was elected a member of the third Committee of Safety. From the fall of 1776 to July 8, 1777, he was in command when detachments of the regiment were on duty at Fort Ann. It is claimed that about this time Yates served on the staff of General Schuyler as a Deputy Quartermaster-general, and that he was afterwards promoted to the rank of Colonel. The evidence to support this claim is contained in letters from General Schuyler, Benedict Arnold, Governor Morgan Lewis, etc., which were at one time in the possession of Judge A.A. Yates of Schenectady. No evidence of this detail and appointment is to be found on the regimental rolls.

After the evacuation of Fort Ann (July 8) he had command of a body of Schenectady militia engaged in felling trees to stop the progress of General Burgoyne's army. He served throughout the campaign, and with General Arnold selected the American position at Bemis Heights. On October 19 he was appointed by the State Committee of Safety one of a committee to repair to Albany to confer with General Philip Schuyler regarding means for checking the advance of the enemy on the northern and western frontiers. He served during the rest of the war in the Quartermaster's Department as a deputy, for most of the time stationed at Saratoga. In June 1779, he was engaged in forwarding the baggage of General Clinton's brigade.

Yates was the first Master of St. George's Lodge No. 6, F. & A.M. (1774-76).

His wife was Jannetje Bradt (August 28, 1743 - March 17, 1823) and they had the following children: Helena Yates Bonett (November 16, 1766 -1819); Eva Christoffel (February 14, 1762 - February 22, 1801); Elisabeth Bradt (May 7, 1763 - January 23, 1824); Joseph Christopher (November 9, 1768 - Mar 19, 1837); Henry Christopher (October 7, 1770 - Mar 20, 1854); Andreas Christoffeise (born January 17, 1773); Annatje (born Mar 12,

1775); Giles (born April 1, 1781); Johannes Barentse (born February 1, 1784); and Jellis Fonda. His wife is buried next to him.

Home of Christopher Yates at 26 Front Street in Schenectady's Stockade neighborhood.

James W. Yelverton

May 16, 1869 - 1949
Location: M 97

James Walker Yelverton was born in Schenectady and was the eldest son of Thomas Yelverton (c.1845-1888), and Leah Little (Walker) Yelverton (1845-1899). He was educated at the Union Classical Institute (now the Stockade Inn) in 1886.

After graduation he worked in the Schenectady County Clerk's office and was appointed Deputy County Clerk, which he held for eleven years. On December 28, 1896, he was appointed by Gov. Levi P. Mortonas as Treasurer of Schenectady County, to fill the vacancy caused by the death of John G.L. Ackerman. He was elected in 1901 and held the position until 1904. He did not run again as he decided to manage his personal affairs.

On November 30, 1901, he married Mary Cochran (Ellis) Veeder (1864-1938), and they had a daughter, Ruth Ellis Yelverton (born March 30, 1903). Mary Ellis was the daughter of Charles G. Ellis (1842-1891), owner of the Schenectady Locomotive Works from 1878 until his death. She had been married to Harmon W. Veeder, who died in 1900, and had a daughter from her first marriage, Mary Elizabeth Ellis Veeder (born 1898).

Yelverton was a Republican member of theNew York State Senate from 1917 to 1920, sitting in the 140th and 141st sessions (31st District), and 142nd and 143rd New York State Legislatures (32nd District).

Yelverton was Director, Vice President and later Chairman of the Board of Citizens Trust of Schenectady. He also was a trustee of the Schenectady Hospital Association, trustee of the First Presbyterian Church, trustee of Vale Cemetery Association, member of the Exempt Fireman's Association and a member of the Schenectady Lodge No. 480, B.P.O.E. He was also a member of the Mohawk Club and the Mohawk Golf Club of Schenectady, and of the leading fraternal and social organizations of the city, including the County Historical Society.

Linda Boyer from the Grand Rapids, Michigan area had a copy of a diary of his that was in code. After years of trying to decipher the code, it was decoded by a professor and was determined to be a Masonic Memory Jogger. It was the rituals used by the Masons and each letter represented a word. The rituals were secret and members were required to memorize them, and this was used literally to jog his memory.

In 1915, when plans were being made to develop Riverside Park in the Stockade, he led an effort, along with 67 other people, to prevent it from being used for "play grounds, baseball and other like sports." citing it would "endanger the public, cause property damage, and in general would be a nuisance to the residents of the city." They lost.

William H. Young

April 22, 1824 - October 31, 1876
Location: U#126

William Henry Young was born in England and lived there until around the age of 12, and then resided in Schenectady. He was married to Anna Alida Barhydt (1825-1889). They had two children, David (?-1835) and Harriet (?-1850).

William enrolled into the 18th New York Infantry on May 14, 1861 at Albany, New York. He was mustered in as Lieutenant Colonel on May 17, 1861. When Col. William A. Jackson, also buried at Vale, died of disease on November 11, 1861, Young was made Colonel of the 18th New York Infantry and took over at the first Battle of Bull Run. Young resigned his position on August 14, 1862.

The following is taken from *The Union Army: A History of Military Affairs in the Loyal States, 1861-65* (Federal Pub. Co., 1908, vol. II).

Mustered in: May 17, 1861
Mustered out: May 28, 1863

Muster-in Roll of Captain M. H. Donovan's Company B Company in the 18th Regiment, (5th Brigade) of New York State Volunteers, commanded by Colonel William H. Young, called into the service of the United States by Proclamation of the Governor, from the 17th day of May, 1861, (date of this muster) for the term of two years, unless sooner discharged.

Eighteenth Infantry. —Cols. William A. Jackson, William H. Young, George R. Myers; Lieut.-Cols., William .H. Young, George R. Myers, John C. Maginnis; Majs., George R. Myers, John C. Maginnis, William S. Gridley. The 18th, the "New York State Rifles," was composed of two companies from Schenectady, four from Albany, one from Dutchess County, one from Orange county one from Ontario County and one from St. Lawrence county. It was mustered into the U.S. service at Albany, May 17, 1861, for a period of two years, and left the state for Washington on June 18, after a month in camp near Albany. Camp on Meridian hill was occupied until July 12, when the regiment was ordered to Alexandria and became a part of the 2nd brigade, 5th division, Army of Northeastern Virginia. It advanced with the army to Manassas, encountered the enemy on the Braddock road, at Fairfax Station and Blackburn's ford, and participated in the Bull Run battle as support for artillery. It was then withdrawn to Alexandria; on Aug. 4, was assigned to Franklin's brigade, later commanded by Gen. Newton; and then went into camp near Fairfax seminary, where the construction of Fort Ward occupied the troops. On March 10, 1862, the regiment was ordered to Fairfax Court House, but immediately returned to camp, and in April, with the 3d brigade, 1st division, 6th corps, Army of the Potomac, moved to Bristoe Station. Again the regiment was ordered to return to camp and it finally reached Yorktown at the time of its evacuation by the Confederate forces. It was active at West Point and in the Seven Days' battles, its loss being heaviest in the battle of Games' mill. It was then stationed at Harrison's landing until Aug. 15, when it was ordered to Newport News and on the 24th reached Alexandria. It was engaged at Crampton's gap, Antietam and Fredericksburg, after which it went into camp near Falmouth, until called upon to participate in the "Mud March" and in the Chancellorsville campaign. At Marye's heights and Salem Church the 18th was closely engaged and lost heavily. This was the last battle of the regiment, which was soon after ordered home and was mustered out at Albany, May 28, 1863, the three years men being assigned to the 121st N. Y. The death loss during service was 39 from wounds and 36 from other causes.

Muster-in Roll of Recruits for (B) Company, in the 18th Regiment, (5th Brigade) of New York State Volunteers, commanded by Colonel William H. Young, called into the service of the United States by ——— from the 26th day of December, 1861, (date of this muster) for the unexpired term of two years, unless sooner discharged.

When he returned he became Superintendent of the Moulders department at Rathbone, Bard Stove Company in Albany, where he and his family lived at 928 Broadway. On June 20, 1865, the Schenctady City Artillery presented Young with a regulation sword and sheath that was very heavily overlaid with gold. Schenectady had a parade that day in his honor.

On October 31, 1876, he was thrown from a horse while attending a Republican campaign parade on Lark Street, just south of Washington Avenue in Albany. Some kids threw a pack of lighted firecrackers in front of his horse. With the sound of the firecrackers, the frightened horse suddenly reared into the air, plunged forward, and threw William. His head struck the curbstone and crushed his skull. He was over 200 pounds and the force was deadly. He was brought into the Charles H. Gaus drug store, at the corner of Washington Avenue and Lark Street, for medical aid. He complained minutes before that he had a spirited horse and was afraid it would kill someone before the parade was over. He was right. The horse had a bad reputation and they were suppose to change it but didn't. William was unconscious and only lived ten minutes until he died. He was only 53 years old.

The Nov 2, 1876 *Saratoga Sentinel* reported it like this:

A Disastrous Demonstration

Tuesday evening there was a mammoth Republican demonstration in Albany, clubs with torches being present from all directions to make an overpowering show. While the march was in progress, Col William H. Young, who had passed through all the perils of the rebellion without harm, was thrown from his horse and killed. He was acting, as one of the aids to the grand marshal, and his horse was frighten by a bunch of power crackers. The Saratoga Starin Guards and colored club from this village were in the parade, leaving here on the 6 o'clock train for that purpose. By some neglect of the managers, provision was not made to take all the members of Capt. Van Dyles' colored club, and the result was that those who were left had a parade of their own, ending with a democratic address at a saloon on Lake Avenue.

It was reported in the *New York Tribune* on November 5 that "The procession at the funeral of the late Col. William H. Young yesterday was the largest ever witnessed in this city." He was buried on the 4th with military honors.

The newspapers also reported the two following resolutions.

At the Lew Benedict Post No. 5 GAR last evening, the following preamble and resolutions were adopted:

Whereas, We are met together at the announcement of the sudden death of our worthy comrade, William H. Young; and

Whereas, We place his name upon the record of "Loss by Death" with feelings of sadness more profound that has ever come to us since our organization, we deem it is just tribute to his memory to give expression to the sentiments of love and esteem which every member of this post entertained towards him because of his nobleness of character and kind brother manner; therefore.

Resolved, That by the death of Comrade William H. Young this organization has lost one of its worthiest members and great friends of whom it is truly said "None knew him but to love him some? him but to praise" and although his many qualities were known and acknowledged by all with whom he came in contact, yet to us, his comrades, those qualities, no high above the average of his fellow man, were exhibited in so marked a manner that our hearts were knit to his as the hearts of David and Jonathan were knit together. In all our undertakings there was none among us more ready to answer a summons to duty, no heart more thoroughly in sympathy with the cause for which we labor, or hand more cheerfully extended in rendering needed assistance than his. His acts will never pass from our recollections while his shall last.

Resolved, That in this hours of woe and deep anguish which has come upon the loving wife and children of our late comrade, we extend them our warmest sympathy, and trust they may had comfort in the knowledge that he, having "fought the good fight" and having "Kept the faith," has entered into "the seat which remaineth for the people of God."

Resolved, that a copy of this action be transmitted to the family of the deceased properly certified by the officers of the Post.

O. Smith, Commander

Wm. P. Barker, Adjutant

In Memoriam

At a meeting of the employees of Rathbone, Sard & Co stove works, held at the foundry the occasion being the death of the lamented William H. Young, the following preamble and resolution were drawn up and adopted:

Whereas, it please an all wise Providence, in His own inscrutable ways, to suddenly removed from our midst one whom we revered and respected, one whom we loved and esteemed throughout the whole period of his connection with us our late foreman, Col William H Young; sad, though bowing in submission to the decree of the Almighty, we yet cannot forbear to testify to the worth and sterling merit of the decease; therefore be it

Resolved, That we tender our heartfelt sympathy to his bereaved wife and children, who mourn the loss of a fond and generous husband and parent, who in their now desolate home weep over the remain of one whom they loved so dearly, Novel, hearty and true, he ever lend a ready ear to a tale of distress, ever opened his charitable heart to its appeals. None feared to unbosom themselves to him, knowing well his generous nature, that his counsel, advice and mean were ever within reach to comfort and succor the needy and afflicted. That we, during the time of our intercourse with him have never cease to regard him but with feelings respect and affection That, bound as we are by ties that could not be severed on earth, we can but inadequately express our sorrow and regret for his untimely demise. Words fail to show forth our regard for him, language seems but tame when we wish to breathe our sorrow and affection. Upright as honestly itself; assiduous and watchful in the interest of his employers; open and fair in all his dealing, and never swerving from the path of duty, he won golden opinions from all, and leaves a blank, deep void, that time cannot fill. A gallant solder, he fought in defense of his country's flag in her hour of distress, nobly periling his life in her service. A good and fervent Christian, his charities and benefactions live after him, bright memorials of his true zeal and constancy in the holy cause of religion. That in him we have lost one to whom we looked for years as an adviser; to whom we confided all our troubles, sure of relief; who never betrayed a trust, but always proved worthy of the confidence reposed in him; one, in whom were centered all the qualities that can make a noble honest and brave man. Christian, soldier, citizen and friend, we deeply mourn our loss, and when years have passed and time may have obliterated many recollections of former days, his memory will live in our hearts fresh and green, his deeds be remember and his name revered.

That we tender these resolutions to his afflicted family, trusting that our word may cheer their heart and were in some matter as a balm for their wounded souls.

That we attend his funeral in a body on Saturday next and by our untied numbers, together with our brother moulders through the city; show not only our own appreciation, but the widespread recognition of his sterling worth in life and the immeasurable regret for his lamented decease.

John J O' Neill,
George Dowaland
James Redfern
Richard Stack
William A Dillon
Michael J McDonald
George Calhoun
Alfred E Dewing
Patrick Grimes
William Dwyer
James Judge-advocate James E Zeilman
Joseph Whalen,

Committee
Albany Nov 2 1876

His headstone was erected by Rathbone Stove Company and business associates.

He was member of Master's Lodge No. 5 F. & A.M. (Albany) and Albany Masonic Relief Associations, as well as a member of the Grace Methodist Episcopal Church, and was on the board of the church.

Monument of Col. William H. Young at Vale.

Appendix 2: General Electric Employees in *The Vale*

This is a partial list of notable General Electric employees buried in Vale Cemetery.

Name	Born	Died	Name	Born	Died
Acosta, William	1881	1961	Newell, Charles	1877	1953
Banker, Louis	1866	1954	Nickle, Clifford	1896	1942
Bartlett, Chester	1881	1953	Norris, William	1890	1967
Broderick, John	1868	1947	Owen, William	1881	1955
Bruce, Robert	1896	1937	Packer, Arthur	1884	1944
Butterfield, Jay	1887	1960	Page, Harry	1881	1959
Cermak, Charles	1885	1956	Parker, Harry	1884	1961
Chambers, Calvin	1869	1942	Peck, Darius	1880	1945
Coulson, Bernard	1877	1964	Peterson, Charles	1867	1944
Day, Winlerton	1872	1951	Plenge, Hervey	1890	1943
Edwards, William	1886	1967	Powell, Earl	1870	1934
Ellis, Ray	1890	1967	Price, Edgar	1875	1958
Erben, Henry	1899	1956	Ratcliff, Bessie	1884	1959
Fabrey, Walter	1879	1950	Reeves, Thomas	1901	1939
Ford, John	1880	1940	Rogers, Glenn	1899	1961
Gandy, Theodore	1882	1952	Rowan, Albert	1873	1937
Hagin, James	1883	1960	Salmonson, Valdemar	1869	1930
Hambly, William	1885	1946	Schiller, Lawrence	1880	1952
Harbison, Charles	1871	1954	Schneider, Henry	1871	1935
Hardman, William	1888	1956	Scudder, Hewlet	1877	1942
Haughton, Frank	1871	1958	Seabolt, Frank	1890	1954
Henningsen, Sophos	1864	1935	Shanklin, George	1889	1961
Hinckle, Leonard	1895	1953	Sheldon, Lucian	1882	1960
Howell, Jesse	1885	1951	Smith, Arthur	1880	1952
Huffmire, Aron	1872	1941	Smith, George	1880	1945
Hull, Edwin	1903	1964	Steenstrup, Christian	1874	1955
Hull, Fred	1886	1931	Summerhayes, Harry	1875	1963
Jackson, Allan	1865	1911	Taylor, William	1884	1927
Jacobs, Harry	1885	1961	Terpening, Earl	1895	1936
Jones, Seth	1885	1955	Taylor, George	1879	1927
Junggren, Oscar	1865	1935	Taylor, John	1876	1941
Knight, Webster	1874	1933	Troy, Matthew	1874	1944
Knowlton, Edgar	1872	1937	Trumbull, Ralph	1887	1934
Kuhn, Howard	1888	1938	Vrooman, David	1870	1954
Link, Henry	1878	1959	Wright, David	1887	1953
Madgett, John	1864	1947	Yates, William	1879	1950
Meyers, Chauncey	1892	1951	Zerbey, William	1887	1935
Mure, Robert	1878	1950	Weaver, Carris	1881	1953
Murray, Robert	1869	1936	Wiesner, Carl	1874	1962
McCollom, Daniel	1866	1949			

Appendix 3: Burials in the Union College Plot

Local historian Frank Taormina, a 1950 graduate of Union, compiled this list of the residents and they are included here with his permission.

Name	Died	Plot	Notes
Aiken, Maud Ripton	1934	X17:17	Daughter of Benjamin Ripton, wife of John Benjamin
Ashmore, Sidney Gillespie	1911	X38:38	Professor of Latin for 30 years
Ashmore, Betsey Howard	1962	X38:38	Daughter of Sidney Ashmore
Bahnuk, Olga Lee Iwanik	1993	X39F	Wife of John Iwanik
Benedict, Julia Jackson	1925	X10:10.2	Wife of Samuel T. Benedict, daughter of Isaac Jackson
Benedict, Samuel T.	1933	X10:10.2	Husband of Julia Jackson Benedict, son-in-law of Isaac Jackson
Bennett, John Ira	1920	X37.37	Professor of Greek for 25 years
Bennett, Lydia Kate	1909	X37.37	Wife of John Ira Bennett
Bennett, William Whipple	1963	X56A	Professor of Economics; urn, disinterred 10/6/78
Berdan, David	1827	XST5	Class of 1821
Blodgett, William Allen	1973	X43:C	Son of Professor Harold Blodgett
Blodgett, Harold		X43:C	Professor of English
Blodgett, Mrs. Harold		X43:C	Wife of Harold Blodgett
Butzel, Henry	1988	X31B	Interred 4/13/88
Chittenden Sr., Rev. Alanson	1853	XXST2	Father of student
Chittenden, Alanson	1852	XST2	Graduated from Union 1852
Clark, Leonard B.	1986	X32C	Professor Emeritus, Biology
Clark, Averill		X32D	Wife of Leonard Clark
Clinton, DeWitt	1924	X37A	Union College Librarian, 1907-1922
Coffin, Harrison			Professor
Coffin, Mrs. Harrison			Wife of Harrison Coffin
Cotton, Maria Louise	1882	X19:19	Daughter of Clarkson Nott Potter
Cotton, Marlette	1949	X10	Daughter of Samuel T. Benedict, granddaughter of Isaac Jackson
Cummins, Earl Everett	1938	X56A:56.5	Professor of Economics, 1931-1938
Dale, Ernest	1972	X43:E	Professor of Biology 1929-1953; Urn
Davidson, Capitola	1969		Wife of President Davidson
Davidson, Carter	1965	X32:A	President of Union, 1946-1965
Dewey, Hartley Frederic	1945	X36:36	Assistant Treasurer, 1908-1931
Dewey, Jennie Greaves	1946	X36:36	Wife of Hartley F. Dewey
Dewey, Ellen	1972	X36:36	Daughter of Hartley and Jennie Dewey
Dewey, Jean P	1989	X36E	Interred in urn
Dewey, Leland G.	1990	X36E	Interred in urn
Doty, Joseph	1980	X43:D	Retired Professor of History
Ellery, Adelaide True	1936	X27A	Wife of Dr. Edward Ellery
Ellery, Edward	1961	X27A	Professor of Chemistry, 1904-1940; 1919-1938; Dean of Faculty; Acting President, 1933-1934
Ely, Esther	1954	X16	Secretary to Dean, Recorder and Registrar, 1909-1933
Farrar, Joseph H.	1836	XST5	Student, Class of 1839
Ferguson, Mrs. Samuel	1943	X18:18	Ellen Margaret Price Ferguson, only daughter of Professor Isiah Price
Fish, Olivia	1886	X9:9	Friend of Mrs. Eliphalet Nott and Mr. Isaac Jackson
Fish, Fannie			Friend of Mrs. Samuel Benedict, no marker
Foster, John	1897	X12:12	Class of 1835; Professor of Natural Philosophy 1839-1897
Foster, Mary Augusta	1919	X12:12	Second wife of John Foster
Fox, Augustus	1975	X44B	Professor of Mathematics, 1929-1965
Garis, Charles F.F.	1957	X34A	Professor of Mathematics, 1903-1919; Dean of the College, 1919-1947

Appendix 3: Burials in the Union College Plot

Garis, Rose Lansing	1958	X34B	Wife of Charles F. Garis
Grover, Betsey Tebbets	1959	X34C	Wife of Professor Frederick W. Grover
Grover, Frederick W.	1973	X34D	Professor of Electrical Engineering, 1920-1946
Hainebach, Hans	1966	X39	Professor of German & French, 1948-1966
Hinman, Nelson H.	1832	XST3	Class of 1832; died of Consumption while still a student
Hale Jr., Edward Everett	1932	X8	Professor of Rhetoric & Logic, 1895-1903; English, 1903-1932; Urn
Hale, Rose Perkins	1963	X8	Wife of Professor Edward Hale, daughter of Maurice Perkins and Ann D Perkins; Urn.
Hoffman, Robert	1961	X17	Son of Professor Thomas E. Hoffman
Hollis, Barbara Piessner	1892	X4:4.2	Daughter of Margaret Lewis and Elias Piessner, granddaughter of Tayler Lewis
Hughes, John Wilbur Jr.	1905	X13:13	Infant son of Assistant Professor Hughes, CE
Hull, Meeker	1835	XST3	Student? Class of 1838, died at age 25?
Iwanik, John	1976	X39E	Professor of Foreign Languages
Jackson, Elizabeth Pomeroy	1882	X10:10.4	
Jackson, George P.	1882	X10:10.1	
Jackson, Gertrude	1864	X10:10.1	
Jackson, Isaac W.	1877	X10:10.4	Professor of Mathematics for 50 years; founder of Jackson's Gardens
Jackson, Phebe	1859	X10:10.3	
Jackson, William A (Colonel)	1861	X10-10.6	Col. 18th infantry Regt., died of illness in Washington D.C. after Bull Run
Jagu, Fernand	1939	X42A	Professor of French for 15 years
Jones, Leonard Chester	1933	X55A	Professor of History, 1921-1933
Jones, Paul S.	1953	X38	Professor of French, German and Spanish
Jones, Yvonne C.		X55B	Wife of Leonard Jones; cremation, no stats
Kellogg, George Dwight	1955	X26	Professor of Latin, 1911-1942; Chairman of Department of Ancient Languages
Kellogg, Mary Collins	1961	X26	Wife of George D. Kellogg
Ketz, Wilford	1991	X45B	Director of Athletics
Ketz, Mabel F.	1988	X45A	Wife of Bill Ketz; interred 12/6/88
Klemm, Edward I	1956	X37A	Son of Professor Frederick Klemm, age two and one half at his death
Landreth, Helen	1981	X23:23	Daughter of Professor Olin Landreth
Lamoreaux, Mary Sharratt	1914	X19:19	Wife of Professor Wendell Lamoreaux
Lamoreaux, Wendell	1907	X19:19	Professor, then Librarian, 1849-1897
Landreth, Eliza Taylor	1917	X23:23	Wife of Olon H. Landreth
Landreth, Henry Olon	1931	X23:23	Professor of Civil Engineering, 1894-1919
Landreth, James T.	1920	X23:23	
Landreth, William T.	1927	X23:23	
Lawrence, Elizabeth Jackson	19225	X10:10	Wife of Col. Samuel Betts Lawrence; daughter of Isaac Jackson
Lawrence, Col. Samuel Betts	1908	X10:10.	Son-in-law of Isaac Jackson
Lewis, Edward Smith	1908	X20:20	Son of Charles F. Lewis
Lewis, Charles F.	1905	X20:20	Son of Professor Tayler Lewis; Civil War Veteran
Lewis, Katherine Smith	1933	X20:20	Wife of Charles F. Lewis
Lewis, Jayne Keziah Payn	1888	X4:4.3	Wife of Professor Tayler Lewis
Lewis, Tayler	1877	X4:4.3	Professor of Greek & Oriental Languages, 1849-1877
Lewis, Tayler, Jr.	1879	X4.4	Son of Professor Tayler Lewis; Civil War Veteran
Ligon, Lois	1972	X45C	Wife of Professor Ernst Ligon
Ligon, Ernst	1984	X45D	Professor of Psychology; Director of Character Research Project, 1929-1962
Magoun, Mary Pearson	1860	X1:1.1	Sister of Professor Jonathan Pearson
Magoun, Stephen L.	1883	X1:1.1	Brother-in-law of Jonathan Pearson
Maras, Joseph T.	1990	X52C	Football Coach; Director of Financial Aid for Students

Name	Year	Plot	Description
Maras, Mildred			Wife of Joseph Maras
March, John L.	1952	X27	
March, Ms. Mildred	1959	X27	Sister of Professor John March
McCombs, Charles Esseltyn	1949	X57	Union Alumnus, Class of 1904; Urn
McCombs, Alice Losea	1951	X57	Wife of Charles E. McCombs
McIlwaine, Theodore	1970	X52	Comptroller; Business Manager, 1939-1970
McKean, Elizabeth Bergfels	1944	X35A	Wife of Professor H.G. McKean
McKean, Horace Grant	1929	X35A	Professor of Rhetoric & Public Speaking, 1905-1926
McNutt, William Allen	1960	X42	Student, Class of 1963
Morrison, Charles N.	1988	X46C	Interred 4/13/88
Morse, David Sherman	1969	X34	Marie Louise Bailey Professor of Mathematics, 1924-1958
Morse, Nellie	1976	X33A	Widow of David S. Morse
Nelson, Marjorie S.	1965	55F	Wife of Professor Alan Nelson (1954-)
Newland, Robert Proudfit	1846	Plot 2:02	Probably grandson of Professor Proudfit
Niemeyer, Adelaide	1975	44C	Mother of Professor Carl Niemeyer
Niemeyer, Carl	1993	44D	
Nott, Eliphalet	1886	Plot 15:15	President of Union, 1804-1866
Nott, Sally Benedict	1804	Plot 05:15.2	First Wife of President Nott
Nott, Gertrude Peebles	1841	Plot 05:15.0	Second wife of President Nott
Nott, John	1878	Plot 5:15.1	Son of President Nott
Nott, Urania Sheldon	1886	Plot 15:15.3	Third Wife of President Nott
Nott, Eliphalet, Jr.	1901	Plot 15:15.1	Son of President Nott
Nott, Mary Ann Lawrence	1911	Plot 5:15.0	Wife of Rev. John Nott
Packard, Alphonsus E.	1854	ST 4	Student, Class of 1854
Pearson, Caleb	1866	X1:1.2	Father of Jonathan Pearson
Pearson, Henry H.	1858	X1,1	Son of Jonathan Pearson (death by drowning)
Pearson, Hetty Libby	1880	X1:1.2	Mother of Jonathan Pearson
Pearson, Jonathan	1887	X1:1.3	Jonathan Pearson, author of the diaries, Professor at Union
Pearson, Mary Hosford	1885	X1:1.3	Wife of Jonathan Pearson
Pearson, William Libbey, MD	1931	X1.1	Son of Jonathan Pearson, Class of 1868
Pearson, Eleanor	1978	X	Wife of Jonathan Pearson III
Pearson, Jonathan III	1991		Director of Admissions, 1950-1970; Director of Alumni Relations
Peissner, Margaret Lewis	1904	X4:4.1	Daughter of Professor Talyer Lewis; College Registrar; Wife of Professor Elias Piessner
Perkins, Annie Dunbar	1922	X8.8	Wife of Professor Maurice Perkins; lived on campus for 47 years
Perkins, Maurice	1901	X8.8	Professor of Chemistry, 36 years; came to Union in 1863; Hon. M.D. Albany Med, 1871
Piessner, Tayler Lewis	1895	X4:4.1	Son of Margaret & Elias Piessner; grandson of Tayler Lewis
Potter, Annie	1842	X15:15	Niece of Alonzo Potter; grandniece of Dr. E. Nott
Potter, Clarkson Nott	1882	X14:14	Son of Alonzo Potter; grandson of Dr. E. Nott
Potter, Sarah Nott	1839	15:!5.2	First wife of Alonzo Potter; only daughter of Eliphalet Nott & Sally Benedict Nott
Potter, Virginia Mitchell	1890	X14:14	Wife of Clarkson Nott Potter
Powell, Jacob A.	1828	ST1	James Augustus Powell, student, Class of 1828
Price, Isiah B.	1884	X18:18	Professor of Mathematics, 1877-1884
Price, Ellen Morton	1945	X18:18	Wife of Isiah Price
Proudfit, Eliza	1876	X2:2	Daughter of Professor Proudfit
Proudfit, Elizabeth Law	1853	X2:2	Wife of Professor Proudfit
Proudfit, Robert	1860	X2:2	Professor of Greek & Latin, 1818-1849; Professor Emeritus until 1860
Ripton, Benjamin Henry	1936	X17:17	Dean, 1899-1919
Ripton, Franeena Nare	1915	X17:17	Wife of Professor Ripton
Rotundo, Joseph	1953	X56A	Professor of Economics & Government, 1929-1953

Name	Year	Plot	Description
Sayre, Mortimer F.	1973	XC33A	Professor of Applied Mechanics
Sayre, Grace	1971	X33B	Wife of Mortimer Sayre
Schauffler, June Van Holland	1927	X41A	Professor First wife of Henry Schauffler, Professor of CE, 1919-1934
Schauffler, George William	1940	X42	Son of Henry & Margurite Williams Schauffler
Schauffler, Mary Reynolds		X42	Daughter of Henry & Jane Schauffler
Schauffler, Alfred H.	1962	X41A	Son of Henry & Jane V. Schauffler; Urn?
Schoppe, Amelia	1858	ST4	Most prolific German author of her day; friend of Mrs. Urania Nott
Schwarz, Winifred M.	1984	X31B	Professor of Physics
Schwarrz, Jeanne M.		X31A	Wife of Professor Winfred Schwarz
Schwarz, Theodore G.	1987	X46B	Associate Professor of Electrical Engineering
Schwarz, Louise F.	1991	X20	Wife of Professor Theodore Swarz
Seede, John A.	1954	X20	Husband of Jane Lewis Seede
Seede, Jane Lewis	1955	X20	Daughter of Charles F. Lewis, Class of 1864; granddaughter of Tayler Lewis?
Stanley, Philip	1963	X56	Professor of Philosophy, 1927-1957; Urn?
Stanton, Benjamin	1878	X5:5	Principal of Union Classical Institute; Professor of Latin, 1854-1905
Stanton, Catherine Coffin	1903	X5:5	Wife of Benjamin Stanton
Stanton, Horace C.	1926	X5:5	Probably son of Professor Benjamin Stanton
Stoller, James Hugh	1955	X28:28	Instructor & Professor of Natural Sciences, 1854-1925
Stoller, Mary Montgomery	1945	X28:28	Wife of Professor James Stoller
Stone, Ruth		X32E	
Taylor, Amy	1968	X33	Widow of Professor Warren C. Taylor
Tidmarch, Charles M.	1993	X38F	Professor of Political Science, 1970-1993
Tolan, Heather P.	1961	X55C	Daughter of Mr. & Mrs. Edwin K. Tolan, Librarian (1962-)
Truax, James Lowell	1894	X7.7	Son of Professor Truax
Truax, James Reagles	1915	X7.7	Professor of English, 1885-1903
Truax, Harriet Watson	1954	X7.7	Wife of Professor James R. Truax
Vedder, John N.V.	1936	X56:56	Professor of Thermodynamics & Mechanics, 23 years
Vedder, Harriet Booth	1958		Wife of Prof John N.V. Vedder; Urn
Webb, Helmer	1970	X43A	Librarian, 1936-1962; Urn
Webb, Mae P.	1988	X43B	
Webster, Isabella McKechnie	1882	X29:29	Wife of President Webster
Webster, Harrison E.	1906	X29:29	Class of 1868; Professor 1869-1883; President 1888-1894
Webster, Jessie R.	1896	X29:29	
Wells, Alice M.	1930	X16:16	Daughter of Professor Wells; gave Wells House to College
Wells, William	1907	X16:16	Professor of Modern Languages, 1865-1907
Wells, Alice Yeckle	1906	X`16:16	Wife of Professor William Wells
Whitehorn, Arthur M.	1869	X3:3.1	Son of Professor Whitehorn
Whitehorn, Matilda Cooper	1888	X3:3.1	
Whitehorn, Henry	1901	X3:3.1	Professor of Greek, 1868-1901
Williams, Clinton	1975	X53F	Professor Emeritus of Engineering Drawing; retired in 1973
Wold, Peter Irving	1945	X13.6	Professor of Physics, 1920-1945
Wold, Mary	1967	X13C	Wife of Peter Wold
Woo, William		X44E	Professor Emeritus, Chinese
Woo, Mrs. William			Wife of Professor William Woo
Wright, Florence Margaret	1907	X21:21	Daughter of Professor Wright
Wright, Margaret Hood	1916	X21:21	Wife of Professor Wright
Wright, Thomas Wallace	1908	X21:21	Professor of Math & Physics, 1885-1905
Yates, Heniretta Cobb	1842	X35:35	Wife of Professor John Austin Yates
Yates, John Austin	1849	X35:35	Professor of Oriental Languages, 1829-1849

Appendix 4: Vegetation Planted in Vale Cemetery

The eastern most section of Vale, Section N, that was developed after 1884, was landscaped and planted with trees and shrubs. The following typed lists, author unknown, contain all the species planted throughout the section, with the exceptions of areas CN, HN and IN.

The variety of trees and landscaping bring an intended feeling of peace and serenity the moment you enter Vale Cemetery. (Courtesy of Richard Vang.)

Strategic plantings provide for interesting settings at The Vale. (Courtesy of Richard Vang.)

Appendix 4: Vegetation Planted in Vale Cemetery

PLANTING LIST,

VALE CEMETERY, SCHENECTADY N. Y.

SECTION A N.

TREES

SCIENTIFIC NAME COMMON NAME,	ABV.	HGT OF TREE	HGT OF TRUNK	CAL. IN INCHES	BB or R	DIAM Of BALL	SPR OF ROOT	QUAN.
Cornus mas Cornelian Cherry,	Cm	7'-8'	3'	1½"	BB	24"	—	3
Prunus serrulata Oriental Cherry (Var. Kwanzan)	Pk	8'-10'	4'	2"	BB	24"	—	2

SHRUBS

SCIENTIFIC NAME, COMMON NAME	No. of CANES	HEIGHT IN FEET,	B.B. or R	SPREAD OF ROOTS,	ABV.	QUANTITY
Rosa hugonis Hugonis Rose,	6	2'-3'	R	14"	Rh	4
Prunis glandulosa, Double Pink Almond,	5	3'-4'	R	18"	Pg	2
Hydrangea aborescens, Snowhill Hydrangea,	8	2½'-3½'	R	14"	Sh	4
Euonymus Alatus, Winged Euonymus,	5	5'-6'	B&B	24"	Ea	2
Rhodotypos kerroides Jet Bead,	5	2½'-3'	R	15"	Rk	5
Syringa persica, Persian Lilac,	5	4'-5'	R	20"	Sp	2
Kerria japonica pleniflora, Kerria Double Flower,	6	2'-3'	R	16"	Kj	8
Deutzia lemoine compacta Dwarf Lemoine Deutzia,	6	1½'-2'	R	14"	Dl	16
Spirea vanhouttei, Vanhouttei Spirea,	6	4'-5'	R	22"	Spv	3
Syringa josikaea Hungarian Lilac,	6	5'-6'	B&B	24"	Sj	2
Philadelphus virginalis, Mock Orange (Double)	5	4'-5'	R	22"	Pv	2
Philadelphus avalanche (Variety of Lemoinei)	5	1½'-2'	R	14"	Pav	18
Chaenomeles japonica Dwarf Japanese Quince,	4	1½'	R	15"	Cjm	6

PLANTING LIST,

VALE CEMETERY, SCHENECTADY N.Y.

SECTION AN

S H R U B S (Continued)

SCIENTIFIC NAME COMMON NAME,	NO. OF CANES,	HEIGHT IN FEET,	B.B. or R	Spread of Roots,	ABV.	QUANTI
Lonicera tatarian, Pink Honeysuckle,	5	5'-6'	R	24"	Lt	1
Rosa setigera Prairie Rose,	6	7'-8'	BB	24"	Rs	1

B R O A D L E A F   E V E R G R E E N S (*)

SCIENTIFIC NAME COMMON NAME	HEIGHT IN FEET	B&B	DIAM. BALL	ABV.	QUANTITY
Rhododendron catawbiense (Hybrids in variety)	4'-5'	B&B	24"	Rhd	23
Pieris floribunda Mountain Andromeda	2'-3'	B&B	16"	Pf	4
Azalea Ghent, (Hybrids in variety)	3½'-4'	B&B	20"	Az	11
Kalmia latifolia, Mountain Laurel,	5'-6'	B&B	24"	Ml	6
Pachysandra terminalis, Pachysandra,	3"	---	4" pots	Pt	80

E V E R G R E E N S

Scientific Name Common Name	HEIGHT IN FEET	B&B	DIAM.	ABV.	QUANTIT
Taxis cuspidata nana Dwarf Jap Yew	2'	B&B	14"	Tn	19
Juniper pfitzeriana, Pfitzer Juniper,	3' spread	B&B	22"	Jf	10
Taxis cuspidata Japanese Yew	3'	B&B	18"	Tc	92
Tsuga canadensis Canada Hemlock,	5'-6'	B&B	24"	Hl	1

<u>NOTE</u> (*) Broadleaf Evergreens must have an acid soil.

PLANTING LIST,

VALE CEMETERY, SCHENECTADY N.Y.

SECTION BN

T R E E S

SCIENTIFIC NAME COMMON NAME	HGT OF TREE	HGT OF TRUNK	CAL. In INCHES	B&B	DIAM.	ABV.	QUANTITY
Cornus kousa, Kousa Dogwood,	6'-8'	3'	1½"	B&B	20"	Ck	2

S H R U B S

SCIENTIFIC NAME, COMMON NAME,	NO. OF CANES	HEIGHT IN FEET,	B&B or R	SPREAD OF ROOTS,	ABV.	QUANTITY
Viburnum acerfolium Mapleleaf Viburnum,	6	2½'-3'	R	14"	Va.	6
Rhodotyphos kerroides, Jetbead,	5	2½'-3'	R	15"	Rk	6
Ligustrum ibolium, Ibolium Privet,	5	5'-6'	R	20"	Li	2
Viburnum dentatum, Arrowwood,	5	5'-6'	R	22"	Vd	3
Acanthopanax pentaphyllum Five Leaf Aralia,	5	3'-4'	R	18"	Ap	12
Viburnum carlesi, Fragrant Viburnum,	4	2½'-3'	B&B	18"	Vc	9
Kerria japonica pleniflora Double flower Kerria,	6	2'-3'	R	16"	Kj	8
Deutzia lemoinei compacta Lemoine Deutzia,	6	1½'-2'	R	14"	Dl	24
Spirea vanhouttei, Van Houttie Spirea,	6	4'-5'	R	22"	Spv	3
Syringa josikaea Hungarian Lilac,	6	5'-6'	B&B	24"	Sj	7
Viburnum tomentosum maresi, Maries Double file Viburnum,	5	5'-6'	R	24"	Vt	5
Philadelphus virginal, Double Mock Orange,	5	4'-5'	R	22"	Pv	2
Philadelphus avalanche, (Variety of Lemoine)	5	1½'-2'	R	14"	Pav	5
Prunus glandulosa, Double Pink Almond,	5	3'-4'	R	18"	Pg	8

VALE CEMETERY, SCHENECTADY N. Y.

SECTION BN

S H R U B S (Continued)

SCIENTIFIC NAME, COMMON NAME,	NO. Of CANES,	HEIGHT IN FEET,	B&B or R	SPREAD OF ROOTS	ABV.	QUANTITY
Kolkwitzia amabilis, Beauty Bush,	6	3'-4'	R	18"	Ka	8
Forsythia intermedia, Border Forsythia,	5	4'-5'	R	20"	Fi	2
Rosa setigera Prairie Rose,	6	7'-8'	BB	24"	Rs	2
Spirea tomentosa, Hardhack Spirea,	5	1½'	R	12"	St	12

B R O A D L E A F   E V E R G R E E N S (*)

SCIENTIFIC NAME, COMMON NAME,	HEIGHT IN FEET	BB	DIAM. BALL	ABV.	QUANTITY
Rhododendron cawtawbiense, (Hybrids in variety)	4'-5'	B&B	24"	Rhd	4

E V E R G R E E N S,

SCIENTIFIC NAME, COMMON NAME,	HEIGHT	B&B	DIAM. OF BALL	ABV.	QUANTITY
Juniperus pfitzeriana Pfitzer Juniper,	3' spread,	B&B	2'	Jf	16
Thuja occid. pyramidalis, American Pyrd.Arbor Vitae,	5'-6'	B&B	2'	Tp	5
Pseudotsuga douglasi, Douglas Fir,	6'	B&B	2½'	Df	1

NOTE (*) Broadleaf Evergreens must have an acid soil.

Appendix 4: Vegetation Planted in Vale Cemetery

PLANTING LIST, SECTION D N
VALE CEMETERY, SCHENECTADY NEW YORK.

TREES.

SCIENTIFIC NAME / COMMON NAME	ABV.	HGT OF TREE	HGT OF TRUNK	CAL. IN INCHES	BB or R	DIAM OF BALL	SPR. OF Root	QUAN.
Betula Alba, Cut leaf weeping birch,	Ba	13'-15'	5'	2"-2½"	R	---	28"	1
Crataegus oxyacantha, Hu. Paulis Scarlet thorn,	Ps	6'-8'	spread 4'-5'	--	BB	24'	--	2
Malus arnoldiana Arnold Crab apple,	Ma	6'-8'	3'	2"	R	---	18"	1

SHRUBS.

SCIENTIFIC NAME / COMMON NAME	No. of CANES	HEIGHT IN FEET	B.B. or R	SPREAD OF ROOTS	ABV.	QUANTITY
Barberi thunbergi, Japanese Barberry,	6	2½'-3½'	R	16"	Bt	12
Acanthopanax pentaphyllum Japanese Barberry,	5	4'-5'	R	20"	Ap	3
Cydonia japonica, Japanese quince,	5	5'-6'	R	24"	Cj	3
Deutzia gracilis, Slender deutzia,	5	1½'-2'	R	12"	Dg	16
Euonymus alatus, Winged euonymus,	4	5'-6'	BB	24"	Ea	7
Euonymus alatus compactus, Hu. Dwarf winged euonymus,	4	2½'-3'	BB	16"	Eac	19
Forsythia intermedia, Border forsythia,	5	4'-5'	R	20"	Fi	4
Lonicera tatarica, White tatarian honeysuckle,	5	5'-6'	R	24"	Lt	11
Philadelphia aurea, Dwarf golden mock orange	5	1½'-2'	R	12"	Pa	14
Prunus glandulosa, Double pink flowering almond,	5	3'-4'	R	18"	Pg	24
Rhodotypos kerrioides, Jet Bead,	4	2½'-3½'	R	16"	Rk	14
Rosa hugonis, Hugonis Rose,	6	2'-3'	R	14"	Rh	5
Rosa Rugoso, Rugosa Rose Grootendorst.	5	2'-3'	R	14"	Rg	8

PLANTING LIST,
SECTION D N
Vale Cemetery, Schenectady New York.

S H R U B S, (Continued)

SCIENTIFIC NAME COMMON NAME	No. of Canes,	HEIGHT IN FEET,	B.B. or R	SPREAD OF ROOTS,	ABV.	QUANTITY
Spirea vanhouttei, Vanhoutte spirea,	6	4'-5'	R	20"	Spv	2
Springa persica, Persian lilac,	4	4'-5'	R	20"	Sp	11
Syringa vulgaris,(hybrid) Ludwig spaeth variety,	5	5'-6'	BB	24"	Sv	9
Weigelia eva rathke, Eva Rathke Weigelia,	4	2½'-3½'	R	16"	Wer	6

E V E R G R E E N S.

SCIENTIFIC NAME COMMON NAME	HEIGHT	B.B.	Diam. of Ball	ABV	QUANTITY
Juniperus chinensis globosa, Globe Chinese Juniper,	3' spread,	BB	2'	Jc.	7
Juniperus chinensis pfitzeriana, Pfitzer juniper,	c3' spread,	BB	2'	Jf.	15
Thuja occidentalis pyramidalis, American pyramid arbor vitaem	6'	BB	2½'	Tp	4
Pseudotsuga douglasi, Douglas Fir,	6"	BB	2½'	Df	2

PLANTING LIST,

VALE CEMETERY, SCHENECTADY N.Y.

SECTION EN

TREES

SCIENTIFIC NAME COMMON NAME,	HGT OF TREE	HGT OF TRUNK	CAL. In INCHES	B&B or R	DIAM. BALL	SPREAD OF ROOTS	ABV.	QUANTITY
Cornus mas Cornelian Cherry,	7'-8'	3'	1½"	BB	24"	24"	Cm	2

SHRUBS

SCIENTIFIC NAME, COMMON NAME,	NO. OF CANES	HGT. IN FEET	B&B or R	SPREAD OF ROOTS	ABV	QUANTITY
Rosa Hugonis, Hugonis Rose,	6	2'-3'	R	14"	Rh	4
Prunis glandulosa, Double Pink Almond,	5	3'-4'	R	18"	Pg	2
Hydrangea aborescens Snowhill Hydrangea,	8	2½'-3½'	R	14"	Sh	4
Euonymus alatus, Winged Euonymus,	4	5'-6'	BB	24"	Ea	2
Viburnum acerfolium, Mapleleaf Viburnum,	6	2½'-3'	R	14"	Va	5
Rhodotypos kerrioides, Jet Bead,	4	2½'-3'	R	15"	Rk	3
Deutzia lemoinei compacta, Lemoinei Deutzia,	6	1½'-2'	R	14"	Dl	14
Syringa josikaea, Hungarian Lilac,	6	5'-6'	B&B	24"	Sj	2
Philadelphus virginal, Double Mock Orange,	5	4'-5'	R	22"	Pv	2
Philadelphus avalanche, (Variety of Lemoinei)	5	1½'-2'	R	14"	Pav	18
Chaenomelis japonica, Dwarf Jap Quince,	4	1½'	R	15"	Cjm	6

PLANTING LIST,

VALE CEMETERY, SCHENECTADY N.Y.

SECTION EN

B R O A D L E A F E V E R G R E E N S. (*)

SCIENTIFIC NAME, COMMON NAME,	HGT. IN FEET	B & B	DIAM. OF BALL	ABV.	QUANTITY
Rhododendron catawbiense, (Hybrids in variety)	4'-5'	B&B	24"	Rhd.	27
Pieris floribunda, Mountain Andromeda,	2'-3'	B&B	16"	Pf	10
Azalea Ghent, (Hybrids in variety)	3½'-4'	B&B	20"	Az	18
Kalinia latifolia, Mountain Laurel,	5'-6'	B&B	24"	Ml	8
Pachysandra terminalis, Pachysandra,	3"		4" pots	Pt	80

E V E R G R E E N S

SCIENTIFIC NAME, COMMON NAME,	HGT. IN FEET	B & B	DIAM. OF BALL	ABV.	QUANTITY
Juniper fitzeriana, Pfitzer Juniper,	3' spread	B&B	22"	Jf	10
Taxis cuspidata, Jap Yew,	3'	B&B	18"	Tc	62
Tsuga canadensis, Canada Hemlock,	5'-6'	B&B	24"	Hl	8
Taxis cuspidata nana, Dwarf Jap Yew,	2'	B&B	14"	Tn	70

NOTE (*) Broadleaf evergreens must have an acid soil.

PLANTING LIST, SECTION F N
VALE CEMETERY, SCHENECTADY NEW YORK.

TREES.

SCIENTIFIC NAME COMMON NAME	ABV.	HGT OF TREE	HGT OF TRUNK	CAL. IN INCHES.	BB or R	DIAM OF BALL	Spr of Root	QUAN
Acer platanoides Norway Maple	NM	10'-12'	6'	$1\frac{1}{2}"-1\frac{3}{4}"$	BB	$2\frac{1}{2}'$	—	5
Crataegus Oxyacantha, Hu.Paulis Scarlet thorn,	Ps	6'-8'	spread 4'-5'	--	BB	24"	—	6

SHRUBS

SCIENTIFIC NAME COMMON NAME	No. of Canes	HEIGHT IN FEET.	BB or R	SPREAD OF ROOTS	ABV.	QUANTITY
Berberis thunbergi, Japanese barberry,	6	$2\frac{1}{2}'-3\frac{1}{2}'$	R	16"	Bt.	12
Euonymus alatus compactus, Hu.Dwarf winged euonymus,	4	$2\frac{1}{2}'-3'$	BB	16"	Eac.	16
Forsythia intermedia, Border forsythia,	5	4'-5'	R	20"	Fi	12
Hydrangea aborescens Snowhill hydrangea,	8	$2\frac{1}{2}'-3\frac{1}{2}'$	R	14"	Sh	5
Prunus glandulosa, Double pink flowering almond,	5	3'-4'	R	18"	Pg	30
Spirea vanhouttei, Vanhoutte spirea,	6	4'-5'	R	20"	Spv	8
Syringa persica, Persian lilac,	4	4'-5'	R	20"	Sp	26
Syringa Hybrid lilacs, Ludwig Spaeth variety,	5	5'-6'	BB	24"	Sv	4
Viburnum carlesi, May flower viburnum	4	2'-3'	BB	12"	Mv	6
Weigelia eva rathke, Eva Rathke Weigelia,	4	$2\frac{1}{2}'-3\frac{1}{2}'$	R	16"	Wer	26

PLANTING LIST,
SECTION P N
VALE CEMETERY, SCHENECTADY NEW YORK.

EVERGREENS

SCIENTIFIC NAME COMMON NAME	HEIGHT,	BB	Diam of Ball,	ABV.	QUANTITY
Juniperus chinensis globosa, Globe Chinese juniper,	3' spread	BB	2'	Jc.	4
Juniperus chinensis pfitzeriana, Pfitzer juniper,	3' spread	BB	2'	Jf.	24
Pseudotsuga douglasi, Douglas Fir,	6'	BB	2½'	Df.	2

PLANTING LIST,

VALE CEMETERY, SCHENECTADY N.Y.

SECTION GN

TREES

SCIENTIFIC NAME, COMMON NAME,	HGT. OF TREE,	HGT. OF TRUNK	CAL. In INCHES,	B&B or R	DIAM. of BALL	ABV.	QUANTITY
Cornus kousa, Kousa Dogwood,	6'-8'	3'	1½"	BB	20"	Ck	3

SHRUBS,

SCIENTIFIC NAME, COMMON NAME,	No. of Canes,	HGT. IN FEET	B&B. or R.	SPREAD OF ROOTS,	ABV.	QUANTITY
Spirea tomentosa, Hardhack Spirea,	5	1½'	R	12"	St	12
Rosa Setigera, Prairie Rose,	6	7'-8'	BB	24"	Rs	2
Prunus glandulosa, Double pink flowering almond,	5	5'-6'	R	18"	Pg	11
Viburnum tomentosum mariesi, Maries Doublefile Viburnum,	5	4'-5'	R	24"	V_t	4
Philadelphus virginal, Double Mock Orange,	5	4'-5'	R	22"	Pv	2
Philadelphus avalanche, (Variety of Lemoinei)	5	1½'-2'	R	14"	Pav	11
Syringa josikaea Hungarian Lilac,	6	5'-6'	BB	24"	Sj	4
Kolkwitzia amabilis, Beauty Bush,	6	3'-4'	R	18"	Ka	13
Forsythia intermedia, Border Forsythia,	5	4'-5'	R	20"	Fi	2
Chaenomeles japonica, Dwarf Jap Quince,	4	1½'	R	15"	Cjm	6
Spirea arguta, Garland spirea,	5	2'-3'	R	16"	Sa	4
Deutzia lemoinei compacta, Lemoinei Deutzia,	6	1½'-2'	R	14"	Dl	18

PLANTING LIST,

VALE CEMETERY, SCHENECTADY N. Y.

SECTION GN

BROADLEAF EVERGREENS (*)

SCIENTIFIC NAME, COMMON NAME,	HGT IN FEET	B&B	DIAM. OF BALL	Abv.	QUANTITY
Rhododendron catawbiense, (Hybrids in variety)	4'-5'	B&B	24"	Rhd	12
Azalea Ghent, (Hybrids in variety)	3½'-4'	B&B	20"	Az	8

EVERGREENS,

SCIENTIFIC NAME, COMMON NAME,	HEIGHT IN FEET	B&B	DIAM. OF BALL	ABV.	QUANTITY
Pseudotsuga douglasi, Douglas Fir,	6'	B&B	2½'	Df	1
Juniperus pfitzeriana, Pfitzer Juniper,	3' spread	B&B	2'	Jf	10
Thuja occidentalis pyramidalis America Pyramid Arbor Vitae,	5'-6'	B&B	2'	Tp	2
Juniperus chiensis pyramidalis, Pyramidal Chinese Juniper,	4½'-5'	B&B	2'	Jc	3

NOTE (*) Broadleaf Evergreens must have an acid soil.

About the Author

Don Rittner is an author, environmentalist, documentarian, historian and archeologist. He has authored close to 40 books and over 1000 articles in science, history, computers and the Internet. He was the former Schenectady County and City Historian (2005-2013) and Albany City Archeologist (1972-79). He headed the construction of The Onrust, a replica of the first fur trading ship built in America (2005-2014). Rittner was the owner of The Learning Factory, an alternative education center from 1996-2001. He was the producer of award winning documentaries, *The Neighborhood That Disappeared* and *ECHOES From The Neighborhood That Disappeared* that documented the displacement of 9000 immigrant families from Albany's South End during the construction of the Empire State Mall during the early 1960s.

Also available from Square Circle Press

Serendipity in Science:

Twenty Years at Langmuir University

An Autobiography by Vincent J. Schaefer, ScD

Compiled and Edited by Don Rittner

ISBN-13: 978-0-9856926-3-6 / ISBN-10: 0-9856926-3-4
428 pages, 7.5" x 9.25", softcover, B&W interior, illustrated
$31.95

www.SquareCirclePress.com

www.ingramcontent.com/pod-product-compliance
Lightning Source LLC
Chambersburg PA
CBHW081216230426
43666CB00015B/2748